THE
WOOD
THAT
BUILT
LONDON

Roberta Fulford

THE
WOOD
THAT
BUILT
LONDON

A *human history of the Great North Wood*

C. J. SCHÜLER

Foreword by Rachel Lichtenstein

SANDSTONE PRESS

First published in Great Britain in 2021 by
Sandstone Press Ltd
PO Box 41
Muir of Ord
Highland
IV6 7YX
Scotland

www.sandstonepress.com

Sandstone Press is committed to a sustainable future.
This book is made from Forest Stewardship Council ® certified paper.

ISBN: 978-1-913207-49-6
ISBNe: 978-1-913207-50-2

Jacket design by Daniel Benneworth-Gray
Typography by Biblichor Ltd, Edinburgh
Printed and bound by CPI Group (UK) Ltd, Croydon, CR0 4YY

CONTENTS

FOREWORD

C. J. Schüler's *The Wood That Built London* is an in-depth history of the woodland that once covered great stretches of what is now south London. This fascinating account reveals how medieval London was built from its timbers and fuelled by the charcoal they produced, before the metropolis expanded to engulf most of this ancient landscape into the surburban townscape. In twelve highly readable chapters, Schüler tells us the stories of this place and its people, from the last great Ice Age, through the arrival of the Normans, the Plantagenet, Tudor and Stuart dynasties, the Industrial Revolution and the Victorian era to the present climate crisis.

This important work of contemporary place writing combines a lively human narrative with rigorous archival research from a wide range of sources, including botanical and zoological evidence, industrial and agrarian history, church records, and even sixteenth-century court witness statements. It preserves the memory of time-honoured landmarks that have long since disappeared, rivers that have vanished underground, place names that recall a rural landscape now buried beneath city streets, and ancient parish boundaries that still shape London's boroughs. The result is a deep mapping of London's ever-changing topography to set beside the work of Peter Ackroyd and Iain Sinclair, and a significant addition to the growing new genre of urban nature writing.

The history of mapmaking in this book makes fascinating reading in itself, as does the detailed account of coppicing and other woodland crafts, revealing the extent to which apparently natural spaces have been shaped by human intervention since earliest times, and how this has created rich, diverse habitats for a wide range of plant and animal species.

This is not just a book about geography and ecology: it is a rich treasure trove of stories about people past and present, characters through the centuries who have in different ways interacted with this place, who have been vividly brought to life and observed with wry detachment by the author. There are not just kings and bishops, but writers and butterfly collectors, land-owners, woodsmen, surveyors, tenant farmers and quarrelsome neighbours. The echoes of these communities retain a ghostly presence in the remnants of woodland familiar to present-day locals. In addition to delving into archives, the author, who has been a conservation volunteer at Sydenham Hill Wood for the past decade, has tramped the surviving pockets of woodland, meeting and recording the stories of professional ecologists, volunteers and local campaigners. These direct encounters with a range of contemporary voices have made the book a collabora-tive project akin to the conservation work that he and his fellow volunteers have undertaken in the woods.

This is a tale for our times, and its implications are not just local but global. Only in recent years have we come to understand the speed and severity of climate change, the crucial role that wood-lands play in protecting us and our world, and how the destruction of such places causes a decline of species diversity which, as the author rightly observes, is accelerating exponentially, weaken-ing the planet's immune system to a dangerous degree.

We exist within nature, and it is all around us, even in the most urban places. During the recent lockdown, travel restrictions have made us acutely sensitised to our hyper-local environment, exploring the wild within the city. This book highlights the importance of these surviving urban woodlands both to an ecosystem in peril as never before, and to our social and psychological wellbeing. We should be thankful to the individuals and public bodies, especially the London Wildlife Trust, who work to protect and promote the recovery of these ancient woodlands, and those, like the author of this important and timely book, whose research and artistry emphasise their enduring value to people and the planet.

Rachel Lichtenstein, London 2021

INTRODUCTION

Standing in the busy streets of South London today, it is hard to imagine that as recently as the eighteenth century, much of this suburban townscape was covered by an expanse of woodland and wooded commons, spreading almost unbroken for seven miles from Croydon to the Thames at Deptford. Its legacy can be found in many local place names: Norwood, Collier's Wood, Honor Oak, Gipsy Hill, Penge, which means 'Wood's End', Woodside, and Selhurst, from the Anglo-Saxon for 'dwelling in a wood'. A survival of the wildwood that once covered much of Britain, from Saxon times until the Industrial Revolution the wood was intensively managed to provide timber for construction and shipbuilding, bark, from which tannin was extracted for leathermaking, and charcoal for London's blacksmiths and bakeries. Its produce helped to build the city that would, in the course of a millennium, whittle it down to a few surviving remnants.

The largest of these can be found at Dulwich and Sydenham Hill, where relict and secondary woodland still covers some twenty-five hectares. Smaller fragments can be found at One Tree Hill in Honor Oak, Biggin Wood, Spa Hill, Beaulieu Heights and Grangewood Park in Norwood, and at Long Lane to the south of Elmer's End. The nearest ancient woodland to central London, they sustain wildlife in the capital, help cleanse its polluted air, and provide city dwellers with access not only to nature but to something rooted deep in our collective unconscious.

Woods occupy a central place in the folklore of many cultures as a scene of mystery, enchantment and transformation. They are the setting for dark fairy tales such as 'Little Red Riding Hood'. They resonate in literature, from Dante's *selva oscura*, a place of confusion and challenge, to Shakespeare's Forest of Arden, a sylvan refuge from the intrigue of the court. 'To enter a wood,' wrote Roger Deakin in his book *Wildwood*, 'is to pass into a different world in which we ourselves are transformed. It is no accident that in the comedies of Shakespeare, people go into the greenwood to grow, learn and change. It is where you travel to find yourself, often, paradoxically, by getting lost.'

Over the centuries, Dulwich Woods have attracted writers and artists such as Samuel Pepys, Byron, Robert Browning, Samuel Palmer and John Ruskin. No fewer than three books by Daniel Defoe have furnished material for this history, though sadly I have found no reference to the North Wood in his most famous work, the *Life and Strange Surprizing Adventures of Robinson Crusoe*. Today, Sydenham Hill Wood, with its faux-medieval folly hidden deep amid the trees, is a magnet for Goths and a popular backdrop for fashion shoots and music videos.

What makes these surviving pockets of woodland so important, aside from their cultural resonance and amenity for local residents, is the fact that their antiquity is attested by both extensive written records and the presence of Ancient Woodland Indicators (AWIs) – species characteristic of areas that have been continuously wooded for at least four hundred years. These include plants such as the wood anemone, a clump of which will expand by just one metre in a hundred years, and many beetles and other insects that, for at least part of their life cycle, are dependent on dead or decaying wood and, because they cannot travel far, rarely establish themselves in new woodland. In recent decades, moreover, scientists have discovered that woodland trees communicate with one another through their root systems, sending electrical and chemical signals to warn other trees of predators so that they may take defensive measures such as secreting toxins to repel them, and even sharing nutrients with those whose ability to photosynthesise is reduced by damage or a shady position.

This process is assisted by the fungi that grow in the forest floor. The toadstools and brackets that we see above ground are in fact only the fruiting bodies; the main body of a fungus is the underground part, or mycelium, a mass of fine filaments known as hyphae. Like fibre-optic cables, these filaments connect the roots of trees in a symbiotic relationship in which, in exchange for nutrients, they assist in the transmission of information and sustenance.[1] Ancient woodland is therefore irreplaceable. You cannot 'offset' the destruction of so complex an ecosystem, which takes centuries to develop, by 'mitigation' planting elsewhere. The fact that a wood is considered ancient does not mean that any of the trees within it are necessarily four hundred years old; simply that it has never been clear-felled and ploughed over within that period. A wood may outlive the individual trees within it by many thousands of years; what matters is the persistence of the ecosystem.

Nor should the antiquity of the North Wood mislead us into thinking that any of its surviving parts are wild, pristine woodland; they have not been that for at least a thousand years, and probably for much longer. Since our Neolithic forebears first crafted flint handaxes and began to clear the wildwood for agriculture, few corners of the British Isles have remained an untouched wilderness. What we regard as natural is actually the result of millennia of interaction between human beings and their environment, and our wildest-seeming landscapes have been sculpted by centuries of husbandry. This book is therefore not only a natural history but a human one, the story of the people who owned the wood, who worked in it, who studied its flora and fauna and, most recently, who fought to save what is left of it. The great events of national and international history – the Norman Conquest, the Dissolution of the Monasteries, the English Civil War, the Industrial Revolution, the enclosure of common lands, the construction of the railways, and two world wars – all affected the woods, and are reflected in these pages.

Since before the Norman invasion, the North Wood was in effect an enormous tree farm, intensively managed and regularly harvested to produce different grades of timber for building, tool making, fencing and firewood. Though much of the wood was in private ownership, commoners had the right to graze livestock such as pigs, geese and chickens there. By trampling and cropping the undergrowth, these animals allowed sunlight to penetrate to the forest floor. The result was a symbiosis of the human and the natural, creating a distinctive biosphere that provided a haven for species not found elsewhere. Since the decline of the woodland economy after the Industrial Revolution, informed, active management has been necessary to reproduce these effects and maintain a balanced ecosystem.

Throughout the surviving parcels of the North Wood, the dominant tree is the sessile oak (*Quercus petraea*). So called because its acorns sit directly on the twig rather than on stems as they do on the pedunculate oak (*Quercus robur*), the sessile oak tends to grow tall and straight, making it suitable for shipbuilding. Across many cultures, the oak is perhaps the most revered of all trees, and resonant with symbolism. The ancient Greeks held it sacred, as did the Druids in far-off Britain. The eighteenth-century poet William Cowper called it the 'king of the woods', and the anthem of the Royal Navy is 'Hearts of Oak'. The pedunculate oak is also known as the English oak, though Germans and Poles also consider the tree a symbol of resilience, strength and national identity.

An oak can live for up to a thousand years; it is said to spend three hundred years growing, three hundred years in stable maturity, and three hundred in slow decline. Each tree supports hundreds of insect species, providing many birds with an important food source, as well as offering nesting spots in its deeply creviced bark. Jays and magpies feed on the acorns, assisting the propagation of the species by burying them some distance from the parent tree and sometimes failing to retrieve them. Oak has long been prized for its strength, and was extensively used in shipbuilding and the construction of timber-framed houses, while the beauty of its grain has ensured its continued use in the making of high-quality furniture. For centuries, the galls (or 'oak apples') produced when parasitic wasps lay their eggs in the leaves, twigs or acorns were the most common source of ink; most of the older documents I consulted while researching this book will, satisfyingly, have been written in oak-gall ink.

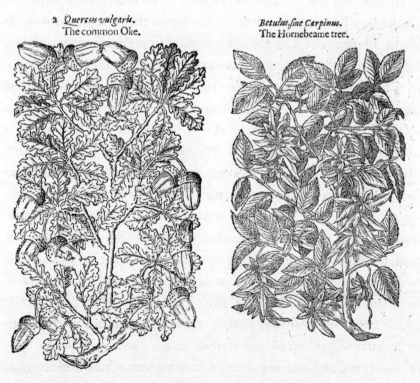

2 *Quercus vulgaris.*
The common Oke.

Betulus, siue Carpinus.
The Hornebeame tree.

The oak and hornbeam, from John Gerard's *Herball*, 1597.

On the heights of Sydenham Hill and Dulwich Woods, the sessile oaks are interspersed with hornbeam (*Carpinus betulus*), a member of the birch family that occupies a similar ecological niche on clay uplands to that of the beech on chalk or limestone. In earlier times it was often confused with the beech or other trees: in Kent, according to the sixteenth-century herbalist John Gerard, 'it is commonly taken for a kind of Elme', while his seventeenth-century successor Nicholas Culpeper felt it necessary to differentiate the beech 'from that other small rough sort, called in Sussex the smaller Beech, but in Essex Horn-beam'. Writing a few decades later, the silviculturist John Evelyn noted that the hornbeam was 'by some called the Horse-Beech, from the Resemblance of the Leaf', and that 'the Places it chiefly desires to grow in are in cold Hills, stiff Ground, and in the barren and most exposed parts of Woods.'

In Britain, the hornbeam is largely confined to south-east England, where it flourishes on the slopes that rise on either side of the Thames, and in the Chilterns. The delicacy of its leaves, especially in the fresh green livery of spring, and its pagoda-like seed-bearing samaras, belie the strength of its limbs, their musculature bulging through the smooth grey bark. Its timber – sometimes known as ironwood – is so hard that it will blunt a woodworker's tools, making it suitable only for applications such as mallets, chopping boards, axles, cogs and pulleys, where durability is more important than fine carpentry. Its high calorific content, however, means that it gives off intense heat when burned, so it was much favoured for the manufacture of charcoal for smelting iron. A hornbeam log does not catch light easily, but added to a fire that is already going strong, it will burn steadily, with a bluish flame, for hours.

For much of its history, this tract of woodland was known as Norwood, or the North Wood, on account of its position in relation to Croydon, the manor to which much of it belonged, and to distinguish it from the forests of the Weald to the south. It is nowadays referred to as the 'Great North Wood', but this appears to be a Victorian invention; I have found no record of it earlier than 1863, in the proceedings of the Surrey Archaeological Society – and there the word 'great' has a lower-case 'g', indicating a prenominal adjective rather than a part of the name itself. By 1898, when the Croydon historian John Corbet Anderson published his book *The Great North Wood*, the name had taken root. It is ironic that, like the River Effra that flowed from its slopes, the wood only acquired the name by which we know it today when it was already fading into the past.

Similarly, the botany and zoology of the woods became the object of scientific study only in the late eighteenth and early nineteenth centuries, just as the Industrial Revolution and the Enclosure Acts were reducing their extent. Prior to that, the records chiefly concerned land ownership, woodland management, and the income it generated. Fortunately, the archives of the Archbishopric of Canterbury and the Dulwich Estate, which between them owned much of the North Wood, survive, and have preserved a record of its stewardship over more than four centuries. Other early evidence survives in the National Archives at Kew, including witness statements in disputes over the ownership of parts of the woods. Much of this documentation is written in secretary hand, the script used by legal and administrative writers in the sixteenth and seventeenth centuries. Designed for speed, its cursive letters often bear scant resemblance to their modern equivalents, and many common words – which, with, parish, person, majesty – are abbreviated. Poring over worn, creased and sometimes torn or worm-eaten sheets of paper or parchment, I learnt, painstakingly, to decipher the hand, bringing the past alive in all its quotidian detail and casual cruelty.

Despite the survival of these valuable records, a word of caution is necessary. Even these archives have frustrating gaps, and others have vanished altogether as a result of fire, damp, mice, mildew, insects, indifference, neglect, and the normal human desire to dispose of seemingly redundant paperwork. How far back do any of us keep our bank statements before consigning them to the shredder? And even where records do survive, as the historian Patrick Collinson has observed, 'it is possible for competent historians to come to radically different conclusions on the basis of the same evidence.'[2]

This is the first full-length history of the woods since Anderson's, though Lucy Neville's 1987 booklet *The Great North Wood* packed a great deal of well-researched historical information into a brief thirty-two pages. I am indebted to both, though once I began to research the subject, it soon became apparent that many aspects of the story – ecological, social, cultural and political – remained to be explored. The purpose of this book is to chart the history of the North Wood and its surviving fragments: their natural and human history, their management, their gradual encroachment by the expanding metropolis, their survival against the odds, and the opportunities and challenges faced by the professional and volunteer environmentalists who maintain them as urban nature reserves today.

On a personal note, I have volunteered at the London Wildlife Trust's Local Nature Reserve at Sydenham Hill Wood since 2011. I have learned the names and habits of many plants and insects, and how to handle ancient tools such as scythes and billhooks. I have taken part in twilight bat surveys on Dulwich and Sydenham Hill golf course, as our handheld detectors amplified the clatter of noctules' and pipistrelles' echolocation signals, and hunched over a fluorescent moth-trap (powered by an ancient car battery) in a damp glade as a curious fox came to investigate. I have seen a kestrel methodically eviscerate a twitching wood mouse on a branch of an oak. I have watched as a dragonfly larva climbed out of a pond up the stem of a flag iris, and the adult burst from its carapace and unfolded its wings to dry in the sun. These experiences have been as enriching as any travel to far-flung parts of the globe, and I would recommend them to anyone.

C. J. Schüler, Herne Hill 2021

MEASUREMENTS, MONEY AND OTHER MATTERS

For much of the period covered by this book, land area was measured in acres, rods (or roods) and perches, and these appear regularly in the historic records quoted in these pages. For the sake of visualisation, an acre is about half the size of a football pitch. There were four rods in an acre, and forty perches in a rod. Confusingly, a rod was also a measure of distance, corresponding to about sixteen and a half feet, or about five metres.

Since the 1985 Weights and Measures Act, however, town planners, councils, developers and environmentalists have used the metric system, though many farmers still prefer to measure the fields they have cultivated for generations in acres. The standard unit of area became the hectare, made up of ten thousand square metres or about two and a half acres. It seems anachronistic, if not downright jarring, to introduce metric units when discussing an era in which place names such as 'Eighteen Acre Field' and 'Forty Acre Wood' were common, so area has been given in acres up to and including Chapter 8; in Chapter 9, both acres and hectares are given; and thereafter hectares are used exclusively.

Readers under the age of sixty or thereabouts may not be familiar with Britain's pre-decimal currency. Until 1971, the pound consisted of twenty shillings, and each shilling was made up of twelve pence. These values were represented as £ s d. Five shillings and sixpence was also rendered as 5/6, or 'five and six'. Trying to provide modern equivalents for historic prices ('about £1,000 in today's money') is a pretty fruitless exercise, however, since inflation has not taken place evenly across the whole range of goods and services. Before the Industrial Revolution, many basic goods such as clothing that can now be obtained cheaply were extremely expensive in relation to the wages of the day.

Until 1753 England used the Julian calendar, which by that time had lagged eleven days behind the Gregorian calendar followed elsewhere in Western Europe. This rarely impinges on this narrative. More problematically, the New Year was considered to begin on Lady Day, 25 March, so Queen Elizabeth I was thought by her contemporaries to have died on the very last day (24 March) of 1602, whereas we would say her death occurred almost three months into 1603. In narrative text, I have converted 'Old Style' dates to modern usage, starting the year on 1 January; when citing historic documents the format 1 February 1606/7 is used.

In transcribing manuscript and printed sources, I have preserved the original spelling and punctuation in all its glorious inconsistency, except for the sixteenth- and seventeenth-century practice of using 'j' and 'i', and 'u' and 'v', interchangeably; these I have altered to their modern equivalents, except for the terminal j then favoured in Roman numerals (e.g. viij).

Plants and animals are classified according to the binomial system devised by the Swedish scientist Carl Linnaeus in the mid-eighteenth century, which remains the standard today. This identifies each organism by genus and species, thus indicating, for example, that the kestrel (*Falco tinnunculus*) is closely related to the peregrine falcon (*Falco peregrinus*) and the hobby (*Falco subbuteo*), but less closely to the sparrow-hawk (*Accipiter nisus*). Since Linnaeus's day, as knowledge has increased, some of the names that he and his followers used have been revised. When citing early botanical and zoological records, I have sometimes given both the old and new forms; elsewhere, to avoid cluttering the text, I have silently updated them.

1

TAMING THE WILDWOOD

c.8000 BC–1485

At the end of the last Ice Age some ten thousand years ago, Britain was connected to continental Europe by a land bridge known as Doggerland across what are now the shallow southern reaches of the North Sea. After the permafrost retreated northwards, the low-lying south was gradually colonised by birch, a pioneer species tolerant of Arctic conditions. As the climate warmed, it was followed in succession by pine, elm, oak, alder, hawthorn, hazel and holly.[1] Among the last species to arrive before the melting glaciers raised the sea level and cut these islands off from mainland Europe were lime, field maple and hornbeam. The trees were followed by large mammals such as deer, bison, wild boar, the wild horse or tarpan, and the huge oxen known as aurochs. These in turn attracted apex predators such as wolves and lynx. Here and there, the wildwood was broken by glades where some great tree had been felled by the wind, and which were kept clear by grazing herbivores.

The wide, sluggish Thames meandered between creeks and marshes over beds of alluvial clay, sedimentary deposits laid down in an ancient sea. Beneath Norwood Hill lies a bed of fossilised oysters, while workmen digging the railway tunnel under Sydenham Hill in the nineteenth century unearthed a rich deposit of marine fossils.² On the southern shore of the river lay the marshes of present-day Deptford; beyond them, at Brockley, a ridge of clay hills began to rise to the south, through Telegraph Hill, Friern Hill and Oak of Honor Hill, reaching twin summits at Sydenham Hill and Norwood. From there, it dropped precipitously towards Croydon, where it met the chalk of the Weald.

At 110 metres (350 feet) above sea level, the Norwood Ridge is scarcely a ripple by Alpine standards, but height is always relative to the surrounding landscape, and its summit is the highest point between Hampstead and the North Downs, commanding sweeping views over London. Until the formation of the London County Council in 1889, the ridge marked the boundary between the counties of Surrey and Kent. It also forms the watershed between two catchment areas: to the west, that of the rivers Effra and Peck, and to the east, that of the Ravensbourne. Springs bubbled from its slopes, creating tributary streams that fed these rivers.

The Peck flowed from the slopes of Oak of Honor Hill, through Peckham Rye (where a short stretch is still visible above ground), to Bermondsey, where it joined the Earl's Sluice, which entered the Thames at Rotherhithe. The Effra was formed of two main branches, the Upper Norwood, which rose just below the summit of the ridge, where Crystal Palace Parade now meets Church Road, and the Lower Norwood, which emerged half a mile away in what is now Westow Park. Though the whole river has long since been channelled underground, the upper branch formed the boundary between the parishes of Lambeth and Camberwell, and the modern boroughs that succeeded them. The tributaries converged near the junction of South Croxted Road and Thurlow Park Road, before flowing north through Herne Hill, Brixton and Kennington. From there, the river probably headed north-east to meet the Earl's Sluice, but by the mid-fourteenth century the monks of Bermondsey Abbey, to alleviate flooding of their farmland, had diverted it to the west so that it now joined the Thames at Vauxhall.[3] On the eastern, Kentish side of the ridge, small brooks such as the Penge Stream and the Willmore flowed into the River Pool, which joins the Ravensbourne at Catford. The larger river then winds its way north to debouch into the Thames via Deptford Creek. Every raindrop that fell on the Kent side of the Norwood Ridge found its way into the Ravensbourne; on the Surrey side, into the Effra or the Peck.

Before the melting ice sheets filled the North Sea and separated Britain from the mainland around 7500 BC, people returned. The first arrivals were Mesolithic hunter-gatherers, pursuing animals, foraging for edible plants, seldom settling in one place for long enough to make much impact on the landscape. Around 4000 BC, however, agriculture reached Northwestern Europe, marking the beginning of the Neolithic era. People began to form settlements, growing early forms of wheat such as emmer and einkorn, and domesticating animals. In the southern parts of Britain, they cleared much of the forest for fuel and building material, carving out fields for their livestock and crops. By the late Iron Age, some 2,500 years ago, most of the wildwood had gone, although the Norwood Ridge, too steep to be easily farmed, retained its tree cover.

The arrival of the Romans in AD 43 led to the rapid growth of Londinium as a commercial entrepôt; by AD 100 it had supplanted Camulodunum (Colchester) as the capital of the province of Britannia. The site was probably chosen because it was the lowest point at which the Thames could be bridged with the technology available at the time; it remained so until the construction of Tower Bridge in the 1890s. At the southern end of the Roman bridge, the suburb of Southwark grew up, keeping close to the riverbank. From here, a road ran through the woods to the south coast, roughly along the line of the present A23. At Croydon, where it crossed the River Wandle, a number of Roman burials have been discovered around the junction of George Street and the High Street, suggesting the presence of a well-established settlement nearby.[4] The Romans may also have introduced a number of plants and animals now widely regarded as intrinsic to the English landscape: sweet chestnut, blackberries, nettles, fallow deer, brown hare and even rabbits, although the archaeological evidence is uncertain and contentious.

Following the Roman withdrawal in AD 410, Britain fell into an extended period of tribal warfare and socio-economic decline. Anglo-Saxons started to arrive from mainland Europe around 450, and by 600 had consolidated their hold on England. Colonised by Jutes from Denmark, north-east Surrey became part of the kingdom of Kent, before being annexed by the powerful Mercian state to the north. Croydon grew in importance: around 800, the Mercian King Coenwulf attended a council there, and a Church synod was held in the town in 809. In 825, the region was annexed by Wessex, and by 871 Croydon – and the woods that lay to its north – had become a possession of the Archbishops of Canterbury.[5]

In 874, the Danes invaded Mercia, driving its king, Burgred, into exile in Rome. In these unsettled times, someone decided to bury their fortune in the North Wood and, for whatever reason, never came back to retrieve it. In 1862, as workmen were cutting the railway line from Thornton Heath to Selhurst, their picks struck a rotting chest, in which they found a bag of coins. In the ensuing scramble for treasure, the contents were dispersed, but a brittle, oxide-fused lump was taken into Croydon where it was sold for silver. On examination, it turned out to be a hoard of about 250 mostly well-preserved Anglo-Saxon coins, together with a few small silver ingots and a part of a silver torc, or neck ornament.

THE NORMAN SETTLEMENT

For much of its history, the Norwood Ridge was border country, straddling the sparsely peopled margins of two counties and five parishes: Croydon, Lambeth, Camberwell, Lewisham and the hamlet of Penge, then a detached outpost of the manor and parish of Battersea. A parish was then – and for most of the period covered in this book – far more than an ecclesiastical division; it was also a civil administrative unit that performed many of the functions of local government, including highway maintenance and poor relief.

Throughout this area, the Domesday Book, compiled in 1086, records a mosaic of fields, pastures, woods, hedges and scattered farmsteads and hamlets. It measured the extent of woodland in each manor not by acreage but by the number of pigs, released into the woods each autumn to forage for acorns or beech mast, that it could feed, a custom known as pannage or mastage. The woodland ecologist Oliver Rackham calculated that the density was often one pig per acre,[6] and while this can provide only a rough estimate – the number of pigs a wood could support would vary according to the mix of tree species, density of cover and other factors – it does suggest the relative amount of woodland in each manor, bearing in mind that there were other areas of forest beside the North Wood.

The woods formed part of six manors: Hatcham, Camberwell, Lewisham, Lambeth, Croydon and Benchesham. The most northerly part lay within the manor of Hatcham, or Hatcham Barnes, to the south of Deptford and west of Greenwich. Now absorbed into New Cross, this all but forgotten district lives on only in the names of Haberdashers' Aske's Hatcham College and the Hatcham Liberal Club. Under Edward the Confessor, it was held by Brixi (or Brihtsige), the Saxon nobleman who gave his name to Brixton. William the Conqueror conferred the manor on his half-brother, Odo, Bishop of Bayeux, from whom it was leased by Gilbert Maminot, Bishop of Lisieux. The Domesday Book records that Hatcham contained woodland for three pigs.

Camberwell was originally one large manor, with woodland for sixty swine. Under Edward the Confessor its lord was Northmann of Mereworth, one of the great Saxon landowners, but after the Conquest William granted the manor to his sheriff Hamon. In the century that followed, Camberwell was split into several smaller manors. The area around the village of Camberwell itself became the manor of Camberwell Buckingham, sometimes called Camberwell and Peckham, a direct tenancy of the king that was held for a time by Robert de Melhent, Earl of Gloucester and illegitimate son of Henry I. Honor Oak may derive its name from a boundary tree that stood at the summit of the hill to mark the southern limit of the Honour of Gloucester; an alternative tradition attributes it to the story that Elizabeth I rested beneath it in 1602.

Among the sub-manors that included or adjoined parts of the woods was Dulwich, first mentioned in a charter of 967 by which King Edgar granted five hides there to one of his thanes, Earl Aelfheah.[7] The name was spelled variously as Dilwihs, Dylways or Dullag, and may derive from the Old English words *dill* and *wihs*, meaning 'the meadow where dill grows'. In 1127 it was granted by Henry I to Bermondsey Abbey. By 1333, its population was recorded as one hundred. Croxted Road, now a broad street of handsome Victorian houses, was then a winding lane lined with large trees, hedgerows and ditches; it is named in a charter of 1334 as Crokestret.[8]

Their proximity to London, with its constant demand for fuel and building material, meant that the woods around Dulwich were an important source of revenue for Bermondsey Abbey, and it guarded its rights to them jealously. In 1235, an Abbey employee, William Gerard, catching a woman taking brushwood from its land, wounded her in the arm and seized her cloak. She took him to the Justice in Eyre, a travelling court

THE NORMAN SETTLEMENT 19

that dealt, among other things, with woodland matters. The court found her guilty of theft, but waived the fine in view of her poverty and jailed Gerard for assault.[9] When Bermondsey Abbey leased the Manor of Dulwich to a London 'pepperer' (a spice merchant) called Thomas Dolsaly in 1359, it specified that the wood would form no part of the lease, but would be retained by the Abbey.[10] In 1530, just five years before the Abbey was dissolved, the monks leased the manor to John Scott, a Baron of the Exchequer, once again excluding the 'great wood called Dulwich woode and Dulwich common hedgerowes and underwoodes, &c.' from the lease.[11]

The name Penge is Celtic in origin, from the ancient British words corresponding to the Welsh *pen* (head) and *coed* (wood).[12] Though it is located on the eastern flank of the Norwood Ridge, it was assigned to the manor of Battersea by King Eadwig in a charter of 957: *Herto ge byreo se pude pe hatte Paenge. seofen milen. seofen furlang. and seofen fet embeganges* ('Hereto belongeth the wood that is called Penge, seven miles, seven furlongs and seven feet in circumference').[13] It was the only significant area of woodland belonging to Battersea, which the Domesday Book assessed as having 'wood for 50 swine'. The whole of the manor of Battersea, including the hamlet and common of Penge, was granted to Westminster Abbey by William the Conqueror.[14]

The manor of Lewisham belonged to the Abbey of St Pierre in Ghent, in what is now Belgium, to whom it had been granted by King Edgar in 964. The Domesday Book records that it had woodland for fifty pigs. Like Camberwell, Lewisham had been divided into several subsidiary manors by 1290, when a new law put a stop to the practice. One of these was Sydenham – the old spelling was Cypenham or Sippenham – which was given by John Besville to the priory of Rochester some time around 1400.[15] The term Westwood, referring to woods to the west of Lewisham, first appears in the thirteenth century; it continued to be used to refer to Sydenham Common until the 1800s, and still features in local street names. In 1414, when Henry V expelled foreign monks from England and confiscated their possessions, the manor was granted to the Carthusians of Sheen. New land was given over to farming, and much of Sydenham's woodland was cleared.

The manor of Lambeth, which extended from the bank of the Thames as far as West Norwood, was held by the monks of Waltham Abbey from the time of Harold I (1035–40), and was regranted to them, 'with all belonging to it; commons, arable lands, meadows, woods and waters', by Edward the Confessor (1042–66). At the time of the Domesday Book it was held by Earl Robert of Mortain, and from 1190 by the Archbishop of Canterbury. To the south, the sub-manor of Milkwood (or Milkwell) and Wickwood occupied some eighty-six acres of woodland on either side of Coldharbour Lane near what is now Loughborough Junction.[16]

Croydon, or Crogedene, is first mentioned in a charter of 809; the name derived from the Old English *croh*, meaning crocus, and *denu*, valley.[17] By the end of the Saxon period, the manor was owned by Harold Godwinson, and following his defeat and death at the Battle of Hastings, it passed to the victor, William I. The Conqueror subsequently bestowed it, along with the forest that extended over its northern part, on Lanfranc, the newly installed Archbishop of Canterbury. The Domesday Book states that '*Archiepiscopus Lanfrancus tenet in dominio Croindene*' (Archbishop Lanfranc holds Croydon in demesne) with '*Silua de CC. porcis*' (wood for two hundred pigs). Apart from a brief interval under the Commonwealth, this extensive domain, which included the largest part of the North Wood, would remain the property of the Archbishops of Canterbury until the nineteenth century.

The manor of Benchesham extended from the centre of Croydon to Beulah Hill. Soon after the Norman Conquest, its tithes were given to the Priory of St Andrew at Rochester by Godfrey de Straenbrook, a grant that was confirmed by successive archbishops.[18] At the end of the thirteenth century, Benchesham was divided into two, possibly as a result of the Second Barons' War of 1264–7. The northern part, 'Northbenchesham', became 'Northborough' and finally 'Norbury'; the southern, 'Suthbenchesham', is now known as Thornton Heath, a name first recorded in 1511. In September 1359, Thomas de Benchesham granted part of the manor to William Walkelate and his wife Joan, namely 'all his lands with all the woods, hedges and appurtenances in Benchisham in the parish of Croydon, to wit all those lands and woods which lie between the land of the said William and the wood called Northwode, and so wholly to the way called Beulestret'.[19] In 1368, the manor was granted to Walter Whitehorse, shield-bearer to King Edward III and Westminster's first recorded Black Rod, which is how it is believed to have acquired the name White Horse.[20]

THE CHARTER OF THE FORESTS

One effect of the Norman Conquest on the management of woodland was the introduction by William I of the Forest Law, under which large areas were set aside as royal hunting grounds, where no commoner was allowed to hunt, fell trees, collect firewood or allow their animals to graze. When the Domesday Book was compiled in 1086, there were already some twenty-five such forests, and under William's successors – avid huntsmen all – the practice continued apace. By the reign of Henry II (1154–89) and his sons Richard I (1189–99) and John (1199–1216), there were no fewer than 143 royal forests throughout England, covering almost a third of the country.

Although the terms 'forest' and 'woodland' are now used interchangeably, they once had quite distinct meanings.

Forest – the word itself was a Norman French import – meant an area reserved for game, and did not necessarily indicate the level of tree cover. While several large royal forests, such as Sherwood and the New Forest, were densely wooded, others were not: the Forest of Bowland in Lancashire, for example, consists of moorland and fells, with few trees on its upper slopes.

The Forest Law was bitterly resented, as it deprived many people of fuel and grazing, and was enforced by cruel punishments including mutilation and death. When the barons forced King John to sign Magna Carta at Runnymede on 15 June 1215, the abuses of royal power it addressed included 'all the evil customs relating to forests'. Two years later, these provisions were expanded to form a separate charter, the Carta de Foresta or Charter of the Forests, which was sealed by William Marshal, Earl of Pembroke, and the Papal legate Cardinal Guala Bicchieri, on behalf of the infant Henry III in St Paul's Cathedral on 6 November 1217. It was at this point that Magna Carta got its name – the 'Great Charter' – to distinguish it from the shorter, more narrowly focused piece of legislation. Both charters were reissued in 1225, when Henry had reached the age of majority, and reconfirmed in 1297. The Charter of the Forests would frame the legal status of much English woodland for at least four centuries, and remained on the statute books until 1971.

The Charter reduced the royal forests to their boundaries at the time of Henry II's coronation, returning the disafforested areas to their previous owners, and abolished capital punishments for offences such as poaching. It also guaranteed the right of free men and women to pasture animals in the woods (known as *agistment*), to allow their pigs to forage for acorns or beech mast (*pannage*), to collect wood for building and fuel (*estover*), to dig peat for fuel and clay for bricks, tiles and pottery, to draw water, to fish, to pick fruit and to gather honey.

Although no part of the North Wood had been designated a royal forest, several of the Charter's provisions had a bearing on it, as they influenced the practices of freeholders such as the Archbishop of Canterbury and the several abbeys that between them owned most of it. A freeholder's rights extended 'only to felling, not to destroying these woods, since the springs must be left in the ground that they may grow to be coverts again'; in other words, it discouraged the grubbing up of woodlands and promoted coppicing, leaving the trees to regenerate. Moreover, the custumal rights to graze animals and collect wood that it enshrined were also practised on freehold properties, and would be invoked in the course of many disputes in the centuries that followed.[21]

The power struggle between the barons and the king erupted into armed conflict again in 1264, when the North Wood appears to have become the scene of an engagement in the Second Barons' War. On 14 May that year, rebel barons led by Simon de Montfort defeated Henry III at the Battle of Lewes, taking him prisoner and forcing him to sign the Mise of Lewes, conceding many powers. Before the barons won the day, however, a contingent of Londoners fighting for them were driven from the field and fled back towards the city. Outside Croydon, they were ambushed and massacred by a detachment of the king's forces from the garrison at Tonbridge. Near the bridge on the London Road over Norbury Brook was an area later known as Battle Close; the Croydon historian Clarence Paget believed that this was the scene of the engagement, and that the North Wood provided cover for the attackers.[22]

A century later, around 1364, someone buried a hoard of gold and silver coins in Biggin Hill Coppice, part of the Archbishop of Canterbury's woods. After the hoard was discovered by a woman digging her garden in the Woodlands Estate, just south of Beulah Hill, in 1953, it was found to consist of fourteen gold and 124 silver coins. The gold was made up of the noble, a handsome 3.5-centimetre coin valued at one-third of a pound, and its fractions, while the silver was mostly groats, worth four pence each. Except for two battered silver pennies of Edward I, all the coins post-dated Edward III's recoinage of 1351, and were thus very recent when deposited. The total face value of the hoard came to £3 15s 10d, the equivalent of several thousand pounds today. What induced the owner to bury such a large sum, and what prevented him or her from retrieving it, we will almost certainly never know.[23]

A coroner's inquest at Croydon declared the find to be treasure trove, and the coins were submitted to the British Museum, which retained a small number while the rest were purchased by the Museum of London. There is a curious postscript to this story. After the finder, Joy Hulme, died in 2013, her husband Jack found a further fourteen coins in an old handbag, and handed them over to the British Museum. Apparently she had held on to them because she was dissatisfied with the amount she had been paid for the hoard. The additional coins were also declared treasure trove.[24]

WORKING THE WOODS

Once much of the wildwood had been cleared for arable and pasture, what remained became an intensively managed resource. Wood was regularly harvested using a technique known as coppicing. This consists of cutting a tree close to ground level to encourage multiple shoots to grow from the stump, or coppice stool, to provide a renewable source of timber. Since the tree already has a fully developed root system, regrowth is rapid, producing a large quantity of round, even, strong and flexible poles. These poles are then harvested at intervals of five to twenty years, depending on the species, after which the cycle starts again.

The practice was described by the Roman writers Cato and Pliny the Elder, but archaeological evidence has shown that it was already more ancient in their day than they are in ours. In waterlogged sites, where timbers are not exposed to the air, they may survive for millennia, and archaeologists are able to date them using a technique known as dendrochronology. Put simply, in a wet summer a tree will grow a wide ring, in a dry year a narrow one. The resulting patterns do not repeat themselves, and are broadly consistent over an entire climatic region such as Northwest Europe. Working backwards from timbers that can be accurately dated by other archaeological evidence or documentary sources, scientists have managed to piece together a chronology stretching back more than twelve thousand years.

As a result, we know that the Sweet Track, a Neolithic wooden causeway across a marsh in the Somerset Levels, was built in 3807 BC. The long, straight crosspieces that support its oak planking appear to be coppice poles.[25] A Bronze Age platform at Must Farm, near Peterborough, is built on oak piles dating from around 1240 BC; during a later phase of construction, around 1000–800 BC, an enclosure of coppiced ash was added.[26] Closer both in time and geographically, archaeological sites from Roman London have produced structural timbers from managed woodlands, along with charcoal that probably originated as coppice poles.[27]

The most frequently coppiced trees were oak, hazel, ash, willow, field maple and sweet chestnut. The cut wood, known as underwood, was used for many purposes, including basketwork, hurdles, the wattle used in the walls of timber-framed buildings, thatching spars, fencing, tool handles, chair and table legs, wheel spokes and axles. Everything was used: bark was peeled to tan leather; leaves were used as fodder for animals, twigs were tied up into bundles known, according to the thickness of the wood, as faggots, bavins or pimps, to serve as kindling or torches. Alongside roads and around fields where livestock grazed, trees were pollarded, a procedure similar to coppicing except that the trunk was lopped at a height of about eight or ten feet above ground so that animals could not eat the young shoots.

As Oliver Rackham observed, 'a wood need no more be destroyed by felling than a meadow is destroyed by cutting a crop of hay.'[28] Far from depleting woodlands, regular coppicing encourages them to regenerate. It is sustainable, avoiding the need to replant, and trees that are regularly cropped tend to live much longer. A well developed root system capable of sustaining a mature tree can put all its energy into producing new shoots, which it does with great speed and vigour. While old trees often retrench naturally, shedding rotten or damaged branches in order to extend their lives, coppicing speeds up the process, increasing the longevity of the tree by up to three times its natural span. It also encourages biodiversity by letting sunlight and rain penetrate to the forest floor, allowing shrubs and wildflowers to flourish, while the close-growing poles provide a haven for insects, which in turn attract birds.

Once we enter the era of documentary record, we know that woods were divided into plots, also known as coppices or copses. These would be cropped each year in rotation, so that by the time the last was felled, the first would have regrown sufficiently to be harvested. This practice helped to foster biodiversity, albeit incidentally, since it resulted in areas with different levels of light and shade and trees at various stages of growth being located in close proximity, each providing a habitat for a different range of plants and animals.

Coppices were marked out by earthen banks, hedges, or both. Hedges could be created either by using existing shrubs or young trees, particularly when woodland was cleared for arable – a process known as assart – or by planting cultivated saplings ('whips') or seed. On reaching the required height, the saplings were – and still are – laid by a technique known as pleaching, or plashing: cutting most of the way through each stem about a foot above ground, leaving a thin layer of bark and cambium, and then bending it almost horizontal, weaving it around the next in line. Any side shoots are trimmed off and threaded into the hedge. New shoots will spring upright from the horizontal pleachers, as the cut saplings are known, and when these have reached a sufficient height, the process is repeated until, after several years, a tall, strong barrier has grown up. Various species of tree and shrub can be used, including hazel, wild cherry, spindle and service tree, though inevitably thorny shrubs such as hawthorn, blackthorn and dog rose are favoured as a deterrent to people and livestock.

Archaeological evidence suggests that the practice of hedge-laying may be almost as old as coppicing. In 2005, the archaeologist Maisie Taylor found a knobbly blackthorn stick in a waterlogged pit in a Bronze Age system of fields and droveways at Fengate, near Peterborough – like Must Farm, part of the wider Flag Fen prehistoric landscape. Radiocarbon-dated to around 2000 BC, it had grown with a series of right-angled bends, indicating that it had been regularly cut and bent over to form part of a hedge.[29] At a Bronze Age site at Shaugh Moor on Dartmoor, archaeologists have found the waterlogged remains of cut hawthorn and rose in a ditch. A surviving pattern of hoofprints suggests that it was part of a stockproof barrier.[30]

The written evidence for hedging is inevitably much later. Julius Caesar, in his *Gallic Wars*, noted that the Gauls 'cut into young saplings and bent them over, and thus by the thick horizontal growth of boughs, and by intertwining with them brambles and thorns, they contrived that these wall-like hedges should serve them as fortifications which not only could not be penetrated, but not even seen through.' Anglo-Saxon charters dating back to AD 800 indicate the presence of hedges in the English countryside. Some of the hedges they document survive today, enabling ecologists to develop the science of hedgerow dating, which allows them to calculate the age of a hedge by the number of species present in a thirty-metre stretch.[31]

For a detailed description of hedge-laying techniques, however, we must wait until the sixteenth and seventeenth centuries.

One of the first printed works on agriculture in English, Anthony Fitzherbert's *Boke of Husbandry* (1534), contains instructions on how 'to plasshe or pleche a hedge':

> If the hedge be of x or xii yeres growing sythe it was first set, thane take a sharpe hatchet, or a handbill, and cutte the settes in a playne place, nyghe unto the erthe, the more halve a sonder, and bende it downe towarde the erthe, and wrappe and wynde theym together, but alwaye so that the toppe lye hyer than the rote a good quantytie, for ells the sappe wyll not renne in to the toppe kyndely, but in processe, the toppe wyll dye, and than set a lyttel hedge on the backe syde, and it shall nede noo more mendynge many yeres after.

Writing some eighty years later, Barnaby Googe, in *The Whole Art and Trade of Husbandry* (1614), describes a 'way of making of a quick-set Hedge, which our Hedgers in the Countrey doe use':

> For setting the young Sets . . . when they be growne to some greatnesse, they cut the Thorne neere to the ground, and being halfe cut and broken a sunder, they bowe it along the Hedge, and plash it. From these cuts spring up new plants, which still as they growe to any highnesse they cut them, and plash them againe: so doing continually, till the Hedge be come to his full height. This way the Hedge is made so strong, that neither Hogge nor other beast, is able to breake through it . . .

Hedges could also be planted from seed. In 1607, John Norden, surveyor of the crown woods in Berkshire, Devon, and Surrey, recommended the following method:

> The berries of the white or hawthorn, acornes, ash keyes mixed together, & these wrought or wound up in a rope of straw, wil serve . . . Make a trench at the top or in the edge

of the ditch, and lay into it some fat soyle, and then lay the rope all along the ditch, and cover it with good soile also, then cover it with the earth, and ever as any weedes or grasse begins to grow, pull it off & keepe it as cleane as may be from all hindrances: & when the seeds begin to come, keepe cattle from bruising them, and after some two or three yeares, cut the yong spring by the earth, and so will they branch and grow thicke . . .

Over the centuries, many regional styles of hedge-laying have developed: some involve driving stakes between the pleachers for additional strength, and some top the hedge with 'hethers', long stems of a flexible wood such as hazel, interwoven three or four deep, to hold the rest in place. In addition to such live or 'quick-set' hedges, dead hedging – the practice of creating a barrier by piling cut brushwood and thorns horizontally between a double row of stakes – was also common. Fitzherbert recommended building a dead hedge on top of a newly planted quickset one to prevent the tender shoots being grazed by livestock.

As we will see in the next chapter, there is abundant documentary evidence that coppicing, pollarding and hedge-laying were all in use throughout the North Wood, corroborated in places by surviving lapsed coppices, boundary pollards and ghost hedges. In order to sustain and renew the rich, biodiverse habitat fostered by these techniques of woodland management, today's reserve officers and volunteers are relearning these ancient crafts and putting them into practice again after two centuries of disuse.

THE COLLIERS OF CROYDON

The woods above Croydon also provided raw material for charcoal, the principal fuel for blacksmiths, glass-makers, bakers and brick and tile kilns until the Industrial Revolution.

A charcoal burner at work in the woods, from John Evelyn's *Sylva: or, A Discourse on Forest Trees,* London, 1679.

The charcoal burners or colliers, as they were known, burned oak and hornbeam coppice poles in conical kilns set up in the wood itself. They were clearly established in the area no later than 1386, when the Lord Mayor of London, James Andreu, ordered that four Croydon colliers, Walter Potyn, William Packe, William Hastere and Hugh le Coupere, be put in the pillory for selling short measures of charcoal.[32]

The place name 'Colliers' has long been associated with the area. A court roll dating to the 11th year of the reign of Edward IV (1471–2) charges a tenant with failing to maintain 'Colliar's bridge' – which presumably crossed Colliers' Water – in good repair.[33] An account dating from the reign of Queen Elizabeth I describes the streets of Croydon as 'deep hollow ways and very dirty, the houses generally with wooden steps into them – and the inhabitants in general were smiths and colliers.'[34, 35]

Edmund Grindal, Archbishop of Canterbury from 1575 to 1583, sued a charcoal burner named Francis Grimes because his kiln at Colliers Water was belching smoke into the archiepiscopal palace at Croydon. Grimes had influential friends in the City of London guilds, however, and the jury acquitted him. John Corbet Anderson mentions an old, ivy-covered house on Parchmore Road near Thornton Heath station that was demolished in 1897. Its gable carried the date 1590, and in the garden was a stone cairn inscribed, 'In Memorium Francis Grimes Collyer'. Grindal's successor, John Whitgift, seems to have found this local industry more a help than an annoyance. When, in 1596, he set about building the almshouses that still stand in George Street, Croydon, the accounts recorded 'a load of wood from Norwood to the Kylne' to fire the bricks.[36]

The name Grimes was traditionally given to colliers on account of their charcoal-besmirched appearance, and the character was a stock-in-trade of sixteenth- and seventeenth-century drama. In *Damon and Pythias*, a comedy by Richard Edwards first performed in 1566, one of the characters is called Grimme the Collier of Croydon. Robert Greene's *Quip for an Upstart Courtier* (1592) contains the line, 'Marry, quoth hee that lookt like Lucifer, though I am black, I am not the Divell, but indeed a collyer of Croydon.' And in 1662, a comedy entitled *Grim, the Collier of Croydon, or the Devil and his Dame* was published by an unknown author identified only as J. T.

The industry persisted well into the eighteenth century. In Emanuel Bowen's 1720 reissue of John Ogilby's popular 1675 atlas of strip maps charting Britain's main roads, beside the route from London to Brighton, a note describes Croydon as 'A large and well-built town encompassed with Hills, well stored with Wood, of which Charcole &c is made grt quantities of it being vended in London.' And as late as 1783, the antiquary Andrew Ducarel noted that 'the town [Croydon] is surrounded with hills well covered with wood, whereof great store of charcoal is made.'

By the end of the Middle Ages, though the surrounding low-lands had been cleared for arable or pasture, the North Wood still stretched across the whole of the range of hills to the east and south of the manor of Dulwich. Norwood, Knight's Hill, Gipsy Hill, Dulwich, Forest Hill, Sydenham and Penge, as well as a large part of Croydon, remained densely wooded. 'Ancient woods,' Rackham noted, 'tend . . . to be in remote places, on parish boundaries and often in the farthest corners of parishes.'[37] Despite its proximity to both London and Croydon, the North Wood was a textbook example of this phenomenon. All across the area it once encompassed, the absence of medieval churches, or any kind of building prior to the sixteenth century, corroborates the documentary evidence that, throughout the Middle Ages, it remained sparsely inhabited.

The wood was a tamer place than it had been, however, as most of the larger mammals had disappeared. Aurochs became extinct in Britain towards the end of the Bronze Age, though they clung on in Central Europe, the last one dying in Poland as recently as 1627. Lynx had gone by the time of the Norman Conquest, wolves by around 1500, and wild boar, once the quarry of kings, had been hunted to extinction by the end of the Tudor period. The European wildcat (*Felis silvestris*), once common throughout Britain, had been exterminated in southern England by the end of the sixteenth century, and today is found only in the Scottish Highlands.

Nor was it a wilderness devoid of human activity: the trees rang with the shouts of woodmen and the crack of their bill-hooks and axes as they pleached hedges and felled coppices, the hollers of swineherds as their pigs grunted and rootled for acorns, and the crackle of fire as the colliers tended their kilns. When the sun sank below the Surrey meadows, the labourers made their way back along the lanes to their homes in Croydon or Lewisham or Dulwich, leaving the woods to the owls, the bats, the foxes and other creatures of the night. But through their industry, the North Wood would fuel – quite literally – the growth of the great city that would ultimately consume it.

2

SURVEYS, SHIPS AND STATUTES

1485–1600

British historians conventionally place the transition from the Middle Ages to the early modern era in the last decades of the fifteenth century. The Earl of Richmond's victory over Richard III at Bosworth in 1485 ended both the Wars of the Roses and the Plantagenet dynasty that had ruled England for three centuries; ascending the throne as Henry VII, he ushered in the Tudor era. Seven years later, in 1492, Columbus sighted land in the Caribbean and their most Catholic Majesties Ferdinand and Isabella of Castile expelled the Moors and the Jews from Spain.

In that momentous year, John Morton, Archbishop of Canterbury and Henry's hard-taxing Chancellor, had a terrier (survey) drawn up of his lands in the Manor of Croydon. Since its purpose was to record the acreage held by each tenant and the rent due, the North Wood, which was directly managed by the archbishopric, did not fall within its scope; but because several of the tenancies bordered the wood, the terrier mentions it several times, giving a fair idea of its extent, and records, often for the first time, place names still in use in the area today.

Archbishop Morton's surveyors proceeded north from Croydon along the London Road, before turning east into Green

This village scene from Hieronymus Brunschwig's *Medicinarius*
(Strasbourg, 1505) illustrates the dependence of early modern
European economies on the produce of woodland management.
Against a backdrop of timber-framed houses, a man weaves withies
around stakes to construct a fence, while another builds a boat. The
furnace and oven of the blacksmith and the baker will have been
fuelled by charcoal from the woods. Wellcome Library, London.

Lane. To their north, they recorded an ancient estate of 120
acres 'in landes called Biggynge', and a little further on a farm of
ten acres on 'land called Beawley'. Beyond it, one Henry Burton
held sixty acres 'upward toward the common called Norwood'.
Morton's men continued along Parchmore Road and what is
now Thornton Heath High Street before turning north up
Whitehorse Road. On the high ground to their left lay the
densely wooded Manor of Whitehorse; the oaks of Grangewood
Park, which occupies part of the former estate, still tower over
Whitehorse Road today. At Easter 1493, the manor was granted
to Thomas Morton, the Archbishop's nephew.[1] The surveyors

then turned east across part of Croydon Common to Long Lane, where they recorded eleven acres of 'lande & woodgrounde buttinge on Longheath Lane', leased to a Mr Heron;[2] this may be the earliest reference to Long Lane Wood. From there, they returned to Croydon via Lower Addiscombe Road.

Half a century later, 'in the 34th yere of the reigne of our most Dred soveraigne Kynge Henrye the eight' (1543), Morton's survey was revised on behalf of Archbishop Thomas Cranmer. The new terrier added little to its predecessor other than to update the names of the tenants and the rents due, although it did identify a track – probably Whitehorse Road – as 'the waie to Northewoode'. In 1552, however, Cranmer commissioned a new survey of the 'utter boundes of the mannor of Croydon' that contains significant topographical detail about the North Wood at this period; the manuscript is now in the Bodleian Library at Oxford, just a few hundred yards from the spot where that 'most reverend father in god', as the document describes the Archbishop, was burned at the stake three years later.

His surveyors, Leonard Perpointe and Thomas Tailour, 'to gether with certayn anceante men as well of the Lordshipp of Croydon and also of divers parrishes adioyning', made the circuit of the entire manor on the 3rd and 4th of May of that year. They started west of Croydon town by an elm tree that grew beside the mill at Waddon, on the border with the manor of Beddington. From here they made their way clockwise around the manor boundary, following a hedge that zigzagged north and north-east between Mitcham Common, Thornton Heath (where they passed a pear tree which, in early May, was probably still clothed in white blossom), Pollards Hill and Norbury. At the corner of a field called Ryecroft, they turned south-east along Streatham Lane (now Streatham Common North), and followed it into the North Wood, where they came to 'a smale hill marked with a round hole'. Here, it seems, the made-up road petered out, for the surveyors advise their readers to follow the 'most used way' for three-quarters of a mile to a landmark called the High Cross – presumably a boundary tree. If the survey is correct, this would have stood on what is now Central Hill, near the junction with Hermitage Road.

From High Cross, they proceeded another half-mile to the Vicar's Oak. This important boundary tree stood just above the source of the Upper Norwood branch of the Effra, and marked the point where the parishes of Lambeth, Camberwell, Croydon, Beckenham and Battersea met on Norwood Hill; the site, at what is now the crossroads of Crystal Palace Parade, Westow Hill, Church Road and Anerley Hill, is marked by a plaque beside the gate of Crystal Palace Park. The immense oak could be seen from ten or twelve miles away and even, according to one observer, from Harrow-on-the-Hill, seventeen miles to the north-west on the far side of London.[3]

At the Vicar's Oak the party turned south along the highway running between Croydon and Penge to the foot of Gravel Hill Way, where an oak grew in an elder bush, and from there they headed west 'without any common pathe or betan way' for the distance of thirty-five rods (about two hundred yards) to another large oak marked with a cross, which grew on the bank of a boundary ditch known as the Bishop's Ditch. They then followed the ditch to the place where, 'yet in mens remem-brance', a great oak called Deadman's Oak had stood until it was felled. From here, they continued south to Penge Corner, where another tree was marked with a cross, and along the ditch that marked the boundary between Kent and Surrey. Pass-ing Ham Farm, near what is now Long Lane Wood, on their right, they began to bear south-west to complete their circuit around Addington and Purley Heath, and back to their starting point at Waddon Mill.[4]

To the north-west, in Lambeth, the road between Brixton and Streatham – today's A23 – was flanked on both sides by deep woods. The fourth edition of John Foxe's Protestant polemic *Acts and Monuments* (popularly known as the 'Book of Martyrs') describes how they afforded a refuge for fugitives. In 1533, when the preacher John Frith, arrested on a charge of heresy, was taken from the Tower of London to Croydon to plead his case before the Bishop of Winchester, his friends plotted his escape:

> You see quoth the gentleman yonder hill before us, named bristow cawsy [Brixton Causeway], 2. miles from London, there are great woodes on both sides, when we come there we will permit Frith to go into the woodes on the left hand of the way wherby he may convey himselfe into kent among his frends for he is a kentish man borne, & when he is gone we will linger an houre or twayn about the high way untill that it somewhat draws towardes the night: Then in great hast we will approch unto Streatham which is a myle and a halfe of, and an outcry in the Towne that our prisoner is broken from us into the woodes on the right hand towardes Waynisworth . . .[5]

Frith refused to flee, however, preferring martyrdom to exile, and on 4 July 1533 he was burnt at the stake at Smithfield.

OUR MOST DRED SOVERAIGNE

In 1513, determined to build a powerful national fleet, Henry VIII established the naval dockyard at Deptford, close to the North Wood with its convenient supply of oak. Henry shared the widespread belief that mature trees needed for shipbuilding were being wastefully felled for uses that could be met by shrubs or coppice wood. This led to the passing of the Statute of Woods in 1543, which laid out strict rules for the felling of timber: twelve standards (or 'stadels') per acre were to be left to grow into mature trees, and coppices had to be enclosed after cutting to protect them from grazing animals.[6]

In 1534, soon after his break with Rome, Henry ordered a valuation of all the Church lands in England and Wales with a view to taxing them. The *Valor Ecclesiasticus*, as it was known, found the annual revenue of Bermondsey Abbey to be £474 14s 4¾d, of which the Manor of Dulwich produced £13 6s 8d.[7] The *Valor* was but a prelude to the wholesale dissolution of the monasteries between 1536 and 1541. After Bermondsey Abbey was dissolved in 1538, Henry sold the Dulwich Estate to a London goldsmith called Thomas Calton and his wife Margaret for £609, but not before he had commissioned a detailed survey of its holdings. It describes the names and acreages of the various coppices in Dulwich, and even lists the age and market value of the trees in each of them, revealing the extent of the woods at the time, and a well-established system of rotational coppicing run by the monks and their tenants.[8]

Dulwich Common covered some 360 acres, of which 130 consisted of 'waste and woodland dystroyed'. Along the southern side of what is now the South Circular, where the sports grounds are located, was a series of coppices leased by the monastery to local gentry. Rigates Green, which covered sixty acres, was encircled by Dulwich Common Wood and belonged to Dulwich Manor. To the east was a wood known as Pere's Grove, held by George Duke. To the south were sixty acres of coppices 'lately felled & enclosed by Thomas Hendleye, John Lynge & William Garner . . . 30 of which are waste, the rest fit only for firewood'. To the south-west, Ling's Coppice covered thirty acres in the area now bounded by South Croxted Road and Alleyn Park, and was leased to John Lynge. To the north of Dulwich Common, the survey presents a patchwork of mixed arable farmland and coppiced woodland. Dulwich Court Farm, on what is now Court Lane, encompassed the twenty-acre

Woodyeares (Woodsire's) Coppice, which was divided into five parcels of six years' growth.[9]

Bermondsey Abbey also owned 'the wood called Mylkewell woodde, in the parish of Lambeth,' near today's Loughborough Junction. This too was seized by the Crown, and leased to the diplomat, courtier and poet Sir Thomas Wyatt in 1540.[10] Westminster Abbey was also dissolved that year, and its manor of Battersea, including outlying Penge, became the property of the Crown, and 'all the woodes of Penge were felled'.[11] At the time of the dissolution, the manor was leased from the abbey by Henry Rydon (variously spelled Ridon or Roydon); on 10 March 1540/1 the Court of Augmentations renewed his lease for a term of twenty-one years, and in 1563 he obtained a further lease of all the 'tymbre trees and pollardes' in the manor of Battersea, including Penge.[12]

A little way to the north-west, 'between Deane Green and the wood called Norwood, and common called Leigham Common', the manor of Levehurst, or Leffhurst, covered much of what is now West Norwood. An inquisition of 1523 stated that it comprised one hundred acres of arable, eight of meadow, fifty-six of pasture and thirty of woods. In 1543 Sir John Leigh sold the manor to Henry VIII, but Archbishop Cranmer claimed he had no right to do so as he did not own the freehold, but had leased the estate from him. A commission set up in 1563 mapped the manor in detail, showing the 'Norwood' adjoining it to the south and east; it is the earliest known map to show part of the North Wood. The commission reported that Sir John had rented the manor from the Archbishop for ten shillings a year, but could not decide whether the adjacent land was freehold or leasehold, possibly because much of it was recently felled woodland whose boundaries had not been accurately mapped. As a result of the dispute, Levehurst Manor seems to have languished in the hands of absentee landlords for much of the next two centuries. [13]

Immediately to the north of Levehurst Manor, at Lambeth Deane, was Knight's Hill, home to the Knight family since the fifteenth century. Henry Rydon – Harry to his family and friends – was married to the daughter of the house, Elizabeth Knight. Her brother John, who had inherited the estate when still young and inexperienced, was 'pitifully snared' by one Sir Thomas Newneham, to whom he became deeply indebted. In April 1558, Newneham obliged him to lease Knight's Hill to him, and forcibly evicted him before he could remove his belongings, leaving him 'most shamfully spoylled dispossessed and disherited of all his substans and welth' – an allegation Newneham denied.

While out hunting in the area with friends on Sunday 12 June, Knight took the opportunity to enter the house, hoping to retrieve some of his things, but Newneham's servants, armed with roasting spits, cornered him in the hall. Fearing they were 'like to have killed him', a friend passed a bow and arrow through the window; after Knight fired a warning shot, the servants fled, but locked him in for the next three hours.

Harry Rydon was entertaining friends at the manor house in Battersea when a boy brought the news of his brother-in-law's predicament. The party, which included Knight's brother (another Henry), had just arrived by river from Lambeth, but immediately set out for Knight's Hill. According to the action that Newneham brought against them in the Star Chamber, they assembled a group of twenty-one 'unrewlie and ryottuus persons . . . beynge all well weaponed wyth bowes arrows Bylles staves pykes swords and bucklers and other weapons', entered the house 'wyth force and armes', and removed various possessions, including a horse and saddle from the stable.

Knight and his fellow defendants strenuously disputed these allegations as 'craftely contryved & wrought by froward and subtill invention', asserting that they had approached the house peaceably to negotiate for his release, and had summoned the village constable and a justice of the peace from Camberwell to prevent any mischief being done. Henry Knight, for his part, denied carrying 'any maner of weapon save onely a dagger which he commonly useth to weare in quiet and peaceable maner', while Rydon, it was claimed, had only a billhook. Whatever really took place that afternoon, Newneham's men eventually agreed to release their prisoner, and Rydon's party made their way back to Battersea.[14]

Frustratingly, we will probably never know whether the court chose to believe Newneham or Knight. The Star Chamber – so called because of the star-spangled ceiling of the room where it met in the Palace of Westminster – was abolished by Parliament in 1641 after Charles I made it notorious by using it to punish his political opponents, and the book containing its judgments, kept separately from the witness statements quoted above, disappeared soon afterwards.

BEATING THE BOUNDS

In the absence of detailed maps, the vicar of each parish and members of his congregation would 'beat the bounds' on Rogation Day (25 April), parading along its borders carrying banners, noting landmarks, which they whipped with sticks of willow, hazel or birch, and cutting crosses on trees. At important places, the priest would recite a prayer, a custom that gave rise to place names such as Gospel Oak in North London, and the Vicar's Oak itself. These perambulations traditionally included both elderly men and teenage boys, the former to remember as many earlier perambulations as possible, the latter to transmit the memory of the present survey far into the future. Sometimes the unfortunate youths were themselves whipped or had their fingers pricked with pins – a practice known as 'giving points' – at significant markers to instil the place in their memories.

Much food and drink was consumed during these processions, to the extent that the preacher Richard Taverner, in his
Epistles and Gospelles (1540), fumed that 'These solemne and
accustomable processions and supplications be nowe growen
into a right foule and detestable abuse . . . which be spent in
ryoting and belychere.' The perambulations to the Vicar's Oak
were no exception. The Lambeth churchwardens' accounts for
1583 record expenses of two shillings and sixpence 'when we
went our perambulation at viccars oke in rogation weke', with
an additional sixpence 'for a drinkinge ye same daye'; the following year, they record another two and six 'layd out in going our
perambulacion to viccars oke' for the 'churchewardens and
other honyst men of the paryshe'; while in 1586 the same sum
was spent 'for makinge honest men drinke when we went to
vicar's oke in perambulacion'. By 1612, the bill had risen to six
shillings and sixpence 'for a kilderkin [an eighty-one-litre barrel]
of bere and other Charges spent on the parishioners at the
Viccars Oke in o^r perambulacion'.[15]

Given the quantities of alcohol downed in the course of these
surveys, it is perhaps not surprising that memories became
blurred and disputes arose. In 1568, or shortly before, Henry
Rydon instructed his men to fell seven acres of the north-western
end of Gravel Hill Coppice, on the edge of Penge Common, for
firewood. Before he could collect the cut wood, Peter Marshe,
woodward to the Archbishop of Canterbury, ordered its seizure,
insisting that the coppice lay within the manor of Croydon.
Under his supervision, some twenty cartloads of wood were
hauled away and stacked in the woodyard of the Archbishop's
palace at Croydon.[16]

The Archbishop, Matthew Parker, was one of the great prel-
ates of the Elizabethan age, a founder of the Anglican Church
and a favourite of the queen, having been chaplain to her mother,
Anne Boleyn. Nine translations from the psalms that he
compiled were set to music by Thomas Tallis; the third of these,

'Why Fum'th in Sight', formed the basis of Vaughan Williams's *Fantasia on a Theme of Thomas Tallis*. Nor was Rydon a poor tenant farmer, but the *de facto* lord of the manor of Battersea, which he leased directly from the Crown. He also possessed a sizeable estate in Beckenham, just over the county boundary in Kent, and lands in Lewisham.[17] The resulting dispute dragged on long after his death in July 1568. An inquiry held at the manor court at Battersea in April 1572 to determine the boundary with Croydon failed to settle the matter,[18] and in 1577 Rydon's widow and heir Elizabeth filed a bill of complaint in the Court of Exchequer, which dealt with civil claims, against Hugh Gouldwell, Randall Snowe, Mathew Dawes and other participants in the confiscation of the wood.[19]

In the spring of 1578, some thirty witnesses made their way from Croydon and Penge to Battersea to give evidence before the Barons of the Court of Exchequer. They were mostly men in their fifties and sixties; land managers, labourers, yeoman farmers, woodsmen. Among the Croydon contingent were Richard Fynche, the vicar, Peter Marshe, and the Archbishop's surveyor George Withers; testifying on Elizabeth Rydon's behalf were Thomas Kempsall and Thomas Holcrofte, MP for Midhurst in Sussex and bailiff of Westminster, who was married to Henry Rydon's daughter Joan.[20] Their statements are sometimes confused – they were, after all, recalling events that had taken place a decade earlier – and often contradictory, depending on which side of the argument they stood. Much of their evidence was hearsay – 'he hathe hearde reporte' – which was not inadmissible at this period.

The dispute hinged on the route taken by the parishioners of Croydon and Battersea to mark out their respective boundaries, and the evidence given in court includes much interesting detail about the topography of the North Wood at this period. The Croydon party proceeded from the High Cross, which stood beside the beaten track from Streatham Lane to the Vicar's Oak, where they would carve crosses on the Croydon side of the trunk. They then turned south down Gravel Hill along a track called Gravelly Way (today's Anerley Hill), keeping the coppice on their right, until they came to a quarry – presumably a gravel pit – where an oak grew in an elder bush. About twenty years previously, however, a Penge man called Robert Lowen (who had since died), had felled the Elder Oak. This act was 'muche misliked' by the Croydon parishioners, who thought he had 'done evill . . . for that it was a boundarye oke of their parishe', and continued to carve their crosses on its stump during their perambulations. From here, they crossed a stile into the lower end of Gravel Hill Coppice and headed south-west to an oak that grew on the bank of the Bishop's Ditch, which ran in a south-easterly direction dividing Croydon from Beckenham and Penge.

Several elderly Croydon parishioners testified that this was their traditional route, which they had taken since the time of William Warham, Archbishop of Canterbury from 1503 to his death in 1532, and continued to follow under his successors Thomas Cranmer and Reginald Pole, and that the priests would regularly read a gospel at both the Vicar's and Elder Oaks. Alice Foden, the wife of a Croydon yeoman and the only woman to give evidence, remembered 'children to have beene beaten at the said Elder ok and to have pointes given them in remembrance of the boundary'. William Jackson, a Croydon butcher, told the court that some fifty years previously, beside the Vicar's Oak, his father 'did there pinche him by the eare, and did byd him remember the boundary oke of Croydon parish'. They and other witnesses insisted that the coppice was part of the Archbishop's common, from which they were accustomed to gather firewood, with one asserting that it 'was never inclosed till of late yeares, sence which enclosure it hath beene reputed and taken that wronge hathe beene done to the See of Cant[erbury] by the enclosing therof'.

In recent years, though, things had started to go amiss with their perambulations. On occasion Richard Fynche, who was appointed vicar in 1560, strayed from the route taken by his predecessors. Once, apparently guided by Sir Nicholas Herne (also spelled Heron), a career soldier who owned a large estate at Addiscombe, he passed from Vicar's Oak along the top of the hill where Church Road now runs to a stile at the upper end of Gravel Hill Coppice, thus leaving the wood on his *left* hand, and descended the hill by a path through the coppice to the Elder Oak. Here, finding the path 'overgrowen with bushes', the parishioners crossed the Bishop's Ditch into Penge. 'Nowe you muste remember,' some of them warned their fellows, 'that wee are owte of our owne boundes, & goe here butt for our ease.'

Fynche and other witnesses told the court that while they were beating the bounds, Thomas Kempsall had stopped them at the stile and prevented them from entering the coppice. Kempsall was a tenant of Rydon, who was godfather to one of his sons, and a beneficiary of his will.[21] John Wakerell of Croydon testified that after Kempsall had turned them away, he heard one of his fellow parishioners mutter, 'Lett the Lordes righte their owne causes we will trouble ourselves no more about ytt.'

Several witnesses recalled an attempt at mediation that had taken place the previous September, around Michaelmas, when the Archbishop's surveyor, John Scott, met parishioners from both Croydon and Battersea at the Vicar's Oak. The Battersea contingent came armed with a 'plotte', or map; the Croydon men attempted to show Scott the route they took on their perambulation from the Vicar's Oak through Gravel Hill Coppice. Once in the coppice, however, 'they stoode still all in a doubte which waie to goe, so that some of them saide if olde Curtesse of Beckenham were here he woulde tell us which waie wee should goe,' and so the issue remained unresolved.

The Battersea parishioners also drew upon precedent to support their claim to the coppice. They perambulated their bounds in the opposite direction to the Croydonites, and insisted that the boundary was a northerly continuation of the Bishop's Ditch they called the Bound Ditch; this ran up Gravel Hill to the Vicar's Oak along the western edge of the disputed coppice, which therefore stood fully within their parish. They too appear to have had trouble forcing their way through the undergrowth and had taken the easier route via Gravelly Way, but only, they insisted, because some of them were on horseback and others were elderly, and they had sent their boys through the bushy terrain along the Bound Ditch to mark the correct border. Several of them attested that the coppice had first been felled in the reign of Edward VI, some thirty years earlier, and that 'the kinge had the profette of the sale thereof'; to challenge Rydon's right to the coppice, therefore, would be to challenge the ownership of his landlord, the queen.

Thomas Holcrofte, giving evidence on behalf of Elizabeth Rydon, told the court that he had been to see Archbishop Parker in his gallery at Lambeth Palace to discuss compensation for the confiscated wood, and that the Archbishop had told him that 'beinge in his Chamber at Croidon and looking owt of his windowe erlie on a morning,' he 'sawe a nomber of cariages loden with woodd brought in to his yeard'. On asking where they had come from, he was informed that it was wood that Roydon had felled, and that Marshe had brought in. 'Before that tyme,' the Archbishop had told Holcrofte, 'he knewe not of the same woodd.'

It also emerged that Archbishop Parker had subsequently written to his steward, Richard Wyndelsey, instructing him to tell Holcrofte that he 'would not mayntaine the parishioners of Croidon against Mr Ridon in the matter . . . touchinge the carrying awaie of wood'. Wyndelsey himself testified that the Archbishop had commanded him to tell Holcrofte that 'he

woulde not mayntaine the parishioners of Croydon to continewe
the wronge don, whereof [he] did complayne'. Whether Parker's
letter was sent before or after Queen Elizabeth visited him at his
palace in Croydon for seven days in July 1573 is unclear, but he
was presumably reluctant to fall out with his sovereign over a
few loads of wood.

In June 1578 the court ruled in Elizabeth Rydon's favour, and
ordered the defendants to make an exact survey of the area.[22]
This was not done, and the following May the court found them
in contempt and breach of its order, and issued an injunction
commanding them to desist from interrupting Rydon in her
quiet possession of the wood.[23] The judgment does not appear to
have gone down well in Croydon; in the margin of Cranmer's
1552 survey, at the point where it reaches the boundary with
Penge, someone has written, 'Here was a coppes wrongfullie
enclosed by the fermer of the manor of Batterseye reproved by
the tennaunts of Croydon and the countree yet sufered so to
remayne for the safgard of the springe.'[24]

At times, these boundary disputes spilled over into physical
violence. In 1588, the Lambeth parishioners appear to have come
under attack while beating the bounds at Vicar's Oak, as the
churchwardens' accounts record the cost of drawing up a letter
'to Sommon Hammond of Penge to appeare before my L[ord] his
grace for molestinge us in our perambulacion'.[25] Almost a
century later, the Lambeth perambulators attempted a bold act
of territorial annexation deep inside a neighbouring parish. On
Holy Thursday (12 May) 1670,

Mr Tompkins ye Parson of Lambeth together with some of
his parishioners came into our outward Court of Gods gift
Colledge in Dulwich and would have marked one of ye Elmes
in their procession as pretending our Colledge did stand in
ye parish of Lambeth, alledging that some of ye boyes of their
parish had marked a tree that stood at ye hither corner about

two yeares before, but ye master and Warden forbad them to
proceed any further therein assuring them upon knowledge
wee stood in ye parish of Camberwell and ye Warden himself
cut out that marke.[26]

Given that the nearest part of the parish boundary lay more than
half a mile to the north of the college, it seems odd that Mr
Tompkins and his flock can have thought themselves within
their bounds. Until the boundary was regularised in 1900,
however, a salient of Lambeth protruded south into neighbouring Camberwell as far as Half Moon Lane. Following its eastern
flank down Red Post Hill they must, for whatever reason, have
failed to turn right into Half Moon Lane and continued straight
on through Dulwich Village until they were turned back by the
dignitaries of Alleyn's college.

TIMBER AND TRAPPING

Along with Bermondsey Abbey, Henry VIII also suppressed
Lewisham Priory and confiscated its lands, including the five-
hundred-acre Westwood. After her accession to the throne in
1553, his daughter Mary brought England back into the fold of
the Catholic Church, and returned the priory to the Carthusians. The friars did not enjoy their restoration for long; after
Queen Mary died on 17 November 1558, her Protestant half-
sister and successor Elizabeth sent them packing again. Her
motive was not only, or even primarily, religious; like her father,
Queen Elizabeth I was keen to ensure a plentiful supply of timber
for shipbuilding, and in October 1559, less than a year into
her reign, she issued directions to her Lord High Treasurer, the
Marquess of Winchester, that the trees in the Westwood, 'near
Lewisham, Kent' should be reserved for the purpose of the
shipbuilding.[27] In the same year, Parliament passed an Act 'that
Timber shall not be felled to make Coals for the making of Iron'

within fourteen miles of the sea or any navigable river;[28] this was followed in 1584 by an 'Act for the Preservation of Timber in the Wilds of the Counties of Sussex, Surrey and Kent'.[29]

A persistent legend, repeated in several local histories, claims that Francis Drake's *Golden Hind* was constructed of oak from Great Stakepit Coppice, which stood just to the north of what is now Beulah Hill in the Archbishop of Canterbury's woods. Given that the ship was built at Plymouth, this is highly improbable, since there was abundant timber much closer to hand. A more likely candidate would be Drake's later flagship, the forty-six-gun *Revenge*, which was built at Deptford in 1577.

The fact that the timber laws had to be re-enacted several times suggests that they were often disregarded. In 1609, James VI and I issued a 'Proclamation for the Preservation of Woods', which complained that 'great spoils and devastations' were being committed 'not only by bordering Inhabitants, but also by woodwards, keepers, and other of our owne inferior Officers'. These abuses included the felling, along with the underwood, of trees reserved for timber under statute. 'For the better maintenance and present supply of the especiall wants of our Navie,' James decreed, 'wee have appointed and authorised our Officers of the same . . . to elect and make choice in every of our Counties assigned for present sale, all such Timber and Trees, as . . . shall be thought fit to be reserved for the especiall use of our said Navie, and the same to marke for that purpose.'[30]

This concern was echoed by the agricultural writer Arthur Standish in his 1613 treatise *New Directions of Experience to the Commons Complaint . . . for the Planting of Timber and Fire-wood*. Printed 'by the encouragement of the Kings most excellent Majesty', it noted that the statutory requirement to leave twelve standard trees per acre of coppice 'is by few men performed' because the shadows they cast inhibited the growth of the underwood.[31]

The Tudor monarchs were concerned not only about the
kingdom's navy, but also its food security. In 1533, after a series
of bad harvests led to rural unrest, Henry VIII's administration
passed an 'Act for the Destruction of Crowes and Rokes' aimed
at protecting the harvest from scavenging birds. 'Innumerable
nombre of Rookes, Crowes and Choughs,' it complained, 'do
daily brede and increase throughout this Realme, which do yearly
destroye, devoure and consume a wonderfull and mervelous
quantitie of Corne and Greyne of all kyndes.' The act instructed
landowners and tenants to offer a cash reward to anyone
bringing in the head of any of the specified 'vermin': two pence
for 'every 12 olde Crowes, Rookes or Choughes' that were
caught.[32]

Under Elizabeth, the legislation was strengthened and its
scope enlarged. In 1566, a new Act for the Preservation of Grain
put a price on the heads of nineteen species of bird and thirteen
mammals:

> For the Heades of everie Foxe or Gray [badger] twelve pence.
> And for the head of everie Fitchers [polecat], Polcatte,
>   Wesell, Stote, Fayre Bade [probably marten] or Wylde
>   Catte one penny.
> For the Heades of everie Otter or Hedgehogges two pence.
> For the Heades of everie three Rattes or Twelve Myse one
>   peny.
> For the Heads of every Moldewarpe or Wante [both names
>   for moles] one half penny.[33]

The two Acts, collectively known as the Tudor Vermin Acts,
initiated a sustained persecution that would last more than
three hundred years. Any species – badger, otter, fox, wild cat,
polecat, pine marten, red kite, hen harrier, green woodpecker,
jay, kingfisher – that competed with humans for grain, fruit,
game birds or fish was to be exterminated. Bullfinches were

targeted for stripping fruit buds, while hedgehogs were slaughtered in the mistaken belief that they sucked milk from the udders of sleeping cows.

The North Wood was no exception. The 1566 Act transferred responsibility for paying the bounty from landowners to local parishes, so the payments were recorded in the churchwardens' accounts. Of the parishes that encompassed the wood, the financial records of Croydon are unfortunately lost as a result of the fire that consumed the church of St John the Baptist in 1867. But where they survive, these ledgers offer a vivid picture of the everyday life of a parish through the humdrum details of its income and expenditure. At St Mary at Lambeth, mother church of an area stretching from the Thames to the high ground of Norwood, the disbursements included the sexton's wages, laundering vestments, 'syxpenny nayles', payment to the bellringers for a peal to celebrate Queen Elizabeth's birthday, 'hollie and Ivie' at Christmas, 'the brecfast and dyner of the Churchwardens & sydemen at the visitacyon at Saynt Mary Overes [now Southwark Cathedral] the Munday next after Michaelmas', and 'item for my dyner at Lundon'. The expenses for 1567–8 include fifteen shillings 'paid to Mathew Allen for to distribute for the preservacion of greyne according to a statute thereof made'. In the following year, eleven shillings and eleven pence was 'pd. out of the Church box for vermyn', and in 1570 the wardens paid ten shillings to one John Fletcher, also 'for vermyn'.

Over at St Giles, Camberwell, a parish that stretched through the woods to the summit of Sydenham Hill, the churchwardens were more specific about the animals killed, most of the victims being hedgehogs. In 1692 they paid fourpence for one; in 1694 they gave Goodman Toombs the same sum 'for a hedgehogg'; and in October 1698 '3 hedghoggs and 1 polecat' earned a parishioner two shillings. The expenses for 1699 reveal a small orgy of killing. In April, 'Mr Brown's drover' was awarded 6d for a badger; in March, the wardens paid 'Goodman Lett for 9

Hedgehooggs Jnº: [John] Hart for one – Buckles boy for One, pd. Wm. Lett for four, Anthony Cock for five George Buddel for foure', which came to a total of eight shillings, while Thomas Nash received three shillings 'for three polecats'. Later that year the wardens disbursed one shilling and fourpence 'for seven hedghoggs', and in 1700 three shillings 'for 3 hedghoggs and 2 polecat'. A massacre of twenty-three hedgehogs in 1701 cost the parish 7s 8d, while in 1702 they paid out one shilling for six badgers.[34] For some reason, a badger only merited twopence while a hedgehog raised twice as much.

It is probably going too far to argue that the Tudor Vermin Acts were responsible for denuding the English countryside of its wildlife; persecution by gamekeepers in the nineteenth century and industrial farming in the twentieth are more likely causes. It may well be that the legislation was no more observed in practice than the Acts for the Preservation of Timber. Arthur Standish certainly believed that people were not killing enough 'vermin' because the rewards were too meagre; increase the bounty, he argued, and the pests would be eliminated once and for all, reducing the need for payments in the long run.[35] The Camberwell accounts appear to bear this out. Catching hedgehogs seems to have been an occasional source of ready cash for the poorer inhabitants of the parish, rather than a sustained activity. Several years go by in which no vermin payments are recorded at all, and the killing of three hedgehogs and one polecat over the whole of 1700 in a parish that covered the southern half of the modern Borough of Southwark is unlikely to have kept pace with the animals' rate of reproduction. The records do, however, afford us a glimpse of fauna – particularly small mammals such as badgers, polecats, stoats and weasels – long since eradicated from the North Wood, at least partly as a result of the legislation.

A ROUGH WASTE PERCELL OF GROUNDE

The Vermin Acts and statutes for the preservation of trees represented a new approach to the countryside, promoted at the
highest level of the state: productivity was to be maximised, and
anything that might reduce it eliminated. This coincided with
increasing pressure from landowners to enclose and develop
common land where, for centuries, local people had enjoyed
custumal rights to graze their livestock and collect firewood.
Just as wild animals were now classified as 'vermin', common
land was perceived to be 'waste' that needed to be improved in
the interests of productivity.

The Tudor monarchs had resisted calls for enclosure, fearing – correctly, as it turned out – that it would give rise to
agrarian unrest. But after the accession of James VI and I in
1603, government began to look more favourably on the practice. In January 1607, the surveyor Raphe Treswell the Younger
drew up a plan of 'A Rough Waste Percell of grounde full of
hills and Fursyes as appeareth belonging to the Kinge's Majestye
And Conteyninge 347 Acres'.[36] The area shown by Treswell was
the Westwood, or Sydenham Common. His sketch closely
matches Rackham's description of a typical common's 'strag-
gling concave outline tapering away gradually into the roads
that cross' it.[37] To the north, Coulton's Wood – elsewhere
described as Coleson's Coppice – had been enclosed by Henry
VIII and awarded to the Calton family. The south-western
corner of Oak of Honor Wood, it occupied the area now
bounded by Horniman Drive, Dunoon Road, Devonshire Road
and Ewelme Road. At the other end of the common, south of
today's Westwood Hill, was Cooper's Wood, enclosed at around
the same time.[38]

Treswell's map was probably created in connection with a
dispute that arose when Henry Newport, a Lewisham landowner and member of the royal household with the resounding

title Yeoman of the Boiling House, approached King James for permission to enclose the common. The local people petitioned James's Secretary of State, the Earl of Salisbury, claiming that 'above 500 poore householders with wives and manye children greatly relieved by sayde Common and would be utterly undone yf yt should be unjustly taken from them.' After an inconclusive commission of inquiry at Greenwich, the case came before the Court of Exchequer in 1608, which found in the parishioners' favour.

Over the next six years Newport and his associates Innocent Lanier, one of the king's musicians, and Robert Raynes, Sergeant of the Buckhounds, held 'secret inquisitions' to work out how to claim the land. In 1614, they succeeded in persuading the king to grant them a sixty-year lease for 347 acres of Westwood, and began to fence off the common, driving off the parishioners' livestock. This time, resistance was organised by the vicar of Lewisham, Abraham Colfe, who led a march of a hundred parishioners through the City of London to present a petition to the king, who passed it to the Privy Council. After Newport's men attacked women gathering firewood, tempers flared and a riot broke out. Cattle were found slaughtered, and the skins of dead sheep were hung from bushes. On 16 October the case came before the Barons of the Exchequer and a jury selected to include no one from any of the neighbouring parishes. They found that Westwood was an ancient common with all the attendant rights, and the attempt to enclose it was thwarted – for the time being.[39]

3

THE WORLD TURNED
UPSIDE DOWN

1600–1700

Newport's attempt to enclose the Westwood may have been defeated, but the new, profit-orientated approach to land management it represented would steadily gain ground over the next two centuries. One of the most popular and influential books of the late sixteenth century was Thomas Tusser's *Five Hundred Points of Good Husbandry* (1573). An expanded version of his earlier *A Hundred Good Points of Husbandry*, it framed practical advice on farming and estate management, bizarrely, in verse. 'The countrie enclosed I praise,' Tusser wrote, 'the tother delighteth not me/ For nothing the wealth it doth raise/ to such as inferior be.' Enclosure, he argued, created 'more worke for the labouring man', while the commons encouraged the poor 'not to live by their wurke/ but theevishlie loiter and lurke'.

It was an argument much repeated over the decades that followed. The surveyor and mapmaker John Norden thought that 'one acre inclosed, is woorth one and a halfe in Common, if the ground be fitting thereto,' though he added the warning that 'Lords should not depopulate by usurping inclosures'.[1] The Surrey landowner Richard Weston, writing around 1650, had no such qualms, vigorously echoing Tusser's sentiments in prose:

I know that poor people will cry out against me, because I call these waste lands; but it's no matter; I desire ingenious Gentlemen seriously to consider, whether or no these lands might not be improved very much by the husbandry of Flanders, viz. by sowing Flax, Turnips, great Clover grass . . . Whether the rottenness and scabbiness of sheep, murrain of cattle, diseases of horses, and in general all diseases of cattle, do not generally proceed from Commons? Whether Commons do not rather make poor, by causing idleness, than maintain them; and such poor, who are trained up rather for the gallows or beggary, than for the commonwealth's service?[2]

Human beings had of course been exploiting and reshaping the landscape for their own ends since the Neolithic, but this was a radical extension of what the American ecologist Aldo Leopold called 'the Abrahamic concept of land' as 'a commodity belonging to us' which it was not only our right but our moral duty – implicit in the term waste – to exploit to the maximum. The King James Bible, published in 1611, explicitly commands us, in Genesis 1:24, to 'Be fruitful, and multiply, and replenish the earth, and subdue it: and have dominion over the fish of the sea, and over the fowl of the air, and over every living thing that moveth upon the earth.'

'The whole Earth,' wrote Richard Surflet in the preface to his translation of Charles Estienne's *Maison Rustique*, 'was once a Tempe, an Eden . . . and the assigned possession and natural inheritance of man and woman, to labour and live in,' but 'through their sinne it was cursed.'[3] As a result of Adam and Eve's fall from grace, the earth was rank with stones, weeds and vermin. It was the husbandman's Christian duty to cleanse the land of such imperfections and return it to an ordered, Edenic state.[4]

'By the observing of these small directions,' Standish advised the 'good Reader' of his *Commons Complaint*, 'thou mayest

performe some part of the cause of thy creation, by giving glorie
to thy Creator, honour, pleasure and profit to thy King, Countrey, and to thy selfe also . . .' Other books on land management
reinforced the idea with scriptural exhortations. Norden, a
staunch Protestant and author of numerous devotional tracts,
prefaced his *Surveyors Dialogue* (1607) with an injunction from
Proverbs 17:2: 'A discreet servant shall have rule over an
unthrifty sonne, and he shall divide the heritage among the
brethren.' Barnaby Googe's *The Whole Art and Trade of
Husbandry* (1614) cites Genesis 3:19 on its title page: 'In the
sweat of thy face shalt thou eate thy bread till thou be turned
againe into the ground, for out of it wast thou taken.'

Developing at a time when England was colonising other
parts of the globe, including Ireland, Virginia and the Caribbean
(Googe himself had taken part in a military expedition to
Ireland in 1574),[5] this mindset was to have far-reaching consequences in which we can trace the origins of our present
ecological crisis. When human society was made up of small
communities separated by wide expanses of untamed land, our
settlements mere pinpricks of light in the vast darkness of the
pre-industrial night, the biblical injunction made sense; since
then, however, we have gone on multiplying and subduing and
exercising dominion to the point where the Earth may never
recover.

Such arguments, moreover, ran in parallel with the development of a biblical justification for slavery. In his *True Discourse
of the Three Voyages of Discoverie* (1577), the mariner George
Best, who had accompanied Martin Frobisher on two of his
journeys to the Canadian Arctic, drew on Genesis to argue that
Africans were the descendants of Ham, whose son Canaan was
cursed by Noah with the words, 'a servant of servants shall he
be.' The theme was taken up by the traveller and poet George
Sandys, treasurer to the Virginia Company, in his *The Relation
of a Journey begun an. Dom. 1610*, where he claimed that

Africans were the descendants of Chus, 'the sonne of cursed Cham; as are all of the complexion, Not so by reason of their Seed, nor heat of the Climate . . . but rather from the Curse of Noe upon Cham.'

These Elizabethan and Jacobean ideologues were the conquistadors of nature. Bible in one hand, billhook in the other, they sought to subdue the Earth and its people to what they saw as God's will – which conveniently coincided with their own interests. In their books and pamphlets we see the 'basic paradoxes' that Leopold identified three centuries later when viewing the environmental degradation wrought on the American Midwest by intensive farming: 'Man the conqueror *versus* man the biotic citizen; science the sharpener of his sword *versus* science the searchlight on his universe; land the slave and servant *versus* land the collective organism.'

It was Norden who first put the North Wood on a printed map. His *Surrey*, originally surveyed in 1595, was engraved by William Kip and published in the antiquary William Camden's *Britannia*, a county-by-county description of Britain, in 1607. The map shows, on a small scale, woods and hills stretching north from Croydon towards Dulwich. To the east are 'Pensgreene' (Penge), 'Lewesham' and 'Peckham Rey'. The River Pool is shown flowing from Penge to join the Ravensbourne at Lewisham, though neither river is named. Norden's survey also provided the basis for John Speede's more detailed *Surrey, Described and Divided into Hundreds*. This magnificent example of Jacobean cartography was engraved by Jodocus Hondius of Amsterdam for Speede's atlas *The Theatre of the Empire of Great Britaine*, published in 1611/12. On both maps, the scattering of trees and hills is pictorial and impressionistic, rather than a precise delineation of the kind found on estate plans, though many details, such as the windmill that tops Sydenham Hill, would be copied for more than a century to come.

No single map of the period shows the whole of the North Wood in detail, however. Instead, we must assemble a composite picture, like a jigsaw puzzle, from those parts of it that appear on estate maps and written descriptions during the course of the seventeenth century. Around 1600, a surveyor, thought to be Raphe Treswell the Elder, prepared a map of the area around Brockley Green on behalf of the London charitable school Christ's Hospital, which owned much of the land. Orientated with north-west at the top, the map is carefully drawn, with the land belonging to Christ's Hospital shaded in yellow and the ownership and acreage of each plot indicated; trees, ponds, houses, a barn and even gates and stiles are sketched in. The main features of today's road layout are already evident, with Brockley Road running from north to south, labelled 'Brokly Lane alias Croydon Lane'; to its east is the irregular polygon formed by Ivy Road (here named Ivy Lane) and Brockley Grove that now encloses Brockley Cemetery. To the south of it, the main road widens into the triangle of Brockley Green.

At the far south of the map, the Hospital owned an eight-acre wood called Ravens Nest; this appears to be the northernmost spur of Oak of Honor Wood. Spreading to the north-west from a narrow frontage of the green is the triangular, nine-acre Gorne Wood; beyond it, the long, narrow strip of Longdowne Wood runs between open fields. Beyond the cornfields to the north are two small woods, the two-acre Barnefield Wood and four-acre Drakes Land Wood. North-east of the Hospital's land, the edge of Hatcham Wood is shown.

Over in Battersea, a survey was carried out in February 1604/5 on behalf of Oliver St John, who had come into possession of the manor on his marriage to Henry Rydon's widowed daughter Joan. A hot-tempered man, St John had been forced to flee the country after killing the navigator George Best in a duel in 1584, and then forged a career as a soldier on the Continent and in Ireland, of which he was later appointed Lord Deputy.

The survey of his lands included a perambulation of 'The Mete and Bounde of the hamlett of Penge', which was, as we have seen, a detached portion of the manor and parish of Battersea. Given the hamlet's location between the manor of Dulwich to the north and the Archbishop of Canterbury's domains in Croydon to the south, this description of its borders tells us as much about these adjoining areas as about Penge itself.

The surveyors began at the hamlet's northernmost point, where it adjoined Rockhills Common, an outlying possession of the manor of Beckenham. From a crossroads 'where sometime a Crosse did stand called Lowcrosse', they followed the Shire Ditch, a tributary of the Pool that formed the boundary between Kent and Surrey, eastwards across what is now Crystal Palace Park, past 'a house of Mr Leighes called Abbette on the north syde'. (The place names Rock Hill and Low Cross are still in use in the area today.)

Passing along Parish Lane, they reached the edge of a wood belonging to 'Lord Ridon'. There they turned south, still following the stream, until they reached the main road from Beckenham. Here, the road crossed the stream over 'Willmoores Bridge', later known as Sheep-Wash Bridge. Standing 'halfe in Kent and halfe in Surrey', the bridge was located where Kent House Road now meets the High Street. From there, they headed south-west along the stream – later known as the River Willmore – which here formed the boundary with the parish of Croydon. With an area of farmland known as the Hursts (another possession of the manor of Beckenham) on their left, they passed around the disputed Gravel Hill Coppice and turned north-west, skirting Croydon Common and crossing 'a greene way that leadeth directly into the high way [which] leadeth from Croydon to Lewisham' – the forerunner of today's A213, part of which is called Green Lane.

Continuing in the same direction across what is now Auckland Road and up Fox Hill, they came to the 'Greate Oake called

Vicars Oake . . . at the partinge of the parishes of Croydon, Lambeth and Camberwell'. From here, a straight road (now Crystal Palace Parade) took them the half-mile back to their starting point at Low Cross, keeping on their left 'a wood of Mr Coltons' which 'lieth within the parishe of Camberwell on the west syde' – the Dulwich Woods, owned by the Calton family (as the name is more usually spelled).[6] The entire circuit measured just over four miles (6.7 kilometres), a distance the surveyors could have walked comfortably in a day.

A few years later, in 1623, the surveyor Nicholas Lane drew up a map of the manor of Beckenham at the behest of its owner, Sir Henry Snellyer, 'with the Demesne Lands Woods Pastures Meadows and Brooks Unto the Same Pertaining'. Several of these outlying parcels of land adjoin the borders of Penge, and confirm the descriptions in the Mete and Bounde. To the north is Rockhills, a triangular, twenty-nine-acre common adjoining the Westwood immediately beyond it; to the east is Abbey Farm, to the south Lord Rydon's Wood and the Hursts. Between these last two properties runs the main road from Beckenham, crossing the stream, and the parish and county boundary, by Willmore Bridge.[7]

To the south, the Archbishop's woods were also surveyed around this time. In the library at Lambeth Palace is a small, vellum-bound exercise book. On the cover, neat capital letters spell out 'WOODS IN KENT'; underneath is written, in a cursive hand, '& In Norwood'. On the last page, under the date 1611, William Somner, woodreeve to the newly installed Archbishop of Canterbury, George Abbot, listed the 'Copises belonging to the Archb'opp of Canterbury lyinge in Norwood & thereabout', giving the acreage of each in the right-hand margin. No figure is given for two coppices, Wickwood and Shelverdine, possibly because the woodreeve was waiting for a report from a surveyor, while Holly Hill is also left blank because it has been 'layd wast':

Wickwood coppise contcyninge

Camberwell rough – cont –	28 acres
Stakepitt great Coppise. cont –	
Stakepitt little Coppise. cont –	} 90 acres
Cleland Coppise – cont –	40 acres
Elderhole Coppise – cont –	50 acres
Cleland little Coppise. cont	16 acres
Gravely hill Coppise. cont	20 acres
Biggin hill Coppise. cont –	36 acres
Windalls Coppise – cont –	16 acres
Shelverden Coppise. cont –	
Bewlye Coppise. cont –	12 acres
Holly hill Coppise. Layd wast	[8]

The names Bewley and Biggin Hill are already present in Morton's 1492 survey, but this is the first known list of all the coppices in the Archbishop's woods, and reveals an expanse of managed woodland covering 308 acres across the parishes of Croydon, Lambeth and Camberwell. Wickwood Coppice was in Lambeth, near today's Loughborough Junction. According to later maps,[9] Cleland (or Clayland), Elderhole and Holly Hill coppices also lay within Lambeth, stretching from West Norwood to where the Vicar's Oak marked the boundary with Croydon. South of the lane running from Streatham to the Vicar's Oak, and north of the road now known as Beulah Hill, were Great and Little Stakepit and Gravelly Hill coppices. The latter cannot be the wood disputed between the Rydons and the Croydon parishioners, since it lies some distance from the border with Penge; the duplication of the name probably reflects the prevalence of gravel throughout the Norwood Ridge. Further east was Windalls Coppice – where Beaulieu Park is now – while Biggin Hill and Bewley coppices lay to the south.

THE FUSTIAN KING OF DULWICH

It was at this period that a new actor – literally – entered the scene. By 1605, Thomas Calton's grandson, Sir Francis Calton, was in financial difficulties and found himself obliged to sell the manor of Dulwich, including 'the wodes upon the waste', for £4,900 to Edward Alleyn. One of the most successful actor-managers of his day, Alleyn (1566–1626) had played the title roles in Marlowe's *Tamburlaine* and *Doctor Faustus* and, with his father-in-law Philip Henslowe, owned the Rose Theatre at Bankside and the Fortune in Finsbury Fields. Along with running the king's bull- and bear-baiting rings on the South Bank, these ventures had brought him considerable wealth, which he used to buy the estate and set up the College of God's Gift, today's Dulwich College, for the education and main-tenance of six poor brethren, six poor sisters, and twelve poor scholars.

The gossipy seventeenth-century biographer John Aubrey wrote that while performing in a play, Alleyn was 'surprised by an apparition of the devil' among the stage demons, 'which so worked on his fancy that he made a vow' to devote himself to charitable causes.[10] Though almost certainly apocryphal, the story may hint at a genuine religious motive, a desire, in today's parlance, 'to put something back'. The frequent thanks to God expressed in Alleyn's letters and diaries, which go far beyond the conventional pieties of the day, leave little doubt as to the depth and sincerity of his Christianity. By the standards of the time, moreover, such a religious impulse need not have been incompatible with a desire to raise his social status from what he self-mockingly described in a letter to his wife Joan as a 'fustian king' to that of country gentleman and lord of the manor.

Between 1606 and 1611, Alleyn enlarged his estate by buying up adjacent properties, and in 1613 commissioned John Benson,

Edward Alleyn, from William Harnett Blanch's *Dulwich College and Edward Alleyn: A Short History*, London 1877. Courtesy of Dulwich College Archive.

a bricklayer of Westminster, to build his college, chapel and almshouses. The work was complete by 1616, when the chapel was consecrated by Archbishop Abbot. But one obstacle remained. Since the Norman Conquest, all land in England was ultimately owned by the king, and held in tenure from him. The right to hold land could be passed on through inheritance, but when a landholder died without heir, it would revert to the Crown. Transferring land from an individual to an institution – a process known as amortisation – was seen as alienating it from the Crown in perpetuity, since unlike an individual, an institution such as the Church might last forever. Such a transfer could therefore only be made with the monarch's express permission, granted in letters patent. The Lord Chancellor, Francis Bacon, was strongly opposed to amortisation, since it deprived the Exchequer of potential revenue, and advised the king not to grant the letters patent. After several meetings with Alleyn, however, Bacon relented, and in May 1619 the letters patent were finally granted.

On 13 September that year, the opening ceremony in the college chapel was attended by Bacon, the Lord Lieutenant of Surrey Sir Edward Cecil, Thomas Howard, Earl of Arundel, and the architect and Surveyor General Inigo Jones. At the banquet that followed, the dignitaries feasted on 'capons in wight broth', boiled pigeons, venison, roast shin of beef, shoulder of mutton with oysters, Westphalia bacon, eels, roast rabbit, roast quail, godwits, partridge and duck, green salad, 'artychock pie' and anchovies. The liquid refreshment included sixteen gallons of claret, three quarts of sherry, the same quantity of 'wight win' and a five-pint bottle of Canary wine. The total catering bill came to more than £200.[11] For Alleyn, it was no doubt money well spent.

According to the statutes drawn up by Alleyn, the college would be governed by a master, a warden (both of whom had to be unmarried men 'of my blood and sirname, and for want

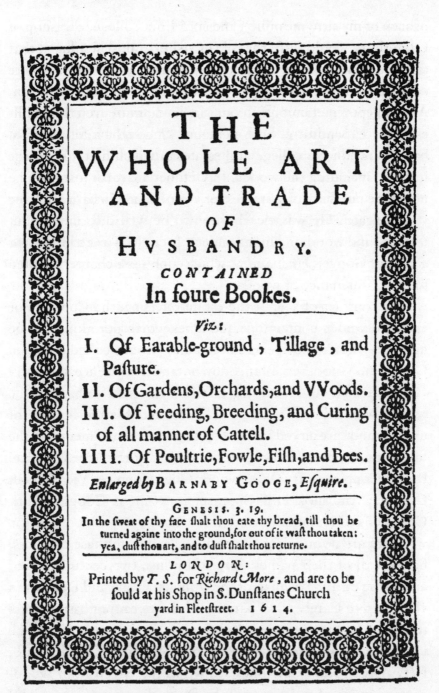

THE WHOLE ART AND TRADE OF HVSBANDRY.

CONTAINED In foure Bookes.

Viz:

I. Of Earable-ground, Tillage, and Pasture.

II. Of Gardens, Orchards, and VVoods.

III. Of Feeding, Breeding, and Curing of all manner of Cattell.

IIII. Of Poultrie, Fowle, Fish, and Bees.

Enlarged by BARNABY GOOGE, *Esquire.*

GENESIS. 3. 19.

In the sweat of thy face shalt thou eate thy bread, till thou be turned againe into the ground, for out of it wast thou taken: yea, dust thou art, and to dust shalt thou returne.

LONDON:

Printed by *T. S.* for *Richard More*, and are to be sould at his Shop in S. Dunstanes Church yard in Fleetstreet. 1 6 1 4.

Title page of Barnaby Googe's *The Whole Art and Trade of Husbandry*, London, 1614.

of such of my sirname onlie') and six fellows. The Archbishop of
Canterbury would fulfil the role of visitor, a post similar to that
of a trustee of a modern charity, to ensure that the statutes were
observed and guard against abuses. An astute businessman,
Alleyn kept a meticulous account in his diary of even the small-
est daily expenditure, both personal ('I bought a felt Hatt &
band') and for his college and estate, in which he took a close
interest, including the woods. In October 1617, for instance, he
noted the purchase of '4 staples for ye woodgates' and 'a Lock for
ye woodgate'. He was clearly keen to be well informed about
farming and woodland management, for in May 1620 he bought
a copy of Googe's *Husbandry*, which contains a chapter devoted
to the maintenance of woods.[12]

The contract of sale of the estate refers to 'the Coppices or
enclosed woods conteininge 400 acres worth per annum to be
farmed – 120£', and specifically names 'woods called Dulwich
Common, Woodsyer, Blanchdowne and Hall Place groves'.[13]
'To be farmed' alludes to the fact that the right to harvest the
woods would be leased or sold. The records of the sale of
underwood preserved in the college archives mention the
following coppices: Peckamin's Coppice; Forty Acre Coppice;
King's Coppice; Fifty Acre Wood; Giles Coppice; Vicar's Oak
Coppice; Ambrook Hill Coppice; Low Cross Coppice; Park
Coppice; and Hamondes Coppice.

There are no maps of the period that locate these coppices,
but several of their names were still in use two centuries later,
appearing on an 1806 map of the Dulwich Estate and Dewhirst's
1841 map of Camberwell parish. While we cannot assume that
their boundaries remained unaltered, their locations can be
identified with reasonable confidence. Starting from the north,
Fifty Acre Wood (sometimes known as the Green Man Wood)
covered much of what is now the Dulwich and Sydenham Hill
golf course; adjoining it, on the crown of the ridge, was Ambrook
Hill Wood, now part of the London Wildlife Trust's Sydenham

Hill Wood reserve; to its west were Peckarmans Wood and Low Cross Wood; the Forty Acre Coppice was situated around the present site of Sydenham Hill Station and the Kingswood Estate; and finally, at the southernmost tip of the manor of Dulwich, Vicar's Oak Coppice extended as far as the famous boundary tree of that name, where it met the Archbishop of Canterbury's woods.

Park, Giles and Hamondes coppices are harder to place, as they are not named on any map. Since the rights to fell Park and Giles were usually sold as a parcel along with Ambrook Hill Coppice, they may have adjoined it. By the late eighteenth century, a new coppice had come into being on the north-east side of Ambrook Hill: Lapse Wood, a name that first occurs as 'the Loppes' in a 1581 court roll, where it appears to be an alternative name for Ambrook Hill.[14] A 1668 survey of the estate gives the combined area of Park, Giles and Ambrook Hill coppices as forty-seven acres;[15] in 1799, the estate surveyor assessed 'The Lapse & part of Ambroke Hill' at slightly over twenty-two acres, and the remainder of Ambroke Hill at twenty acres, making a total of forty-two acres.[16] Allowing for a certain amount of conversion to farmland, Park and Giles coppices may therefore have been amalgamated some time in the eighteenth century to form Lapse Wood.

In the statutes for the governance of the college that he drew up shortly before his death in 1626, Alleyn ordered 'that twentye acres of woode be felled and sold yearly, such wood falls to be made at seasonable times, and in accordance with the laws and statutes of England [i.e. the Acts passed under Henry and Elizabeth], for the preservation of timber trees, such trees to be of the growth of ten yeares.' He also stipulated 'that no timber-trees shall be sold to any person or persons whatsoever, but to the tenants of the lands belonging to the said college in Dulwich, for the building or repayring of their tenements,' and that the master of the College should:

have yearley for his owne use in his chamber two hundred faggots; the warden shall have yearley two hundred faggots: for his owne spending; the fower senior fellowes shall have yearley one hundred and fifty faggots a piece for their owne spending; the six chanters or junior fellowes one hundred faggots a piece for their owne spending; all the said to be brought home to the said College at the charge of the said College between the 1st September and the 1st of All Saints yearley, to be kept in a stack and delivered by the bailie to the master, warden, and fellowes by half hundreds or quarterns as they shall desire . . .[17]

One coppice was to be felled each year when the new growth was ten years old, providing both fuel to warm the school and – through the sale of the rights to harvest the wood – income for the foundation.

As prescribed by Alleyn, the cultivation in Dulwich Woods conformed to the 'coppice and standard' pattern decreed by the 1543 Statute of Woods. The first such recorded sale was made by Alleyn himself in 1626, just days before his death on 'the 25th daie of November beeinge Saterdaie about 8 of the clocke at night'[18], and his second wife Constance (daughter of the poet John Donne) to William Sewer, a yeoman of Deptford, granting him the right to:

the woods, underwoods, trees, and bushes in Gileses Coppice, Dulwich, except fifty wavers, and twelve of the best and fairest trees or staddles to be left standing on every acre, for the sum of two pounds ten shillings for every acre.[19]

All subsequent sales were made by the master, warden and fellows. On 16 January 1630, for example, they sold Sewer, a regular customer:

all the woods and underwoods of the Wood or Coppice comonly called Kings Coppice conteyning forty acres more or lesse with libertie to fell cut downe and carry away the same, excepting all bushes and furzes and all manner of runting and grubbing whatsoever, and all timber trees, and fifty wavers and twelve stadles to be left upon every acre of the premises, and except so much wood as the College shall have occasion to use for their own firing, at the rate of forty-five shillings an acre.[20]

Some coppices, however, were converted to farmland soon after Alleyn bought the estate. On 3 May 1620, he noted in his diary that he had paid just short of £20 'for ye grubing of Lings Copice', while a covenant to pay tithes dated 29 August 1626 describes Cokers as 'heretofore copice woods and lately converted into earable and tillage'.[21]

The sale of wood from the remaining coppices continued to provide an income for the college for the next two centuries. In January 1632, for example, the woods and underwoods in Peckarmans Coppice were sold to the Southwark innkeeper Richard Windever and the Dulwich yeomen James Nelham and Faver Fox at forty-eight shillings an acre;[22] in December 1637, Fox paid £20 for the wood in Giles Coppice;[23] and in November 1638 William Sewer bought the wood and underwood in Fifty Acre Wood, which was 'of about ten years' growth', for two payments of £57 10s.[24]

The underwood in the coppices was sold and felled between November and February each year. Over the course of the seventeenth and into the eighteenth century, a clear pattern of rotational coppicing emerges from the deeds of sale: the Fifty Acre Wood, felled in 1638, 1648, 1658 and 1668; then the Forty Acre Wood, in 1639, 1650, 1659 and 1668; King's Wood in 1651, 1670 and 1680 (the records for 1660–61 are missing); Peckarmans

Wood, 1632, 1642, 1652, 1662; Vicar's Oak Coppice, 1652, 1663, 1674; and Ambrooke, Park and Giles coppices, 1645, 1654, 1665, 1685 (1675 is missing). After 1703 the records cease, to resume briefly from 1780 to 1788, when the same sequence is still evident.[25]

Alleyn was not the only one to realise that income generated by woodland could be used to fund a charitable school. In 1614, the Worshipful Company of Haberdashers purchased the manor of Hatcham for much the same reason. The deed of sale included 'that great wood, woodland, and ground, called or knowne by the name of Hacham Great Wood, or The Great Wood . . . conteyning by estimacion fourescore acres'.[26] An estate map made for the Haberdashers in 1619 shows an irregular area of woodland about three-quarters of a mile across and a mile from north to south, between Telegraph Hill and the future site of Nunhead Cemetery.[27] Haberdashers' Aske's Hatcham College still flourishes in the area, with sites at Pepys Road and Jerningham Road.

HAVOC IN THE WOODS

During the reign of Charles I (1625–49), the Court paid frequent visits to the woods for hunting. Anthony Holland, one of the king's yeomen-huntsmen, was instructed to order the inhabitants of the area 'that they forbeare to hunt, chace, molest, or hurt the king's stagges with greyhounds, hounds, gunnes, or any other means whatsoever.' Holland was further authorised 'to take from any person or persons offending therein their dogges, hounds, gunnes, crossbowes, or other engynes.'[28]

In 1642, the long-festering dispute between Charles and Parliament over who held ultimate authority in the land and what form of religion the country should follow erupted into open warfare. On 4 January, the king arrived at the House of Commons with eighty heavily armed troops to arrest five of his most

prominent opponents, including John Hampden and John Pym.
Warned of his arrival, they had taken a boat to the City of
London. The king followed them there, but the City authorities,
staunchly Puritan supporters of Parliament, refused to hand
them over. With London in uproar, the frustrated monarch left
to muster an army in the north. It was the start of eleven years of
civil war that would ravage England, Scotland and Ireland – killing a greater percentage of the population than the First World
War – and wreak havoc in the woods.

In April 1643, Parliament ordered the sequestration of the
property of 'delinquents', as the king's supporters were called,
and of fourteen bishops, including the Archbishop of Canterbury. A high churchman and close ally of Charles I, Archbishop
William Laud was an object of particular hatred for the Puri-
tans, and had been imprisoned in the Tower of London on a
charge of treason since the beginning of the Civil War. Those
parts of the North Wood belonging to him as lord of the manor
of Croydon now came under the control of the newly established
Sequestration Committee for the county of Surrey.

As the social order broke down, bands of people began to
pillage woods and forests around London, a situation aggra-
vated by the shortage of coal from Newcastle, which was held
by the Royalists. In May 1643 the Sequestration Committee
ordered that the Archbishop of Canterbury's woods be protected
from 'rude & disorderly people cominge from London &
elswhere'. Their objective was not to defend the Archbishop's
property, but to control the removal of wood and ensure that it
was targeted at the enemies of Parliament; the order also
reflected a concern that people were not just helping themselves
to firewood but taking whole timber trees. In July, Parliament
appointed officers to take wood from estates owned by the king,
the bishops and their royalist supporters within sixty miles of
London, and distribute it to the poor. They appear to have
encountered some resistance from Croydon people accustomed

to collect firewood from the Archbishop's lands, for in August the committee paid £2 16s 'to Captain Ghest's souldiers for their paines and charges, for that it was informed there would be opposition in going to the woods'.[29] By September 1644, however, the Commons had become concerned that the nation's timber stocks were becoming dangerously depleted, and ordered a committee to consider suspending the ordinance for providing wood to the city.[30]

In 1644 the master, warden and fellows of Alleyn's College of God's Gift came into direct conflict with Parliament, initiating a dispute that only ended with the Restoration. Three of the fellows had declared their support for the king, as a result of which they were dismissed; the prolonged absence of the fourth meant that all four positions were vacant. On 3 May, the Committee for the Safety of the County of Surrey prohibited the master and warden from replacing the fellows, and on the 23 May the Committee for Plundered Ministers – a body set up by Parliament to compensate vicars dispossessed by the Royalists and to eject incumbents it considered unsuitable – appointed a minister and schoolmaster in their place, but without the status of fellows. The College was ordered to pay them twice the usual fellows' salaries and food allowance.

A further difficulty arose concerning the role of the Archbishop of Canterbury as visitor. Archbishop Laud was beheaded in January 1645, and in October the following year, Parliament abolished archbishops and bishops throughout England and Wales. In 1654 the master and warden petitioned Oliver Cromwell, pointing out that without fellows and a visitor, they were unable to fulfil their obligations under the founder's statutes, or renew the leases on which the College's income depended. In response, Cromwell appointed a Corporation of thirty visitors to oversee the governance of the College. [31]

Alleyn's successors still collected rent from his old theatre, the Fortune, so the Estate had suffered financially since

Parliament banned plays and playhouses in September 1642. For a while, the actors continued to perform in defiance of the regulation, but in February 1648, Parliament issued a new, more draconian 'Ordinance for the utter suppression and abolishing of all Stage-Plays and Interludes', ordering the city authorities 'to pull down and demolish, or cause or procure to be pulled down and demolished all Stage-Galleries, Seats, and Boxes'.[32] By Christmas, the rents were in arrears by £1041 1s 5d.[33]

In 1647, when Parliamentary forces commanded by Sir Thomas Fairfax were stationed at Putney and Fulham, a company of ten soldiers under the command of Captain Atkinson was billeted in the college, where they caused considerable damage, destroying the chapel organ and, according to legend, melting down lead coffins for bullets. The College later received nineteen shillings and eight pence in compensation. [34]

Despite these disruptions and depredations, the coppicing of Dulwich Woods continued according to the established pattern throughout the Civil War and the interregnum. (Curiously, the sales continued to be made in the name of 'the Master, Warden, four Fellows &c.', even when there were no fellows.) There was one significant change, however. Since Alleyn's time, the coppicing rights had mostly been sold to yeoman farmers in Kent and Surrey: in December 1640, for example, a Camberwell yeoman called John Redding bought the wood and underwood in Forty Acre Coppice, for £3 5s an acre, of which £50 was to be paid in advance.[35] But in May 1645, the college sold 'all the wood and underwood in Giles Coppice, Dulwich' to a London fishmonger called William Lock for £20;[36] and the following year, Lock bought the wood and underwood in Low Cross Coppice for an unrecorded sum.[37]

We should not envisage Lock in a white apron selling whelks from a stall. He was a Freeman of the City of London, a prosperous wholesaler who also owned a bakery in Southwark;[38] the kind of City merchant who formed the bedrock of Parliament's

support. From then on, he became the sole purchaser of the
Estate's woods. In January 1649/50 Lock bought the right to fell
Forty Acre Coppice for £3 an acre, of which £50 was to be paid
up front; in January 1650/1 he bought the wood and underwood
in Kings Coppice; in November 1652, Peckarmans Coppice; in
1653/4 Vicar's Oak Coppice; and in December 1654, Ambrook,
Park and Giles coppices.[39] After Lock's death in 1656, the wood-
falls were regularly sold to one Anthony Allen, 'Citizen and
Baker of London';[40] following the restoration of the monarchy
in 1660, however, the sales reverted to local yeomen such as
Richard Clowder of Beckenham and Thomas Cranwell of
Dulwich.[41]

In Croydon meanwhile, a survey undertaken by Edward Boyer
for Parliament in March 1646 found that the wood, 'late the
property of the dissolved Archbishopricke', consisted of 830 acres
in which the people of Croydon 'have herbage for all manner of
cattle, and mastage for swine without stint', but 'such havoc had
been committed in it', that it contained only 9,200 oak pollards
and eighty timber trees. It listed the following timber and underwoods, with their value in pounds and shillings:

Woods and underwoods groweing and being upon Biggin great coppice aforesaid . . .	lxxi £.
Woods and underwoods groweing and being upon Bewdley coppice aforesaid	xxii £.
Timber and pollards there.	vii £. x s.
Woods and underwoods groweing and being upon Windalle's coppice aforesaid.	xxi £. v s.
Timber and pollards there.	x £.
Woods and underwoods groweing and being upon Shelverden's coppice aforesaid	xxi £. xi s.
Timber and pollards there	vi £.
Woods and underwoods groweing and being upon Great Stakepitt aforesaid	xxxv £. xii s.

One hundred and fifty small trees, or	xxx £.
thereabouts, being timber and pollards	
growinge and being upon Great Stakepitt	
aforesaid Woods and underwoods growing	
and being upon Gravelly Hill coppice aforesaid	xliiii £.
Thirty small timber trees and pollards there	lxxv £.
Woods and underwoods growing and	xxix s.
being on Little Stakepitt aforesaid	
Timber and pollards growing and being	iiii £. x s.
there Eighty timber trees growing and being	
upon one wood called Norwood, lying in the	
parish of Croyden, and part thereof in the parish	
of Lambeth	l £.
Nine thousand two hundred oaken pollards,	
with the tops and lops, growing and being	
upon the wood aforesaid, which wood	
containeth eight hundred and thirty trees	mmccxl £. [42]

Over the parish boundary, the Parliamentary survey found that:

There belongeth allsoe to the said Manner of Lambeth a
Common Wood called Northwood conteyninge by estimac[i]
on about three hundred Acres adjoining to an other parte of
the said Wood call'd Northwood which lyeth within the
Parish of Croyden. The division whereof begins at the East
end of the lane called Stretham Lane and from there upp to a
place called highcross and up to an Oke called Viccars Oke
leavinge the Parish of Croydon all the way on the South and
the Parish of Lambeth on the North . . .

The Lambeth woods contained about 6,300 trees, mostly oaks
that were pollarded every thirty years; the herbage, bushes and
thorns were 'claymed by the Tenants of Lambeth as belonginge
to their Tenem[ts] and soe have bin from tyme to tyme enioyed by

them'. Within the wood were three enclosed coppices, Elderhole (seventy-seven acres), Great Clayland (forty acres) and Little Clayland (thirteen acres), totalling some 130 acres. 'Usually' felled after ten years' growth, they were then enclosed for seven years to protect the young shoots from browsing livestock, 'and then the commoners have had their common therein for three yeares till ye next fall'. At the time of the survey, Elderhole Coppice was of eleven years' growth, Little Claylands was of ten years' growth, and Great Claylands was of two years' growth. The manor also owned a parcel of common land 'neere unto Bristow Cawsey' [Brixton Causeway], some common woodland at Knights Hill, and three closes: Milkwood, Wickwood, and Camberwell Ruffe.[43]

In 1647, the manor of Croydon was granted to Sir William Brereton, one of Parliament's most effective generals, as a reward for his successful campaigns in the north of England. Brereton, a convinced Puritan who had travelled in the Netherlands and written approvingly of enclosure,[44] allowed farmers to grub up some of the coppices for agriculture and suspended the traditional right of pasture in the woods. A post-Restoration pamphlet lampooned his 'prodigious stomach', alleging that he had turned the Archbishop's chapel into a kitchen.[45] On the restoration of the monarchy in 1660, the Archbishopric was reinstated and the manor and its woods returned to the Church, though Brereton was permitted to remain in residence at the Archbishop's palace until his death in April 1661.

The new authorities, like the Parliamentary surveyors before them, were keen to blame the previous regime for the state of the woods. Reviewing William Somner's 1611 ledger, the Archbishop's woodreeve assessed the damage inflicted during the Civil War and the interregnum, using the blank left-hand margin to record the extent of each coppice in 1663. Ironically, the total acreage appears to have increased, but this is only because the wood-reeve has included the figures for Wickwood and Shelverden omitted by his predecessor. Once these are accounted for, the overall picture is one of decline. Great and Little Stakepit coppices have shrunk from a combined acreage of ninety to sixty; Elderhole Coppice is down from fifty to forty acres; while Little Clayland and Gravel Hill coppices, which between them covered thirty-six acres in 1611, now amounted to just twenty-four. And though Wickwood Coppice is included in the tally, beside it is written 'grubbed in y ill times'. At the bottom of the page is the terse note, 'These Woods put out of ye former order by the Rebells'. [46]

Like his Tudor predecessors, Charles II – or his ministers – worried about the scarcity of timber for the Navy. According to the Commissioner of the Navy, Peter Pett, the royal forests were 'almost wholly cut down and decayed'. In 1662, Pett addressed 'Five Quaeries' to the newly founded scientific institution the Royal Society, as to how the supply of timber could be improved and secured. Among the Society's founding members – alongside such luminaries as Isaac Newton and Christopher Wren – was the civil servant, diarist and horticulturist John Evelyn (1620–1706), who lived at Sayes Court, close to the Royal Dockyard at Deptford. He responded with a paper presented to the Society, which he expanded over the next two years to form his great work *Sylva, or a Discourse of Forest-Trees and the Propagation of Timber in His Majesty's Dominions*. Its exhortation to landowners to plant trees echoed the views of Standish and others, while its chapter-length studies of individual species anticipated the scientific botany of the following century. His advice on coppicing, to 'Cut not above half a foot from the ground. Nay the closer, the better, and that to the south, slope-wise,' so that rainwater will run off and not rot the stool, remains valid today.

Civil war was followed in 1665 by plague. Looking back across almost sixty years, the novelist Daniel Defoe painted a grim picture of an event that had haunted him since childhood:

I have been told that several that wandred into the country on
Surry side were found starv'd to death in the woods and
commons, that country being more open and more woody
than any other part so near London; especially about
Norwood and the Parishes of Camberwell, Dullege, and
Lusume [Lewisham], where it seems no Body durst relieve the
poor distressed people for fear of the infection.[47]

The woods became a burial ground for plague victims. In
1673, the inhabitants of Croydon issued a petition against their
vicar, Dr William Cleiver, for his 'unparalleled extortions' of
excessive tithes, which had reduced many parishioners to
destitution and which, they alleged, he spent in 'houses of
debauchery, particularly a blind, beggarly, disorderly ale-house,
in a by-place within the parish of Newington, infamous for
entertainment of lewd persons'. Among the charges against
him was that:

Several poor people having, in the time of the late dreadful
sickness, buried relations in the woods, the said Doctor, in
the time of their necessity, was far from extending his charity
towards their relief that he forced them to pay unreasonable
fees for their burials, as if they had been buried by him in the
church-yard. Those that would not comply with him he sued
and extorted great sums of money from them . . .[48]

The case was brought before the Archbishop of Canterbury and
King Charles II himself, with the result that Cleiver was eventually removed from office.

London had scarcely recovered from the plague when almost
the entire area within its ancient walls was consumed by fire.
The conflagration broke out at Thomas Farriner's bakery in
Pudding Lane shortly after midnight on Sunday 2 September
1666, and raged for four days through narrow lanes lined with

timber houses. Although we don't know where Farriner obtained his fuel, many London bakers were supplied by the colliers of Croydon, which raises the prospect that the North Wood, having contributed much to the growth of the city, may have now played a part in its destruction.

A GREAT WOOD CALLED NORWOOD

In Dulwich, meanwhile, a 'terrier of the lands, tenements and woods belonging to God's Gift College' drawn up in 1668 showed that it owned seven areas of woodland totalling 268 acres:

The College Woods	Acres
Vicar's Oak Coppice cont	32
Kings Coppice cont	39
Fourty acres Coppice cont	25
Low Cross Coppice	32
Peckamans Coppice	44
Giles's Coppice The Park & Ambrook Hill	47
Fifty Acres Coppice	49
	268[49]

The woods were a lucrative asset that the Estate, like the monks of Bermondsey before it, was keen to defend. Its accounts for 31 March 1668 record a payment of two shillings to 'our men when they went before the Lord Scott with Holmes and another man for cutting poles in our woods and hee sent them to Bridwell and their they were whipt'.[50] Less than a month later, on 23 April, there is a payment for 'a Mittimus [warrant] and expences when our men went with Robert Budder before the Lord Scott for cutting wood in Peckamans copies, they were to cary him to Bridewell but hee runn away from them.'[51] And on 22 August 1691, the college spent £1 14s 8d prosecuting 'several Inhabitants of Camberwell for carrying away severall great quantities of wood . . . under couler of Tyth pretended to be due to Mr Bowyer'.[52]

The coppices were marked out by ancient boundary trees and pleached hedges. In his logbook, John Hamond, the college's woodman from 1687 to 1691, recorded that for much of the time between mid-December and April, he 'plisht wood'. He also 'made bavins in the wood', 'cut some faggit wood' and 'cutt up Runts'.[53] When a wood is graded, the largest trees are taken and the runts are left as seed stock. The trees left standing come in different sizes, and for the next cut the logger selects the largest of the runts. The Hamonds appear to have been a long-established local family; a John and Thomas Hamond had both testified in the Rydon case a century earlier, and Hamondes Coppice was listed as part of the Manor of Dulwich when Alleyn bought it.

In 1678, Archbishop William Sancroft's woodreeve (identified only by the initials IT), commissioned the surveyor William Mar to produce a map of the Archbishop's woods around Croydon 'as a Small acknowledgement of great and Condescending favor'. Mar had produced estate plans in Surrey and Oxfordshire, and was probably the same William Marr who served as a Parliamentary surveyor of Crown Lands, worked in London, Middlesex and Surrey from around 1640 to 1685,[54] and contributed to John Leake's 'Exact Surveigh of the Streets Lanes and Churches Contained within the Ruines of the City of London' that recorded the devastation left by the 1666 fire.[55]

Mar's plan charts a great swath of woodland extending some three miles from West Norwood to what is now Norwood Junction, and covering more than 1,300 acres. It is exquisitely drawn on a long sheet of parchment, a medium favoured for maps of this type because it is durable and hard-wearing; despite being almost 350 years old, the map is remarkably well preserved, although its folds, creases and other signs of wear suggest that it was regularly used in the field. By seventeenth-century standards, it is accurately surveyed, showing each coppice within the woods, together with its acreage. The wooded areas are painstakingly filled in with tiny sketches of trees, each casting a shadow to the north-west to suggest an early morning vista.

In the parish of Croydon, the largest coppice, Great Stakepit, covered 116 acres; Biggin Hill Coppice, immediately to the south, seventy-eight acres; Bewlye Coppice, to the south-west, twenty-five acres; and Windalls Coppice twenty-nine acres. Beyond these, a 571-acre woodland is labelled 'Croydon Woods called Norwood'; on it, a later hand has pencilled 'open common'. Cutting into it from the north is a nineteen-acre triangular enclosure, with farm buildings, labelled Shelverdine, alias Goat House – a name that survives today in the Goat House pub in Norwood. To the west of Biggin Hill, the partly wooded Croydon Common extended over 111 acres. To the north, the map indicates that eighteen acres of Gravelly Hill Coppice, about half its total extent, had been grubbed up. Although Mar did not mark watercourses on his map, the undulating border that divides Great Stakepit Coppice from Gravelly Hill and Little Stakepit to the north appears to correspond to the Lower Norwood branch of the River Effra. Among the pencilled additions of later date is a 'new road' running between Great Stakepit and Biggin Hill Coppices; this is today's Beulah Hill.

In the Parish of Lambeth, there appears to be some confusion over the names of the coppices. The westernmost, with its distinctive 'panhandle' extending towards Knight's Hill, is labelled Cleyland Coppice and covers seventy-six acres; immediately to its east is the fifty-one-acre Elderhole Coppice. This reverses the acreage given for the two coppices in the 1646 Parliamentary survey. On the Norwood enclosure map of 1808, the names are the other way round, with the larger coppice to the west called Elderhole and its eastern neighbour Claylands.

Since this concurs with the 1646 survey, it would appear that either Mar mistakenly transposed the names, or for some reason they were switched. Here too, the lower branch of the Effra forms a boundary, in this case between the coppiced woods and Lambeth Common to the west. To the east of the ambiguously labelled coppices, the twenty-nine-acre Holly Hill is shown as sparsely wooded, confirming the earlier observation that it had been 'layd wast'. Immediately to its north stands the mighty Vicar's Oak, where the Archbishop of Canterbury's woods met those of the Dulwich Estate.[56]

The woodreeve's duties were spelled out in detail in the instructions given by Archbishop William Wake to William Stobbs in February 1715:

> The Wood-Reeve must be one that well understands the Nature of Wood and Wood-Lands, and to order the felling, cutting out, making up, stripping, setting, runting, coaling, Racking, &c. To provide Workmen, Colliers, &c. and to apportion every Man his Employment. To contract with them and to pay them weekly, according to the several Rates agreed upon; and that before any Account can be had of them, what their work will come to; which except he understands as well as themselves, he will be sure to be cheated. He must see every Man's work to be well done; provide Teams, order their Loadings, and see to the Delivery; otherwise the Wood will be carried to wrong Places, and no Account given of it, which is a usual Thing, and the Wood-Reeve's Loss. For this Purpose he must constantly attend early and late, both by himself and others; for one alone is not sufficient to look after every Workman, which at somctimes are near twenty at a Time in several Places, and some at great Distances, to prevent the common Cheats and Abuses usually practised by the Woodmen, Colliers and Carters. Gates and Fences he must look after for Preservation of the Springs; and take Care

to punish Offenders, Woodstealers, Trespassors, and the like. For what is sold he must likewise provide Teams and Chapmen, keep Account to whom, and take Care whom he trusts, and either to collect the Money, or perhaps be made answer it himself. He must from Time to Time observe the Steward's Orders. And at the End of the Year give an Account of his Office.[57]

A similar job description was issued by Joseph Allen, the master of Dulwich College, to his woodman in 1746. Like the Archbishop, Allen was particularly anxious that his supervisor guard against fraud by the workmen he employed:

In the month of November the Woodman and Bayliff attend the Master or Warden to that Part of the Wood, that is next to be felled, and there every man takes his Pitch (as their Phrase is) that is every One goes through and marks his part, that he is to fell: after that they proceed to one of the Publick houses at Dulwich where they Dine, the College allowing one Shilling to every Man, that pitches for his Dinner: it is necessary to observe that Ten or twelve Men are sufficient for any of the Woodfall, otherwise there will be a greater Number imposed to the Prejudice of the College.

Every Day that they Work, they are allowed to carry home a bundle of Wood; but in Stripping Season they take the best flead Pole, that they can choose, and carry it home; it is customary in many places to allow 3d instead of a Pole every night during the Stripping Season, and one Bavin for every fifty that are made instead of a Bundle of Wood every Night. I think it would be much better for the College if it was so regulated, as it would prevent a great deal of fraud.[58]

The Archbishop's possessions were only part of the North Wood at this period. To the north, as we have already seen, were the

Dulwich Woods. To the north-west, Streatham Common extended over 111 acres. To the north-east, over much of Penge, Mar's map shows woodland belonging to Sir Walter St John, a descendant of Oliver St John then in possession of the manor of Battersea. Directly adjoining the Archbishop of Canterbury's woods to the south was White Horse Wood, which then covered eighty acres and belonged to one Thomas Morton, who owned the Manor of Benchesham.

In 1678, as William Mar was mapping the Archbishop's woods, John Aubrey visited Croydon while compiling his perambulation of Surrey, and left this account:

> In this parish lies the great wood, call'd *Norwood*, belonging to the See of *Canterbury*, wherein was an antient, remarkable Tree, call'd *Vicar's Oak*, where four Parishes met in a Point. This Wood wholly consists of Oaks. There was one Oak that had *Misselto*, a Timber Tree, which was felled about 1657. Some Persons cut this *Misselto*, for some Apothecaries in *London*, and sold them a Quantity for Ten Shillings, each time, and left only one Branch remaining, for more to sprout out; One fell lame shortly after: Soon after, each of the others lost an Eye, and he that fell'd the Tree, about 1678 (tho' warned of these Misfortunes of the other Men) would, notwithstanding, adventure to do it, and shortly after broke his Leg; as if the *Hamadryades* had resolved to take an ample Revenge for the Injury done to that sacred and venerable Oak.[59]

4

FAITH OR SCIENCE?

1700–1790

On the night of 26–27 November 1703, a powerful storm blew in off the Atlantic and smashed into southern England, bringing down thousands of chimneys, destroying buildings and wrecking ships in the Channel. It obliterated the recently constructed Eddystone lighthouse, killing its designer, Henry Winstanley, and five other men. At the naval dockyard at Deptford and in the Pool of London, ships were torn from their moorings and slammed into one another. Throughout the country, and off its shores, some eight thousand people, the majority of them seamen, were killed. Queen Anne, forced to shelter in the cellars of St James's Palace as its chimneys came crashing down, described it as 'a Calamity so Dreadful and Astonishing, that the like hath not been Seen or Felt, in the Memory of any Person Living in this Our Kingdom'.

Kent and Surrey were severely affected. The church steeple at Brenchley was blown down, the market hall at St Mary Cray destroyed, and the walls surrounding Greenwich Park collapsed. Daniel Defoe – who advertised for eyewitness accounts in newspapers all over the country to rush out a book, *The Storm* – rode around Kent counting fallen trees but, 'being tired with the Number, I left off Reckoning after I had gone on to 17,000; and tho' I have great reason to believe I did not observe one half the Quantity.'[1]

John Evelyn wrote in his journal:

> The effects of the Hurricane and tempest of wind, rain, and
> lightning through all the nation, especially London, were
> very dismal. Many houses demolished, and people killed. As
> to my own losses, the subversion of woods and timber, both
> ornamental and valuable, through my whole estate, and about
> my house, the woods crowning the garden mount, and grow-
> ing along the Park meadow, the damage to my own dwelling,
> farms, and outhouses, is almost tragical, not to be paralleled
> with anything happening in our age.[2]

When the fourth edition of his book *Sylva* appeared in 1706,
Evelyn added a dramatic recollection of the storm:

> Methinks that I still hear, sure I am that I feel, the dismal
> groans of our forests, when that late dreadful Hurricane,
> happening on the 26th of November, 1703, subverted as many
> thousands of goodly Oaks, prostrating the trees, laying them
> in ghastly postures, like whole regiments fallen in battle by
> the sword of the conqueror, and crushing all that grew
> beneath them.[3]

For many, the great storm was an act of God, a judgement on a
sinful nation; for the small but increasingly influential group of
scientists associated with the Royal Society, it was a meteorological phenomenon to be understood by rational enquiry. This
shift from an essentially medieval world-view to a modern one
would lead to the North Wood being mapped with greater accuracy, produce the first botanical and zoological records of the
species found there, and usher in the Industrial Revolution that
would eventually destroy it.

Although parts of the wood had been mapped in detail on
estate surveys such as Mar's Norwood Plan, these were unique,

hand-drawn documents that remained the private property of the landowner for the purpose of recording ownership and facilitating management. The printed – and therefore public – maps of the seventeenth century, such as Speede's *Surrey,* depicted the wood in a sketchy, impressionistic manner, and do not provide an accurate record of its extent. In 1695 Edmund Gibson published a new edition of Camden's *Britannia*, and commissioned the cartographer Robert Morden to provide new maps. Morden's map of Surrey shows an expanse of woodland stretching south from Knight's Hill and east from Streatham. His map of neighbouring Kent, however, offers a different view, with the woods spreading either side of the road that runs from Croydon to London via Dulwich.

The woods are charted with greater accuracy on *A New Map of the County of Surrey* (1729) by the London map and globe maker John Senex. Using hachures to indicate the hilly topography, Senex shows a band of woodland stretching from Knight's Hill to 'Pens Common', with a lighter scattering of trees extending north via Honor Oak to Hatcham. Alleyn's College is shown at the apex of the triangle formed by College Road, Gallery Road and Dulwich Common.

It was a German cartographer, however, who first put the name 'North Wood' on a printed map. In his *Delineatio ac Finitima Regio Magnae Britanniae Metropoleos Londini* (Delineation of London, Metropolis of the Kingdom of Great Britain, and its Environs, *c*.1730) the prolific Augsburg mapmaker Matthäus Seutter shows the wood stretching south from Knight's Hill to Streatham, with a further band of trees extending east towards Sydenham. Sydenham Hill is still topped by its windmill; to the north are Dulwich College, Dulwich Wells and Lewisham.

The North Wood is also named on the magnificent twelve-sheet chart of *The Country Near Ten Miles Round London*, published by the French-born Huguenot cartographer John

Rocque in 1746. One of the most valuable sources revealing the extent of the woods at this period, it records fields, farms and woodland now engulfed by the metropolis, with the North Wood stretching for more than three miles from the Green Man pub at the junction of Dulwich Common and Lordship Lane to White Horse Wood. East of Dulwich and north of Sydenham, he shows a wooded hill named Oak of Arnon, today's Honor Oak, with Wood Lane (now Wood Vale) running to the west of it. To the south, what is now Upper Norwood is still a furze-covered waste extending from Croydon to Penge Common.

Rocque's range of ten miles around London excluded the southernmost portions of the woods, but shortly before his death in 1762, he produced a fine map of Surrey at a scale of two inches to the mile, showing parish boundaries and land use. Completed and engraved by Peter Andrews, it was published in 1768 by Rocque's widow, Mary-Ann. While the terrain in Kent is left blank, the two maps together form a comprehensive survey of the woods in the mid-eighteenth century. To the south of White Horse Wood, and separated from it by open fields, the Surrey map shows the small Dragnel Wood, a fragment of which survives alongside the railway at Selhurst Junction. About two miles to the east, a more substantial area of woodland, the Eighteen Acre Wood, extends either side of Long Lane; adjoining it to the south is Ham Wood. Parts of these woods still exist in Long Lane Wood, to the south of Elmer's End, and the nearby Glade.

From the mid-seventeenth century the wooded ridge started providing opportunities for leisure, as medicinal springs were discovered at Streatham and Sydenham, in today's Wells Park. On 2 September 1675, Evelyn, after visiting Dulwich College, 'came back [to Deptford] by certain medicinal spa waters, at a place called Sydnam Wells, in Lewisham parish, much frequented in summer.'[4] Defoe, writing around 1724, 'saw Dullige or

Sydenham Wells, where great crouds of people throng every summer from London to drink the waters.'[5]

Some time before 1714, John Cox, landlord of the Green Man, was given permission by the Dulwich Estate to cut a path through the Fifty Acre Wood, 'reserving for shade on each side half a rood of wood, unfelled' to bring customers to his inn from Sydenham Wells.[6] The oak-lined avenue is clearly shown on Senex's map, and Rocque labels it 'Green Man Walk'; today it is called Cox's Walk. In 1739, Cox's grandson Francis discovered a mineral spring in the grounds of the Green Man, and established a spa to rival Sydenham Wells, complete with pleasure gardens, a bowling green, sports facilities and other entertainments.

The therapeutic reputation of the area received a further boost in 1744, when the Scottish physician and poet John Armstrong published *The Art of Preserving Health*, a best-selling book of medical advice in verse, in which he advised readers toiling in 'the busy town . . . for power or gold' to 'lose the world amid the sylvan wilds/ Of DULWICH, yet by barbarous arts unspoil'd.'

Another attraction for visitors was the sizeable Roma community that lived in the woods. When they first appeared in the area is unknown, but they were clearly established by 1668, when Samuel Pepys recorded in his diary: 'This afternoon my wife and Mercer and Deb went with Pelling to see the Gypsies at Lambeth and have their fortunes told; but what they did, I did not enquire.' Their regular encampment was the area now known as Gipsy Hill in Upper Norwood. 'The Gypsy House,' wrote the topographer Daniel Lysons around 1790, 'is situated on a small green in a valley surrounded by woods. On this green a few families of gipsies have pitched their tents for a great number of years during the summer season. In the winter they either procure lodgings in London or take up their abode in some more distant counties.'[7]

Around the turn of the seventeenth and eighteenth centuries, Margaret Finch, widely famed as Gypsy Queen, settled there, and received many visitors. When she died in 1740 at the age of 109, it was found that, because she had spent so long sitting cross-legged with her chin on her knees, her limbs could not be straightened. Her remains were placed in a deep square box and carried to Beckenham Churchyard, where her funeral was attended by a large crowd of people from all walks of life. Her cottage on Gipsy Hill was still standing in 1808. She was succeeded by her niece Bridget Finch, whose burial on 6 August 1768 is recorded in the register of Dulwich College chapel. The title was then inherited by her niece, Margaret's granddaughter, who was recorded as living next door to the Gipsy public house in Norwood in 1786. Such was their fame that in 1777 a panto-mime entitled *The Norwood Gipsies* was produced at Covent Garden. In 1799, the young Lord Byron, then a pupil at Dr William Glennie's academy (which by then occupied the site of the Green Man), would often make his way up Cox's Walk to visit the gypsies in Dulwich Wood.

A NATURAL HISTORY OF THE ENLIGHTENMENT

The science of natural history as we know it today has its roots in the second half of the seventeenth century, and it is to this period that we owe the earliest records of the flora and fauna of the North Wood. Modern Europe's first scientific academy, the Royal Society, was founded in London in 1660 with the aim of 'improving natural knowledge', and its members would meet to discuss mathematics, astronomy, physics, botany and zoology. Less formally, enthusiasts of the new sciences would gather in London coffee houses, taverns and apothecaries' shops, where celebrated academicians, aristocratic amateurs and self-educated tradesmen could meet on equal terms to discuss their shared enthusiasm. The botanists gathered at the Temple Coffee House and the Rainbow Coffee House in Fleet Street, while entomologists such as Joseph Dandridge, Peter Collinson and Moses Harris met at the Swan Tavern in Cornhill. Noting that the word chrysalis derives from the Greek *khrusos*, gold, they called themselves the Society of Aurelians, from the Latin *aureolus*, or golden.

The members of these scientific clubs cultivated extensive networks of correspondents who would send them specimens from all over Britain, Europe and even as far afield as India and North America. They would also mount expeditions to collect plants and insects themselves, usually from villages within a day's ride of the capital, and Dulwich and Oak of Honor woods appear in several of their observations.

Among the founding members of the Royal Society was the physician and botanist Christopher Merrett, a contributor to Evelyn's *Sylva* and the author of one of the earliest surveys of the flora and fauna of Britain. First published in 1666, and reprinted the following year, after the Great Fire of London destroyed most of the original print run, his *Pinax Rerum Naturalium Britannicarum* included an alphabetical list of some one hundred plants found across the country. Many species are associated with generic habitats rather than specific sites: enchanter's nightshade, for example, he records '*in locis humidis & umbrosis*' (in damp and shady places). Where precise geographical locations are given, they are sporadic rather than systematic. '*Betulus* sive Carpinus, the *Horn-Beam tree*' he records only 'On the West of Primrose-Hill, and *Hamsteed* Woods', though one Samuel Harris noted it 'on a walk from London to Dulwich' in 1725.[8] Despite a few reports from around Croydon and Addington, and a sighting of buckthorn (*Rhamnus solutibus*, now *R. cathartibus*) 'near *Lewsham* in *Kent*', Merrett and his collectors appeared to have been better acquainted with the woods around Hampstead and Highgate than those south of the Thames.

A far more significant Fellow of the Royal Society was the clergyman and natural historian John Ray (1628–1705). The Cambridge-educated son of a blacksmith, he was born in Black Notley in Essex, where his mother was a traditional herbalist. Among his many publications on botany, zoology, religion and morality was the *Historia Plantarum* (History of Plants, 1686), in which he was the first to formulate the concept of species:

> After a long and considerable investigation, no surer criterion for determining species has occurred to me than the distinguishing features that perpetuate themselves in propagation of seed . . . Animals likewise . . . preserve their distinct species permanently; one species never springs from the seed of another nor vice versa.

This might seem self-evident to us today, but it was not self-evident to Ray's contemporaries, who believed, for example, that wild geese hatched from barnacles. It was a crucial insight that prefigured and made possible the work of Linnaeus and Darwin. Towards the end of his life, Ray turned to the study of insects, collecting specimens from 1690 onwards. His *Historia Insectorum* was almost ready for the press when he died. Published posthumously in 1710, it contains the first entomological record from the North Wood, the observation that the Duke of Burgundy fritillary (*Hamearis lucina*) 'is pretty common about Dulwich'.

Among Ray's many correspondents was the London apothecary James Petiver (*c*.1665–1718). His shop in Aldersgate Street became a meeting place for collectors, and a repository of plant and animal specimens from all over the world. Although he regretted his lack of 'Academicall Learning', Petiver's research earned him a Fellowship of the Royal Society in 1695. On his death, his vast – and chaotic – collection was bought by his friend Sir Hans Sloane, the Irish-born naturalist, slave owner and founder of the British Museum, and many of his specimens are still in the Natural History Museum today.

It was Petiver who coined the name fritillary, from the Latin word for a chequered dice box, and his *Papilionem Britanniae Icones* (1717) described eighty British butterflies, including a white admiral (*Limenitis camilla*) 'found about Dullidge and Wickham near Croyden', a marsh fritillary (*Euphydryas aurinia*) observed in 'the Oak of Honour Woods near Dullidge, about the end of May and beginning of June', and the Glanville fritillary (*Melitaea cinxia*), which he named the 'White Dullidge Fritillary' because it was 'found in the *Wood*, thereabouts in May'. This butterfly is now named in recognition of Eleanor Glanville, one of the collectors who sent Petiver specimens and who first identified the species near her Lincolnshire home.

Entomological research suffered a major setback in March 1748 when a fire ravaged the area around Cornhill in the City of London, including the Swan Tavern where the Aurelians were holding a meeting. The members narrowly escaped with their lives, but their notes and specimens were all destroyed in the blaze. Disheartened, the group disbanded, and it was not until fourteen years later that Harris's nephew, also named Moses, decided to revive it. A skilled artist and engraver, he published *The Aurelian, or Natural History of English Insects* in 1766. Harris's illustrations combine artistic beauty with scientific accuracy, but their arrangement is bizarre to the modern eye. Each of the forty-one plates shows one or two butterflies in every stage of their development, a couple of moths, with sometimes a few beetles thrown in for good measure. The selection may have been an aesthetic choice, but could also have been dictated by the book's publication as a partwork; each instalment needed to have something for every interest.

The Aurelian includes an early sighting of the purple hairstreak at One Tree Hill (it can still be found there, and at Sydenham Hill Wood): 'They fly high, delighting to settle on the

Leaves of the Oak, and are commonly taken in Plenty in *Oak-of-Honour* Wood, near *Peckham*, in Surry'; two Camberwell beauties – 'one of the scarcest Flies of any known in England' – caught in 'Cool Arbour Lane' near Camberwell in August 1748, and delightfully named the 'Grand Surprize'; and the clouded yellow (*Colias crocea*), then known as the saffron, 'seen about Deptford, Peckham, &c. from June till September'. The only dragonfly to make it into *The Aurelian* was the broad-bodied chaser (*Libellula depressa*), along with its fearsome nymphs – an omission Harris rectified handsomely in his later book *An Exposition of English Insects* (1780).

It is not until the second half of the eighteenth century that we see a systematic development in the recording and classification of plants and animals. Building on the work of John Ray, the Swedish scientist Carl Linnaeus (1707–78) streamlined the cumbersome and haphazard Latin names invented by earlier scientists and established the binomial system in use today. The first English botanical work that claimed to employ the Linnaean taxonomy – though it did so inconsistently, incorporating many older classifications – was the *Plantae Cantabrigienses* by John Martyn, published in 1763. Martyn was Professor of Botany at Cambridge University, and though his book – as its title states – was primarily concerned with the plants of Cambridgeshire, reports from several other counties, including Surrey, were included at the end. In addition to the list of plants drawn up by Martyn's friend Harris on his walk nearly forty years earlier, there are the results of a fungus-gathering expedition 'about Dulwich' undertaken by the two men in October 1724. Apart from one agaric, the ten species recorded are mostly of the genus *Amanita*. The general list of 'plants' for Dulwich may also have been drawn up by Harris, since it consists mostly of fungi, including *Agaricus piperatus*, or peppery inkcap, *Boletus luteus* (now *Suillus luteus*), *Peziza punctata* (nail fungus) and *Clavaria hypoxylon* (now *Xylaria hypoxylon*), or candlesnuff, which still grows plentifully in Sydenham Hill Wood today. The only herbs listed for the area are generally found in meadows rather than woods: *Lathyrus nissolia* (grass vetchling), *Inula pulicaria* (small fleabane) and, on the common, a thistle, *Carduus acaulos* (now *Cirsium acaule*).[9]

The rapid acceptance of Linnaeus's system of nomenclature in Georgian England was largely due to the efforts of Joseph Banks (1743–1820). Banks corresponded with Linnaeus, was among the first British scientists to adopt his system of classification, and when he joined James Cook's first voyage to New Zealand and Australia in 1768, did so in the company of Linnaeus's pupil Daniel Solander. On his return in 1771, Banks assisted George III in establishing the Royal Botanic Gardens at Kew, and in 1778 was elected President of the Royal Society. Like that of Hans Sloane, Banks's career embodies the role played by the scientists of the eighteenth century in the consolidation of the British Empire and the Atlantic slave trade. When Cook's expedition landed in Tahiti, Banks came upon the breadfruit plant (*Artocarpus altilis*); realising that it could be a cheap source of food for slaves on the Caribbean plantations, he later instigated William Bligh's ill-fated voyage to transplant the shrub halfway around the world. In New Zealand, Banks was involved in skirmishes in which nine Māori were shot dead, and after landing at Botany Bay with Cook, he became a prominent advocate for the establishment of a penal colony in New South Wales.

Banks's interest in botany was fostered early in life by visits to the Society of Apothecaries' Physic Garden, near his mother's house in Chelsea. In 1777, William Curtis, the Garden's director, embarked on an ambitious project to record all 'such plants as grow wild in the environs of London' using the Linnaean system. Beautifully illustrated with engravings by James Sowerby, Sydenham Edwards and William Kilburn, *Flora Londinensis* appeared in six large volumes between 1777 and 1798.

Banks was among its subscribers. Despite the financial backing
of the Earl of Bute, a former prime minister, amateur botanist
and patron of the arts, the project nearly bankrupted Curtis,
obliging him to launch the more popular and profitable *Botanical Magazine*, which is still published today. Of the two projects,
'One brought me pudding,' he remarked, 'the other praise.' The
purpose of the *Botanical Magazine* was to familiarise gardeners
with the exotic plants that Banks and others were importing to
Britain from around the world. This international horticultural
trade would have a far-reaching effect on the botany of these
islands, including the North Wood, where the rhododendron *R.
ponticum*, introduced to the UK from Spain in the 1760s, would
become an invasive species.

It is to the *Flora Londinensis*, however, that we owe the first
detailed records of the indigenous botany of the North Wood. In
addition to flowers such as wood anemone, enchanter's nightshade and herb-Robert, which he found in woodland all around
London, Curtis recorded nine species in Honor Oak Wood, four
in and around Dulwich Wood, and one in Norwood. On the
clayey soil of Honor Oak, he observed three species of hypericum, or St John's wort: *H. androsaemum* (tutsan), *H. hirsutum*
and *H. pulchrum*. Hoary ragwort (*Senecio erucifolius*) was 'no
where more abundant than about the Oak of Honour Wood',
Lathyrus sylvestris grew there sparingly, while *Stachys arvensis*
flourished in the surrounding cornfields.

In Dulwich Wood, lily of the valley (*Convellaria majalis*)
flowered plentifully in May and June. Of the bluebell (*Hyacinthoides non-scripta*), he noted that 'our meadows, woods, and
hedge-rows, are beautifully decorated with the blossoms of this
plant in the spring'. The drooping flowers of the wild English
bluebell, he observed, 'obviously distinguished' it from a 'very
similar' recently introduced species, 'which is much more common
in gardens, and flowers at the same time; a plant overlooked by
LINNAEUS; but named by Mr. BANKS *Scilla campanulata*.' This

is the Spanish bluebell (now classified as *Hyacinthoides hispanica*), and his observation that both species could be found together in gardens suggests that hybridisation – a cause for concern among environmentalists today – may already have been taking place in the eighteenth century.

In addition to a moss, *Hypnum purum*, which grew plentifully in Honor Oak Wood, Curtis recorded several species of fungus, including *Agaricus glutinosus*, *A. floccosus* and *Phallus impudicus* (common stinkhorn). 'In the months of August, September, and October', he wrote, 'this singular Phenomenon of the Fungus tribe makes its appearance in Woods, Hedgerows, and Hedges . . . Near London it has been found in Coombwood, and Norwood.' One toadstool particularly excited him, a *Boletus lucidus*, now generally known by its Chinese name, Lingzhi:

> In the month of November, 1780, I fortunately found the fine specimen of this Boletus . . . in the Wood adjoining the Oak of Honour, near Peckham; on first discovering it, the top of the Pileus and stalk were of so bright a colour, and so beautifully polished, that I scarcely knew whether I had found a natural or an artificial production, a view of its under side, however, soon convinced me it was natural; it grew out of a rotten hazel stump.[10]

Towards the end of the eighteenth century, the area came to the attention of the Anglo-Irish zoologist Edward Donovan. His *Natural History of British Insects*, published in thirteen volumes between 1792 and 1808, lists six species from the North Wood. The blotched emerald (*Comibaena bajularia*), a green-winged moth that feeds on oak, 'appears to be a local species. It has been found for many years past in the month of June, near the Oak of Honor, by Peckham. We have never heard that it has been taken in any other place in England.' On account of the location, the blotched emerald was known as 'maid of honor moth'. The jewel beetle *Anthaxia salicis* (then known as *Buprestis salicis*) was found by 'a person on whose veracity we can rely . . . on the bark of an old willow tree, between Dulwich Common and Norwood' in June 1794. Another beetle, the iridescent green *Chrysomela marshami*, was found in Norwood, as were several moths. The 'beautiful little' pearl grass-veneer moth (*Catoptria pinella*) was found there in June 1798.

For an accurate identification of the dominant tree in the North Wood, however, we must turn to John Martyn's son and successor in the Chair of Botany at Cambridge. In his *Flora Rustica* (1792), Thomas Martyn appears to have been the first to recognise that it was not the pedunculate or English oak (*Quercus robur*), but the sessile oak (*Q. petraea*). Examining a branch sent to him by a Mr White of Norwood, of a tree that was 'by no means uncommon' in the area, he noted that it bore the 'essential characters' of the Durmast (an old New Forest term for *Q. petraea*), including 'sessile clustered acorns'.[11] However, his observation that the leaves bore a greater resemblance to those of an English oak suggests that White's specimen may have been a naturally occurring hybrid.

PROFIT AND LOSS

Hand in hand with its religious function, the See of Canterbury was very much a business, with extensive landholdings through-out England and beyond, and institutional links to slavery: founded in 1701, its missionary arm, the Society for the Propagation of the Gospel in Foreign Parts, of which successive Archbishops served as President, owned plantations in Barbados.

While the Dulwich Estate sold the rights to harvest its coppices, the Archbishop of Canterbury's woodreeves continued to manage the felling and sale of the underwood directly until the second half of the eighteenth century. The woodreeve Henry

(Harry) Margitts supervised the felling of Bewley Coppice in 1724; Windalls and part of Great Stakepit in 1725; the rest of Stakepit in 1726; Gravelly Hill in 1727; Elderhole in 1729; half of Claylands in 1730, and the rest the following year. Biggin Wood was also cropped in two batches, in 1732 and 1733, and in 1734 the cycle began again with the felling of 'Buly', and Windalls the year after.[12]

In 1761, however, there was a change in the way the Arch-bishop's woods were managed. That year, the 'coppices of underwood . . . known by the several names of Claylands, Big-gins, Bewley, Windals, great Stakepit, Little Stakepit, Gravelly Hill and Elderhole . . . containing in the whole 341 acres' were leased to William Newton of Lambeth for a rent of £55 a year. The lease specified that the underwood was to be felled 'only as hath been heretofore customarily practised,' and that 'all Timber trees and Timber like trees . . . ought to be left standing and growing therein upon the felling of the said Coppices'.[13]

The effect was to free the Archbishopric from the responsibil-ity of managing the woods, and the attendant financial risk. In a good year, the Archbishop had cleared a respectable profit. The felling of Windalls Coppice in 1725, for example, raised £172 from the sale of timber and underwood. After deducting £105 13s to cover the repair of fencing, payments to workmen and the woodreeve's annual salary of £20, there was a balance of £66 7s. The wood cut from Gravelly Hill in 1727 generated a clear profit of £48 6s 6d after these expenses had been met. But when half of Claylands was felled in 1730, the wood raised £79 5s which, after deducting £55 16s expenses, left a profit of just £23 9s, and the downward trend continued in the years that followed. Under the new arrangement, the Archbishop would receive a guaranteed income of £55 per annum from the woods while, in return for the proceeds from the sale of timber, the lessee shouldered the expense of maintaining and felling them. Moreover, the lease specified that all 'hazel, hollies Willows,

Bushes and Thornes' should be delivered to the Archbishop's palace at Lambeth each Michaelmas. As we have seen, this brushwood had previously been 'claymed by the Tenants of Lambeth', so the removal of this custumal right was a significant development, and a sign of things to come.

5

INDUSTRY AND ENCLOSURE

1790–1850

The Age of Enlightenment did not look altogether favourably on woodlands. To a mindset that valued rational self-interest, they seemed a relic of a primitive past, a place of darkness, disorder and superstition. The word savage is derived, via the medieval French *sauvage*, from the Latin *silvaticus*, 'of the woods'. Edward Gibbon was characteristic of his era when, in his *History of the Decline and Fall of the Roman Empire* (1776–88), he repeatedly evoked the 'thick and gloomy woods' from which savage hordes emerged to harass the peaceful inhabitants of the settled lands. He praised the Romans' clearance of large areas of woodland as a civilising endeavour, and lamented how, after their withdrawal in 410, much of Britain 'returned to its primitive state of a savage and solitary forest'.

Although the influential landscape gardeners Lancelot 'Capability' Brown and Humphry Repton admired veteran trees and often incorporated them in their designs, their appreciation of woodland was primarily scenic. Their parks and gardens, while intended to look natural, were artfully constructed to conjure an idealised rural idyll, a process that often involved creating artificial lakes and moving large quantities of earth to produce contours pleasing to the eye. Copses and spinneys were retained, reshaped or planted to frame a vista, and intended to be admired from a distance.

Reason marched hand in hand with commerce. The completion of the first Blackfriars Bridge in 1769 made Camberwell,
Dulwich and Sydenham more easily accessible to merchants and
bankers from the City of London who could afford to keep a
horse and carriage, and the agrarian landscape of the area developed into a mosaic of small country houses set amid paddocks
and landscaped parkland: Bell House (1767), Belair House (1785)
and Tappen House (1803) in Dulwich Village all date from this
period, while at the northern tip of King's Coppice, Kingswood
Lodge was built for the solicitor William Vizard in 1811.

Both Senex and Rocque's maps of Surrey show a road leading
south from Dulwich Common to Penge, but it appears to have
been little more than a track through the woods, known as Locus
Lane. In 1787, John Morgan, the proprietor of Penge Place, which
stood at the northern end of Penge Common, was given permission by the Dulwich Estate to widen and surface the road at his
own expense.[1] It was known as the Penge or Dulwich Road until
the 1870s, when it was renamed College Road to mark the
construction of the school's new premises. To recoup his costs,
Morgan set up the toll gate that still exists on College Road.

By now, the Industrial Revolution had made coal and iron
readily available, reducing demand for charcoal and timber, so
parts of the wood were grubbed up for farmland. Many ancient
trees were felled, and large tracts of woodland assumed the
appearance of open common. At the Dulwich Estate, John
Dugleby, surveyor from 1785 to 1804, was alert to the changing
circumstances and keen to ensure that the land remained profitable. The Fifty Acre Wood, which extended to the Green Man
on John Cary's 1786 *Actual Survey of the Country Fifteen Miles
Round London on a Scale of One Inch to a Mile*, was the first to
go. On 17 September 1790, Dugleby wrote, 'I have this day
surveyed the Green Man Wood & am of the opinion that it will
be of Advantage to the College to grub up the underwood on
each side of [Cox's] walk & to leave a space of Ground on each

side of the Walk 25 feet wide measuring from the center of the walk . . .' Cleared of trees, he calculated the land to be worth £7 7s an acre, with 'the tenant to bear the expense of clearing the wood'.[2] Forty Acre Wood was grubbed up a few years later, creating open fields between Low Cross and King's coppices.

Dugleby also considered the pollards that lined the fields, roads and common to be unproductive, and during his twenty-year tenure, had more than three thousand of them felled and replaced by nursery-grown standards.[3] In 1799, he reported the acreage of the woods as follows:

The Lapse & part of Ambroke Hill	22a. 1r. 26p.
Ambroke Hill (remainder)	20a. 0r. 28p.
Peckermans No. 1	28a. 3r. 22p.
Peckermans No. 2	28a. 1r. 23p.
Low Cross	31a. 2r. 20p.
Vicars Oak East part	20a. 0r. 00p.
Vicars Oak West part	20a. 0r. 00p.
Kings Coppice No. 1	19a. 3r. 22p.
Kings Coppice No. 2	20a. 2r. 22p.
Total	212a. 0r. 09p.[4]

This was almost fifty acres less than was shown in the terrier of 1668, reflecting the recent conversion to arable.

THE NEW CARTOGRAPHY

It was at this point, when the North Wood, though reduced in extent, had not yet succumbed to the urban expansion of the nineteenth century, that improvements in surveying technology gave rise to the most accurate and detailed maps of the countryside around London so far. The principle of triangulation – recording the angle of a distant object to either end of a measured baseline

Pl. III.   *Philos. Trans. Vol.* LXXX. *Tab.* VII. *p.* 172.

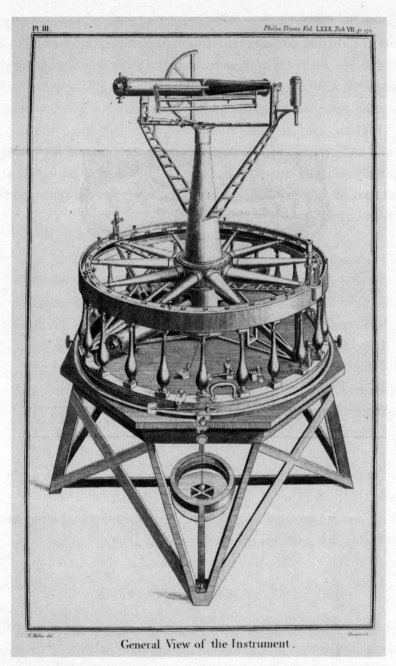

General View of the Instrument.

Jesse Ramsden's theodolite, engraved by Thomas Milne, from
William Roy's 'Account of the Trigonometrical Operation, whereby
the Distance between the Meridians of the Royal Observatories of
Greenwich and Paris has been determined', in the *Philosophical
Transactions of the Royal Society,* Vol. 80, 1 January 1790.

to calculate its distance from the observer – had been understood since the ancient Greeks, but the equipment available was insufficiently precise to use it over long distances. Only after the development of the theodolite did it become a viable technique for mapping large areas with greater accuracy than before.

Once again, Joseph Banks was a prime instigator. In 1783, as President of the Royal Society, he received a memorandum from Jean-Dominique de Cassini, Director of the Paris Observatory, whose father, grandfather and great-grandfather had pioneered the triangulation of France. Cassini suggested that a joint trigonometric survey be conducted to resolve discrepancies between measurements taken by the Greenwich and Paris observatories. The following year, Banks commissioned the military engineer Major-General William Roy to take charge of the operation, and in 1784 Roy measured out a five-mile baseline on flat ground on Hounslow Heath (now under Heathrow Airport), using a steel chain precision-engineered by Jesse Ramsden, the leading instrument maker of the day.

From there, with the aid of a large theodolite also made by Ramsden, mounted on a portable scaffold and transported in its own carriage, he constructed a series of triangles across Surrey and Kent to Dungeness, and – using white lights – over the Channel to Dunkirk. One of Roy's triangulation stations was at Norwood, 'towards the Croydon end of the heights'; on his map, it corresponds to the present site of the transmitting station on Beaulieu Heights. From this one-hundred-metre elevation, he could take sightings over the swaying canopy of the North Wood to Hanger Hill in Ealing, Hundred Acres on Banstead Downs, the Royal Observatory at Greenwich and Severndroog Castle on Shooters Hill.[5]

Roy died in 1790, however, shortly after completing his triangulation; by 1793 Cassini had been thrown out of his observatory by the French revolutionary government, and Britain and France were at war. Fortunately Roy's careful measurements were not in vain: as he had always intended, they came to form the basis of a survey of the whole of Britain. Starting from his Hounslow baseline, the Board of Ordnance – the forerunner of the Ministry of Defence – embarked on its Principal Triangulation of Great Britain in 1791, and the Ordnance Survey came into being.

Before it could issue any maps itself, two important surveys based at least in part on its co-ordinates were published. Between them, they show the full extent of the North Wood in the 1790s. The first to appear was Joseph Lindley and William Crosley's *Map of the County of Surrey, from a Survey made in the years 1789 and 1790*, which was published in 1793. The son of a Halifax solicitor, Lindley had worked at the Royal Observatory and taken part in Roy's London–Paris triangulation; Crosley was an estate surveyor with an extensive practice in the north of England, and may also have been a Yorkshireman.[6]

The trigonometrical observations were made by Lindley, while the on-the-ground surveying was mostly undertaken by Crosley, using a plane table and a measuring wheel, as the chain he tried at first stretched and broke in use, and 'was soon found too tedious'. Lindley's first trigonometrical station was General Roy's old observation post on Norwood Heights, and he himself surveyed the roads 'from Dulwich to Sydenham, down Lordship Lane to Goose Green, and from thence to Camberwell, the roads also on the east side of Dulwich Common, by the Gipsey House, Mr Morgan's road to Penge Place, and Penge Green'.[7]

Lindley and Crosley's map shows the arc of Dulwich Woods curving around the Kent border, with Morgan's new road running through them to Penge Place. Beyond it, the tree cover broadens out, and is clearly labelled North Wood. On its eastern flank, 'Timber Hill' overlooks Penge Common; to the east lies Knight's Hill Common; to the south, beyond Bulay Farm and Beggars Hill, is Whitehorse Farm.

Thomas Milne was not directly employed on the survey, but seems to have been associated with it: he drew the illustrations

of instruments for Roy's report in the *Philosophical Transactions of the Royal Society*, and in 1794 mapped Norfolk for
the royal cartographer William Faden, who would later publish
the first Ordnance Survey maps. A surveyor with twenty years'
experience working on estates in Scotland, Milne had moved to
England in 1785, where he established himself as a cartographer.
By 1791, his reputation was such that George Adams, in his
Geometrical and Graphical Essays, described him as 'one of the
most able and expert surveyors of the present day', noting his
skill in using the theodolite. Milne himself contributed two
chapters, 'Mr. Milne's Method of Surveying' and 'Observations
on Plotting', to the book, as well as drawing all its illustrations
and specimen surveys.[8]

Milne's contribution provides an insight into his method of
surveying:

> Having two assistants provided with a pole each, to which
> are attached plumb lines for keeping them perpendicular,
> and a third assistant for carrying the theodolite; I proceed to
> plant the instrument where I began to measure, or at any
> other angular point in the circuit; if the wind blows high, I
> choose a point to begin at that is sheltered from it, so that the
> needle may settle steady at the magnetic north, which is
> indispensably necessary at first setting off, at the same time
> taking care that no iron is so near the place as to attract the
> needle.[9]

Using Roy's published triangulation tables, his own surveys, and
information he may have gleaned though his connections, he
published *Milne's Plan of the Cities of London and Westminster, circumadjacent Towns and Parishes &c, laid down from a
Trigonometrical Survey taken in the Years 1795–9* in 1800, a
year before the first Ordnance Survey map, of Kent, appeared.
(The entire first series was not complete until 1870.) Milne's

map, printed on six large sheets on a scale of two inches to one mile, covers an area of about 260 square miles, from Heston in the west to Greenwich in the east, and from Finchley in the north to Norwood in the south. With its sound basis in triangulation, it is the first map of the Greater London area that can be neatly superimposed on to a modern street plan, and the first to show the extent of the North Wood with precision.

Milne engraved and published the map himself, using letters and colouring to indicate land use: arable land is marked with the letter 'a' and tinted yellow; meadow is marked 'm' and shaded light green; paddocks and parks are marked 'p' and coloured pink; woodland is dark green and marked 'w'. Arable fields on common land are designated by the letters 'caf' and coloured brown, while common meadows are marked 'cmf' and coloured light green. Hills are shown by hachures. The result is an accurate and up-to-date picture of a changing landscape on the eve of enclosure.

The southernmost parts of the North Wood lay beyond the edge of Milne's map, but the main body of it is shown on Sheet 5, with the westernmost coppices on Sheet 3. The wood is still ringed by the commons of Dulwich, Sydenham, 'Pinge' and Norwood. The Fifty Acre Wood has gone, leaving Cox's Walk a tree-lined avenue through open fields. Further south, arable fields and pasture push through from Dulwich to Penge, separating the northern and southern parts of the wood. Great Stakepit Coppice is still wooded, as is Biggin Hill Coppice, though Biggin Wood is now detached from it and surrounded by pasture and arable land. To the north, Oak of Honor Wood has shrunk to about half the extent shown on Rocque's 1745 map, with its lower slopes converted to arable, presumably the cornfields observed by Curtis. To the west, part of Coleson's Coppice remains, though detached from the main wood. While Rocque's map showed only one road through Oak of Honor Wood, following the line of today's Forest Hill Road before turning south to skirt the eastern flank of the hill, Honor Oak Road now cuts a swath through the middle, with villas set in substantial parkland marching up the hill on either side. It was around this time that the name Forest Hill came into use to designate the burgeoning settlement.[10]

Strangely, only a few copies of Milne's map, numbered and signed by him, were printed, and only one set of all six sheets survives; presented to King George III, it is now in the British Library. It is alarming to think how closely the single most informative map we have of the North Wood came to being lost altogether. Maybe Milne never intended the map for wider circulation, although it has been speculated that the Ordnance Survey, or William Faden, may have invoked copyright law to prevent its publication.[11] Instead, maps of the London region by Cary and Faden, first published in 1786 and 1788 respectively and compiled from county maps up to thirty or forty years old, continued to be reprinted into the reign of Queen Victoria, with new developments such as canals and railways added to their outdated and often inaccurate cartography.

Conversion to farmland and private gardens was not the only process reducing the extent of the woods; demand for gravel for roadbuilding and clay for brick and tile making was altering the very contours of the ground on which they stood. Evidence given in the Rydon dispute suggests that gravel was being quarried in Penge as early as the 1560s, if not before. Mar's Norwood Plan of 1678 shows that the Gravelly Hill Coppice in the Archbishop of Canterbury's woods had been partially grubbed up, and Rocque's 1745 map marks a gravel pit on the edge of Knight's Hill Common. On 30 June 1797, Dugleby, anticipating that 'gravel will become a scarce article when that part of Norwood in Croydon Parish is enclosed,' noted that 'there appears to be a considerable quantity of that article in the Woods called Vicars Oak & the Woods next Sydenham Common . . .' On 22 August, he inspected Vicar's Oak and Low Cross woods, and reported that 'digging down about 3 feet and about 10 feet from the hedges' he found 'very good gravel in Vicar's Oak fit for that purpose & am of the opinion that enough to cover the said Road [the new road to Penge] will do very little Hurt to the Wood as the price may be hereafter increased by the road being made good.'[12]

Clay was dug on the south side of Dulwich Common from the seventeenth century, if not earlier, leaving the pond that can be seen today; Rocque's map shows a 'Bree Kill' (brick kiln) on the site. By 1702, there was a tile kiln on Ambrook Hill,[13] and in 1738, seventeen acres on the western flank of Oak of Honor Hill were leased to a brickmaker, who set up a kiln there, extracting his raw material from the hillside.[14] And at the end of the nineteenth century, Anderson noted that 'The beautiful green hillock, from time immemorial known as Biggin Hill, having fallen into the hands of the brickmaker, is, on account of the excellence of its clay, now rapidly diminishing.'[15]

THE END OF THE COMMONS

The reduction of the extent of the woodland was accelerated by the practice of enclosure. Throughout the seventeenth and eighteenth centuries, landowners had been making periodic attempts to fence off commons on which local people without land of their own were allowed to graze livestock and gather firewood. In 1754, locals tore down fences and asserted their right to gather fuel in Cooper's Wood, and in 1792 one Michael Bradley, a father of four, was shot in the leg by a landowner, Samuel Atkinson, for exercising common rights in Coleson's Coppice. Infection set in, and Bradley subsequently died. By the time the coroner's court had returned a verdict of manslaughter, Atkinson had absconded, and seems to have escaped punishment.[16]

In the late eighteenth and early nineteenth centuries, a series of Enclosure Acts formalised the removal of these common lands from public ownership, allowing them to be broken up into allotments and sold to private landlords. In 1797, the Croydon Enclosure Act was passed. Biggin Hill Coppice was sold by the enclosure commissioners to pay their salaries and expenses; divided into long rectangular plots, most of the land was bought by City businessmen to construct suburban villas.[17] White Horse Wood, meanwhile, was enclosed by John Cator, who had bought the manor ten years previously. By 1800, the wood was completely surrounded by fields. On Cator's death in 1806, his nephew John Barwell Cator sold the estate to John Davidson Smith, who partitioned it into small plots and sold them for development, leaving only the central triangle of woodland.[18]

Enclosure Acts for Dulwich, Lambeth and Norwood followed in 1805, 1806 and 1808 respectively. Following the Dulwich Enclosure Act, the governors commissioned a survey of the estate from the land agent William James, who reported that:

> The woods and Coppices, since the introduction of Coal, are no longer necessary for the supply of Fuel for the College, and on this account in the last Bill a Clause was introduced impowering the College to grant the same or a part thereof on Building Leases. The produce of this Land does not give an Annual profit of more than 15/ per acre, and being at a great distance from the College, it is very liable to depredations.[19]

Sydenham Common – the Westwood so fiercely defended by Abraham Colfe and his parishioners two centuries earlier – was finally enclosed in 1810. The commons of Croydon and Lambeth contributed 1,350 acres to the burgeoning suburb of Norwood, where the former Lord Chancellor Edward Thurlow had purchased Leigham Manor in 1789. Thurlow commissioned the architect Henry Holland to build him a house at Knight's Hill, but when the project ran over budget, he refused to move in. 'He was first cheated by his architect,' commented another Lord Chancellor, the Earl of Eldon, 'and then he cheated himself; for the house cost more than he expected, so he never would go into it. Very foolish, but so it was.' After Thurlow died in September 1806, his executors pulled down the mansion and sold the lands for development.[20] His connection with the area, unhappy though it was, is commemorated in the naming of Thurlow Park Road.

The politician and diplomat Sir John Stanley first visited the area in 1789, to call on the political hostess Mary Nesbitt, whose portrait by Joshua Reynolds can be seen in the Wallace Collection. The mistress of Augustus Hervey, 3rd Earl of Bristol, she had inherited Park House on his death in 1779. The house stood amid fields carved out from the north-western corner of Great Stakepit Coppice, on the future site of the Virgo Fidelis convent:

> The house had swelled itself out from a cottage, by additions to it by Lord Bristol, and after his death by Mrs. Nesbitt, into a comfortable and spacious villa, with stables &c. Lord Bristol in his rides had been struck with the picturesque and peaceful character of the woody recess in which the cottage stood, divided by a space of cleared land, enclosed from Norwood Common. He purchased the place, and obtained from the Archbishop of Canterbury a grant of several acres, at that time covered with wood, so that there were meadows and pasture fields, a garden and pleasure ground of nearly half a mile in length, all within a ring fence. The common was covered with gorse, and extended from the crown of Norwood hill towards the west, to the Dulwich Road on the south, crossing a valley to cultivated lands, with only here and there a dwelling on them.[21]

The Norwood Enclosure Act of 1808 unleashed a wave of development. By the time the first Ordnance Survey map of the area, part of the 'Old Series', was published in 1816, Great Stakepit Coppice had disappeared (except, ironically, for the fragment purchased from the Archbishop by Lord Bristol, which survives today as Convent Wood), as had Elderhole and Clayland coppices. Thomas Allen's *History and Antiquities of the Parish of Lambeth* (1826) recorded that 'Formerly the major part was common woodland; this has been grubbed up, and neat commodious villa residences built thereon.' When Penge Common was enclosed in 1827 at the request of Barwell Cator, the philosopher John Stuart Mill lamented that one of 'the two finest pieces of natural scenery within twelve miles of the capital' – the other being Addington Hills – was 'now in preparation for being cut up into citizens' boxes and bits of garden ground'.[22]

John Davidson Smith also bought Bewley Coppice, on Spa Hill, where a mineral spring enabled him to establish Beulah Spa, which opened in 1831. Designed by the celebrated architect Decimus Burton, the spa grounds included about twenty acres of enclosed woodland, and offered spectacular views as far as Banstead Downs and Windsor Castle, while stagecoaches ran between Charing Cross and Beulah Spa three times a day.[23] Some time around 1830, Biggin Wood House was built in the northern part of Biggin Wood, and occupied by a corn merchant called Hugh Bowditch; after his death in 1870, it was purchased by James Epps, a well-known manufacturer of homeopathic cocoa.[24]

In 1836, control of all lands belonging to bishoprics in England and Wales – including the Archbishop of Canterbury's lands in Croydon – was transferred to a new corporate body, the Ecclesiastical Commissioners, with the aim of distributing the revenues throughout the Church as a whole. The new commission thus became one of the largest landlords in the area, and began releasing land for house building, accelerating the development of suburbs such as Norwood and Selhurst. West Norwood Cemetery opened in 1836 on Knight's Hill, on farmland that was once part of the North Wood. Although much of the site was cleared, a number of mature trees were retained in the landscaping. A tree survey performed by the Parks Agency in 2005 identified one oak thought to date from 1540 to 1640, while core samples showed that fourteen more oaks and an ash also pre-dated the foundation of the cemetery.[25]

In 1801, an Act of Parliament had been passed authorising the construction of the Croydon Canal. Opened in 1809, it ran from the Grand Surrey Canal at New Cross through Brockley, from where a chain of locks carried it up the eastern slope of Honor Oak Hill, further reducing this outpost of the North Wood. Some woodland still remained, however. 'After passing Sydenham Common towards Deptford,' wrote a contemporary observer, the canal

> enters a large wood, and passes it for near three quarters of a mile, presenting the most rich and delightful scenery, with fine views, at intervals of the new and elegant houses on Forest Hill, that rise directly up from the canal. Several of the paddocks belonging to these houses, are now extended down to the canal; and fancy boat-houses and pleasure-houses have been built on its banks, so as to tender a walk along it truly delightful.[26]

From Honor Oak, the canal continued via Penge to Norwood, from where another series of locks took it downhill to Croydon. Barges carrying stone, lime, fuller's earth or timber ran from Croydon to Deptford, and returned to Croydon laden with coal. To keep the canal supplied with water, reservoirs were constructed on Penge Common and at South Norwood; although the Penge reservoir has long since been filled in, the latter forms the centrepiece of South Norwood Lake and Grounds.

THE NORTH WOOD, *c.*1560–1800

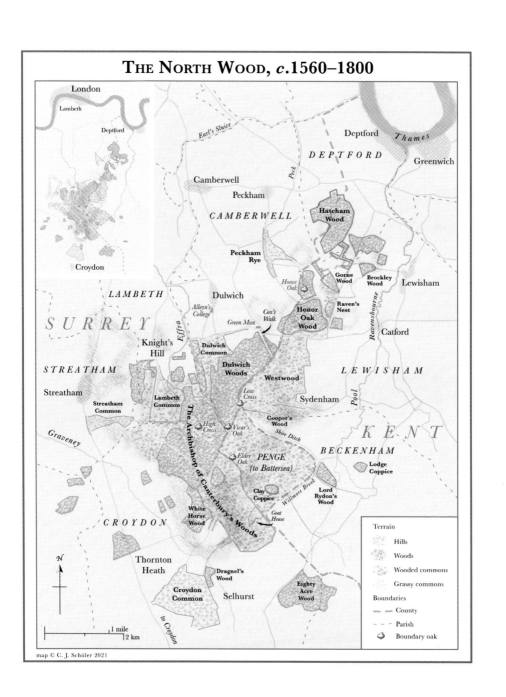

London
Lambeth
Deptford
Croydon

Earl's Sluice

Deptford

Thames

DEPTFORD

Greenwich

Camberwell

Peckham

Peck

CAMBERWELL

Hatcham Wood

Peckham Rye

Gorne Wood

Brockley Wood

Lewisham

Honor Oak

LAMBETH

Dulwich

Honor Oak Wood

Raven's Nest

Alleyn's College

Green Man

Cox's Walk

S U R R E Y

Knight's Hill

Elfra

Dulwich Common

Ravensbourne

Catford

Dulwich Woods

Westwood

L E W I S H A M

STREATHAM

Streatham

Low Cross

Sydenham

Pool

Streatham Common

Lambeth Common

The Archbishop of Canterbury's Woods

High Cross

Vicar's Oak

Cooper's Wood

Shire Ditch

K E N T

Graveney

BECKENHAM

Elder Oak

PENGE (to Battersea)

Lodge Coppice

Willmore Brook

Clay Coppice

Lord Rydon's Wood

Gott House

White Horse Wood

C R O Y D O N

Thornton Heath

Dragnel's Wood

Eighty Acre Wood

Croydon Common

Selhurst

to Croydon

N

1 mile
2 km

Terrain

Hills
Woods
Wooded commons
Grassy commons

Boundaries

County
Parish
Boundary oak

map © C. J. Schüler 2021

This miniature for the month of November in *Les Très Riches Heures du Duc de Berry* (c.1485) illustrates the practice of pannage, as herdsmen release pigs into the woods to feed on acorns or beech mast. Musée Condé, Chantilly.

The calendar page for February in the *Psalter of Lambert le Bègue* shows a man using a billhook to prune a tree. British Library, Additional 21114 f.1v.

Part of a hoard of silver and gold coins of Edward III deposited in the North Wood around 1365 and unearthed on Beulah Hill, Upper Norwood in 1953. The coins are now in the Museum of London. © Museum of London.

Archbishop John Whitgift's Hospital of the Holy Trinity in Croydon was founded in 1596 to provide almshouses for the poor. According to the original accounts, at least some of its bricks were fired with 'a load of wood from Norwood'.

Monument in St Mary's Church, Battersea to Oliver St John, 1st Viscount Grandison (1559–1630) and his wife Joan Holcrofte (c.1550–1631), the daughter of Henry Rydon and widow of Thomas Holcrofte. Through their marriage, St John acquired the lease of the manor of Battersea, including Penge, and in 1627 he bought the freehold from the Crown. The portrait busts were sculpted by Nicholas Stone the Elder.

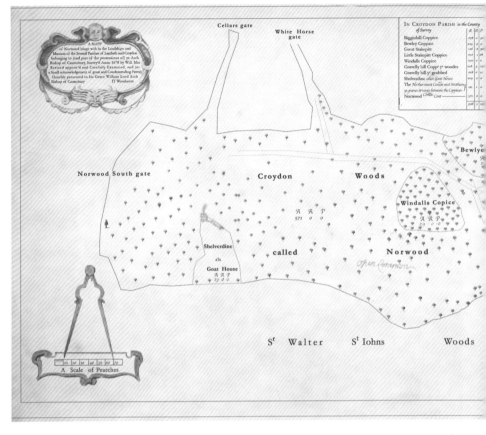

A modern facsimile of the surveyor William Mar's map, commissioned by Archbishop William Sancroft's woodreeve in 1678, of the woods in Croydon and Lambeth, showing each coppice with its acreage. The adjoining woods in Penge are still owned by a member of the St John family. The original parchment map is now in the Museum of Croydon.

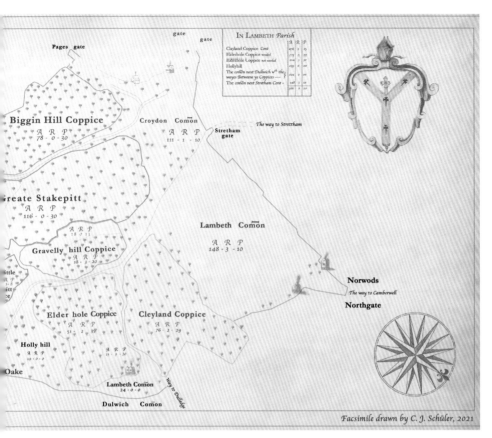

IN LAMBETH *Parish*	A	R	P
Clayland Coppice *Cont*	076	2	25
Elderhole Coppice *wodd*	051	0	015
Biddehole Coppice *not wodd*	016	1	15
Hollyhill	030	0	00
The *comon* next *Dullwich* w[ch] the 3 wayes *Betweene ye Coppices*	004	0	00
The *comon* next *Strettham Cont*	148	3	10
	301	0	10

Pages gate

gate gate

Biggin Hill Coppice
A R P
78 - 0 - 30

Croydon Comon
A R P
111 - 1 - 10

Stretham gate

The way to Strettham

Greate Stakepitt
A R P
116 - 0 - 30

A R P
18 - 0 - 11

Lambeth Comon
A R P
148 - 3 - 10

Gravelly hill Coppice
A R P
18 - 3 - 20

Little
R P
itt
ce

Elder hole Coppice
A R P
51 - 2 - 35

Cleyland Coppice
A R P
76 - 2 - 29

Norwods

The way to Camberwell

Northgate

Holly hill
A R P
10 - 0 - 0

A R P
18 - 3 - 30

Oake

Lambeth Comon
24 - 0 - 0

Way to Dullidg

Dulwich Comon

Facsimile drawn by C. J. Schüler, 2021

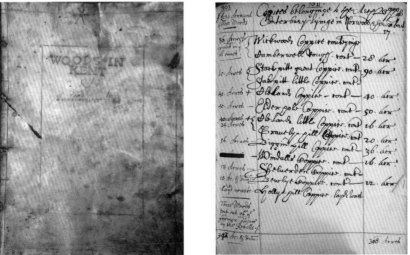

This vellum-bound notebook contains the woodreeve William Somner's survey of the woods owned by the Archbishop of Canterbury in Kent and Surrey in 1611. The final page lists the coppices 'in Norwood & thereabout', with their acreages. In the left hand margin, his successor has assessed their condition in 1663, noting the damage done during the Civil War and the interregnum. Courtesy of Lambeth Palace Library.

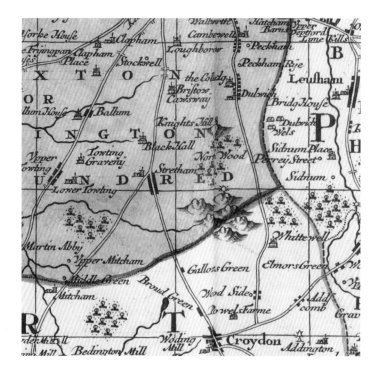

It was the German cartographer Matthäus Seutter who, around 1730, first placed the name 'North Wood' on a printed map, though his depiction of its extent is sketchy. Alleyn's college and the mineral spa at the Green Man, named 'Dulwich Wells', are also shown.

The celebrated London cartographer John Senex's *New Map of the County of Surrey* (1729) shows the woods with greater accuracy, including the tree-lined Cox's Walk running from the Green Man to Sydenham Wells, here named 'Dulwich Wells'.

To the Hon.ble Richard Bateman
This Plate is humbly Dedicated by his most Obedient Servant Moses Harris.

This plate from a 1778 edition of *The Aurelian* by Moses Harris shows a selection of woodland moths and butterflies in their larval, pupal and adult forms. Figures a to f depict the oak eggar moth (*Lasiocampa quercus*), g to l the brimstone moth (*Opisthograptis luteolata*), m to o the clouded yellow butterfly (*Coleas croceus*), and p to s a china mark moth (*Elophila sp.*), and t to u, the wood white butterfly (*Leptidea sinapis*) on hawthorn leaves.

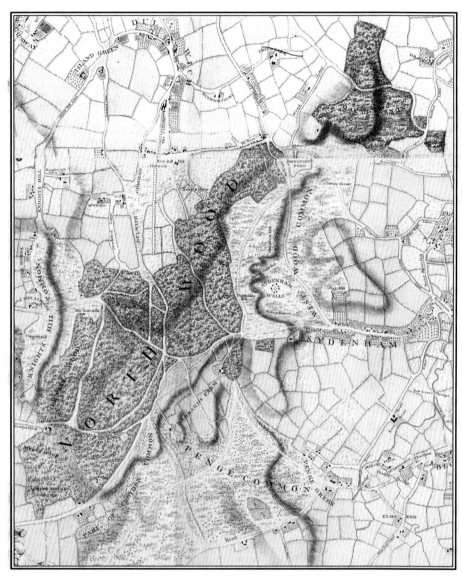

A detail from John Rocque's *An Exact Survey of the citys of London
Westminster ye Borough of Southwark and the Country near ten miles round*
(1746), showing the North Wood, the adjoining commons, and 'Oak of
Arnon' wood to the north.

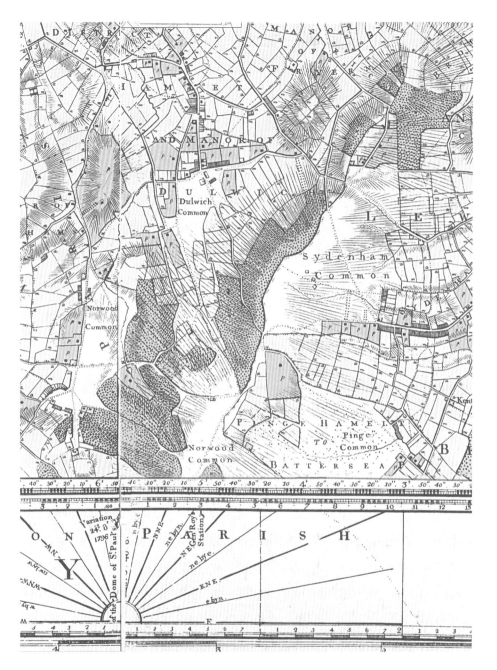

This detail from *Milne's plan of the cities of London and Westminster, circumjacent towns and parishes &c* (1800) shows the extent to which the North Wood had shrunk since Rocque surveyed it half a century earlier.

When the French Impressionist Camille Pissarro stood on the Cox's Walk footbridge in 1871 to paint this train approaching from Lordship Lane Station, the railway was less than a decade old and the embankments were treeless, though part of the woods can be glimpsed to the left. Now, with the branch line long gone, the trees have reclaimed the scene. Courtauld Institute of Art.

The Camberwell-based artist John Arthur Poulter (1824–1921) made this watercolour of *Dulwich Wood and Common* in 1870. From the South London Gallery Collection/Southwark Art Collection, Southwark Council, London.

Pissarro's view of the newly built St Stephen's church on College Road, Dulwich, shows part of Low Cross Wood to the left. Apart from the disappearance of the Crystal Palace, seen in the background, the view is scarcely altered today. A replica of the painting hangs in the church.

Poulter continued to paint the woods until near the end of his long life; his *Study of Trees in Dulwich Wood* dates from 1914. From the South London Gallery Collection/Southwark Art Collection, Southwark Council, London.

These rare early photographs of Dulwich Woods (top) and Cox's Walk (above) appeared in F. D. Power's *Ornithological Notes from a South London Suburb* (1910).

These early 20th-century postcards depict Cox's Walk (top) and the footbridge that carries it across the branch line through the woods (above).

Alderman David Stone, the original occupant of Fairwood, one of the villas on the upper slope of Sydenham Hill Wood, commissioned James Pulham & Son to build this folly in its grounds during the 1870s. The Gothic 'ruin' is constructed of brick clad in Pulhamite artificial stone.

One of the last canals to be built, it was made obsolete by the coming of the railways within a few years of its completion, and closed in 1836. The watercourse was filled in to form the trackbed of the London & Croydon Railway, which opened in June 1839 – a harbinger of the changes about to engulf the woods.

PLEASURE IN THE PATHLESS WOODS

Despite the Enclosure Acts and its proximity to the expanding metropolis, the area retained its rural character well into the nineteenth century, an expanse of woodland, heath, scrub, pasture and isolated farms, where nightingales sang and the churring of nightjars could still be heard at dusk.[27] Writing at the end of the nineteenth century, Anderson recalled that within living memory, Upper Norwood:

> where not covered with oak-woods, was a furze-clad waste, with here and there a patch of cultivated ground. There was however a considerable breadth of pasture-land between the upper and lower portions of the hamlet, respectively within the parishes of Croydon and Lambeth; but the former was still surrounded on the south and east by thick woods, in which rabbits and hedgehogs burrowed; where sang the nightingale: and the cooing of the ring-dove mingled with a melody, arising from throats of innumerable other feathered warblers. The houses with which the northern slope was beginning to be dotted stood at long intervals, and there were not half-a-dozen shops in the place.

The stretch of Beulah Hill between All Saints' Church and Spa Hill, then called Leather Bottle Lane, was little more than a path between Stakepit and Bewley's coppices, known as 'between the woods', while today's Parchmore Road was a green lane, lined with ancient pollard oaks, which became impassable in winter. As late as 1832, the countryside was still sufficiently open for the Surrey Stag Hounds to ride from Sutton across Mitcham Common and Biggin Wood to Penge Common, where they finally brought down their deer.[28]

By the late eighteenth century, the poets and painters of the Romantic movement had come to reject the ethos of the Enlightenment; viewing the growth of industrial capitalism with disgust, they sought solace and inspiration in the works of nature. 'There is a pleasure in the pathless woods,' wrote Byron in *Childe Harold's Pilgrimage*, 'Society where none intrudes . . .' He was not the only writer or artist enthralled to discover this rural idyll within sight of the metropolis. Walking on Peckham Rye when he was about ten years old, William Blake looked up to see 'a tree filled with angels, bright angelic wings bespangling every bough like stars.'[29] In 1824 his disciple, the landscape painter Samuel Palmer, wrote in his sketchbook:

> When you go to Dulwich it is not enough on coming home to make recollections in which shall be united the scattered parts about those sweet fields into a sentimental and Dulwich looking whole. No. But considering Dulwich as the gate into the world of vision one must try behind the hills to bring up a mystic glimmer like that which lights our dreams. And those same hills . . . should give us promise that the country beyond them is Paradise.[30]

The Scottish poet Thomas Campbell settled on Peak Hill in Sydenham in 1804, when the area was still rural. After viewing his new home, he wrote to his friend James Currie:

> When arriving at the height of Sydenham the whole glory of London spread itself before us like a picture in distant but distinct perspective. Fifteen miles and more of the peopled

shores of the Thames lie in that prospect; St Paul's in the centre – Westminster towers on the left. I think we even traced a white sail at the very verge of the landscape . . . This view is within a short walk of my intended home. A common, but not a naked one, in the heart of a lovely country, rises all round it. I have a whole field to expatiate over undisturbed; none of your hedged roads and London out-of-town villages about me, but 'ample space and verge enough' to compose a whole tragedy unmolested.

In the summer of 1806 Campbell was visited by the surgeon Sir Charles Bell. They 'rambled down the village,' Bell recalled, 'and walked under the delightful trees in moonlight.' At the Greyhound in Sydenham, 'Tom got glorious in pleasing gradation, until he began to swear I was the only anatomist worth a d—n. His wife received him at home, not drunk, but in excellent spirits. After breakfast we wandered over the forest; not a soul to be seen in all Norwood.'[31]

Campbell was also friends with Byron and Dr Glennie, whom he would visit in Dulwich. On one such walk in March 1809, he witnessed a coppice being felled. 'The wood cutters had finished demolishing Dulwich, or rather Sydenham Wood, down from Heron's Gate,' he wrote to his friend Fanny Mayow. 'There will now be no nightingales to sing to us; and you will be obliged, instead of listening to the truly best poet of the grove, to be contented with the best that can be had.'[32]

Robert Browning (1812–89), who grew up in Camberwell, used to go for long walks in the woods by night. His biographer William Sharp records that the young poet composed parts of his early works 'Paracelsus' and 'Strafford' 'in these midnight silences of the Dulwich woodland'.[33] John Ruskin (1819–1900), who lived on Denmark Hill, left a nostalgic description of the area as it was when, in his youth, he surveyed it from Herne Hill:

On the other side, east and south, the Norwood hills, partly rough with furze, partly wooded with birch and oak, partly in pure green bramble copse, and rather steep pasture, rose with the promise of all the rustic loveliness of Surrey and Kent in them, and with so much of space and height in their sweep, as gave them some fellowship with hills of true hill-districts . . . But then, the Norwood drew itself in sweeping crescent good five miles round Dulwich to the South, broken by lanes of ascent, Gipsy Hill and others; and from the top, commanding views towards Dartford, and over the plain of Croydon.[34]

In his poem 'A Sketch From Nature', datelined 'Sydenham Wood, 1849' and published in the Pre-Raphaelite magazine *The Germ*, the poet and sculptor John Lucas Tupper lyrically described the woods at the close of day:

> The air blows pure, for twenty miles,
> Over this vast countrié:
> Over hill and wood and vale, it goeth,
> Over steeple, and stack, and tree:
> And there's not a bird on the wind but knoweth
> How sweet these meadows be.
> The swallows are flying beside the wood,
> And the corbies are hoarsely crying;
> And the sun at the end of the earth hath stood,
> And, thorough the hedge and over the road,
> On the grassy slope is lying:
> And the sheep are taking their supper-food
> While yet the rays are dying.
> Sleepy shadows are filling the furrows,
> And giant-long shadows the trees are making . . .

INFAMOUS DESPERADOES

The first half of the nineteenth century was the last period (except for the blackouts during the two World Wars) when the night sky above the woods was truly dark. Gas-fuelled street lamps were first introduced in central London in 1807, and by the middle of the century they had begun their relentless march through the suburbs. For the time being, however, while a nocturnal rambler might have seen the glow of the city on the northern horizon, overhead the Milky Way still streamed through the immense canopy of stars. So dark was the sky that between 1837 and 1839, the aurora borealis was seen above Dulwich Woods no fewer than seven times.[35]

The very darkness and remoteness that attracted artistic spirits to these wooded hills also made them a lawless, dangerous place, roamed by footpads and highwaymen and traversed by smugglers carrying contraband from the Kent and Sussex coasts to London:

> These strange looking horsemen rode along in the dusk, carrying a small barrel in front, and another behind, and leather bottles also, fastened to their belts, all full of Hollands or brandy. May not Leather Bottle Lane, in this neighbourhood, have acquired its peculiar nomenclature from having formerly been often used by these bold defiers of the law, when pursuing their hazardous adventure of plundering the revenue?[36]

In 1802, Samuel Mathews, an old man who worked as a gardener and lived in a cave he had dug on the border of Dulwich Woods and Sydenham Common, was dragged from his shelter, robbed and murdered.[37] The brutal killing of this inoffensive man lingered long in local memories; more than twenty years after the event, W. H. Lance, a resident of Dulwich Grove, came across the site of Mathews's cave while walking in the woods:

> I seated myself on a bank, shaded by one of the trees which once waved its branches over the hermit's cave: he had been murdered there, a crowd of recollections rushed upon my brain; his cave had fallen to decay, a heap of sticks and leaves lying in a hole, the only indication of its site; the dreary shade of desolation there showed most drearily; the birds seemed to whistle near it none but the most plaintive notes . . . To preserve the remembrance, for at least a few years, I cut the form of a cross on the bark of a tree which once formed a part of his residence.[38]

The year after Mathews was murdered, one Mr Thropwaite, returning to London by carriage, was robbed of £15 at gunpoint by a lone highwayman between Sydenham and Dulwich.[39] In 1817, *The Times* reported that 'Norwood and its vicinity have of late been infested with as infamous a band of desperadoes as any that have plagued the country for many years,' an armed gang whose crimes included stealing cattle, poultry and farm equipment.[40] Twenty years later, two pistol-wielding footpads were terrorising Sydenham with 'several very daring attempts at highway robbery'.[41] Even in the 1840s Norwood Lane (now Norwood Road) was so lonely that it inspired fear in a young man walking home from his work in London,[42] while on winter nights, Dr Leese, who lived on Central Hill, used to discharge a pistol to make it known that he had firearms in the house.[43]

On 11 September 1841, under the headline 'Robin Hood Redivivus', *The Spectator* reported that 'a juvenile gang' had been meeting in Sydenham Wood, from where 'they sallied forth to plunder the larders of neighbouring gentlemen'. A policeman reported that 'provisions of every description, from venison down to a pig's head', provided them with 'sumptuous suppers', after which they slept on the grass. The 'Maid Marian' of the group, a girl of fifteen, had been captured by the police and was to be sent to the Magdalen Hospital, an institution for the rehabilitation of prostitutes in St George's Fields, Southwark.

A few years later, a brutal crime took place in the woods. On 20 September 1849, Lambeth Magistrates Court heard that at about quarter to ten the previous night, William Hunt, a butcher living on Dulwich Common, after hearing his dog bark violently, had gone to the back door and found a young woman with her hands, face and clothes covered with blood. When he asked who had done this, she replied that it was her husband. Hunt took her to the house of his neighbour Edward Rae, a surgeon, who attended to her wounds and arranged for her to be taken to Guy's Hospital.

Later that night, police arrested her common-law husband, Stephen Alfred Jordan, a painter said to be eighteen or nineteen years old, at his lodgings in St Andrew's Road, Brixton. There was blood on his shirt and under his fingernails; in his pockets were a loaded pistol and about a dozen bullets. At a further hearing, his victim, Sarah Frances Ewings, had recovered sufficiently to be brought to court from hospital in a cab. She testified that she had known Jordan for about a year and a half, and was 'in the family way' by him. He had arranged to meet her at St Matthew's Church in Brixton, and then persuaded her to walk with him to Penge Common in order to catch a train to Croydon, where he said he had found lodgings for them both. As they passed through Dulwich Wood, he cut her throat with a razor and beat her about the head with the butt of his pistol.[44]

At the Old Bailey on 29 October, Jordan was found guilty of assaulting Sarah Ewings with intent to murder her, and sentenced to death.[45] When it was discovered that he was in fact only seventeen, his sentence was commuted to life imprisonment, and he was transported to Australia.

The woods, though diminished in size, continued to be economically productive into the middle of the century, albeit on a smaller scale. A Dulwich Estate map of 1806 shows the woodland compartments, giving their area in acres, roods and perches: Cox's Walk, 1: 3: 0; Lapsewood, 18: 1: 32; Ambrook Hill Wood, 21: 3: 30; East and West Peckarmans Woods, 28: 0: 0 and 20: 1: 30 respectively. To the south are First and Second Low Cross Woods, 15: 3: 6 and 21: 0: 4; East and West Vicar's Oak Woods, 16: 2: 11 and 20: 3: 30; Hither and Further King's Woods, 20: 3: 30 and 19: 0: 14. (The name Hither Wood – and a fragment of the wood itself – survives in a small square surrounded by housing just west of College Road.) A nursery, located where the Kingswood Estate now stands, covered a little over one acre. This made up a total wooded area of just over 206 acres, and the pattern had changed little when Dewhirst published his map of the Parish of St Giles Camberwell in 1841.

Around 1850, the Dulwich Estate's Wood Record listed the materials being harvested and sold: poles; small poles; birch trees; birch poles; old posts; bavins; bakers' bavins; potters' bavins; fine wood; roughwood; hurdles; cloth props; props; stakes; hethers; bushes; hollys; earthers; pea bows; bean poles; withes; pimp spreys; stivers; and canhoops.[46] At times, the growing appreciation of the woods as a place of sylvan tranquillity came into conflict with the economic interests of their owners. In August 1842, a correspondent wrote to the *Gentleman's Magazine* to complain about the clear-felling of trees in Dulwich Woods:

In one of the sweetest spots about London, along the road from town to Beckenham, whole acres of the Dulwich woods have been laid bare: a number of ornamental birches, about 50 years old, which crowned the hollow side of the hill, of very little value, are cut down; and thriving young oaks, not worth the bark which has been stripped from them, but

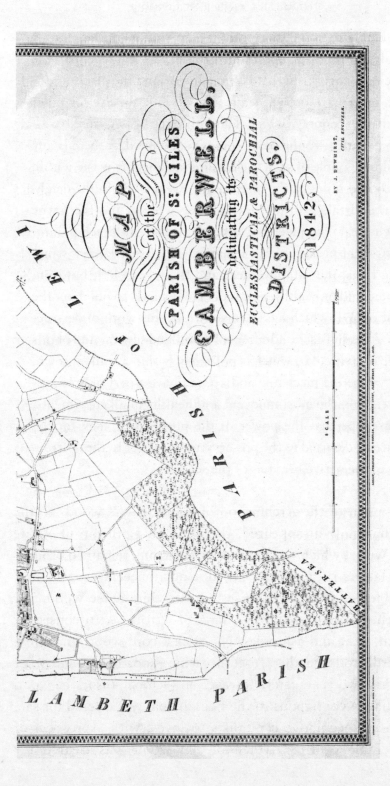

The southernmost portion of J. Dewhirst's map of the parish of Camberwell (1842), showing the coppices within Dulwich Woods.

invaluable to stand as timber, are at this moment lying by
hundreds literally upon the ground, as evidence of the
unseemly barbarism that is spreading round the place.

A large bare brown heath now offends the eye for miles
about the country, which a month back was covered with
very beautiful young oaks. It may be doubted, if there is any
similar example of such useless and melancholy waste within
a hundred miles of the metropolis. Every body in the neighbourhood takes an interest in these woods, and the havoc
which has taken place has been the subject of much painful
remark: the prospect has been materially injured; a few strag-
gling trees, indeed, have here and there been left, but thin,
stunted and unhealthy, as if more particularly to point out the
want of skill which has been shown in this work of destruction. As enthusiastic admirers of woodland scenery and of this
place in particular, which is positively within a walk of town,
and where the mechanic and artisan have a sort of prescrip-
tive right in the most innocent and healthy of all enjoyments,
let us hope that the power of the proprietors, may for the
future be diverted to the preservation, and not to the destruction of the native beauties of the scene . . .

While much of the Archbishop of Canterbury's woods to the
south had now disappeared, the remaining portion of White
Horse Wood, which was in private ownership, remained productive as late as 1857, when a Croydon auctioneer, George Bance,
offered for sale 'on the Premises, Great White-horse Wood, at 1
for 2, the PRODUCTION of 20 acres of WOOD-LAND consisting
of birch, oak, and ash poles, pea-sticks, cord-wood, thatching
and hurdle rods, heathers, together with 15,000 bakers and other
bavins'.[47] Two years later, however, in October 1859, 'the wood
immediately contiguous to the Beulah Spa' was offered for sale
'to enable speculative capitalists to invest with a prospect of
considerable profit'.[48] Much of the wood was cleared for

development, but the central triangle (which now forms Grange-wood Park) was purchased by the industrialist Charles Hood, who had a substantial villa, Grangewood House, built there in 1861, retaining many of the oaks in its grounds.

The enthusiasm with which the expanding middle classes of the nineteenth century embraced natural history as a pastime led to the proliferation of specialist magazines such as *The Zoologist* and *The Phytologist*, and has left us with a more detailed record of the flora and fauna of the North Wood than at any earlier period. Daniel Cooper's *Flora Metropolitana* (1836), subtitled *Botanical Rambles within Thirty Miles of London* and aimed at 'the student in practical botany', included a substantial list of plants to be found around Norwood. Dominant among the trees were sessile oak and hornbeam, while many species now recognised as Ancient Woodland Indicators flourished in the understorey, including wood anemone, lily-of-the-valley, herb-Robert, wood avens, butcher's-broom and the St John's wort *Hypericum androsaemum*.[49]

In the 1840s, the Godalming-based naturalist John Drew Salmon set about cataloguing the plants of Surrey with the assistance of a number of correspondents who would report their finds to him. The book, unfinished when he died in 1859, was completed by James Brewer, secretary of the Holmesdale Natural History Club, and published as *Flora of Surrey* in 1863. Salmon himself recorded the wild service tree in Low Cross Wood, and whitebeam, lily of the valley and wood spurge (*Euphorbia amygdaloides*) in Dulwich Woods. Among his plant-spotters was J. S. Mill, a keen amateur botanist who, throughout the 1840s and 1850s, regularly reported his observations to *The Phytologist*; and it is to Mill that we owe the first record of wild cherry (*Prunus avium*) in Dulwich Woods, where it can still be found in abundance.

This sylvan environment supported a rich population of saproxylic (wood-loving) beetles. In his *Illustrations of British*

Entomology, James Francis Stephens recorded *Megatoma undata*, 'on walls near Dulwich, in June'; the brown powderpost beetle *Xylotrogus brunneus* (now *Lyctus brunneus*), taken in July 1826 'out of a wasp's nest at Dulwich'; *Pseudocistela ceramboides*, a large brown beetle that lives in decaying wood, at Sydenham Wood; *Nemosoma elongatum*, 'in plenty during March and April last, in an old elm rail near Sydenham-wood'; and the metallic green wood-boring beetle *Trachys troglodytiformis* at Norwood. Of the jewel beetle *Anthaxia salicis*, previously noted in the area by Donovan, he says, 'This beautiful insect has been taken on some willows in Lordship-lane, near Dulwich.'

In his volume devoted to lepidoptera, Stephens recorded that the six-striped rustic moth (*Lytea umbrosa*) was 'occasionally taken near Birch-wood, and I have twice found it in Sydenham-wood at the end of July'.[50] To Stephens's findings, William Wood's *Index Entomologicus* added pink-barred sallow (*Xanthia flavago*) in 'woods at Sydenham', and pink under-wing (*Limacodes testudo*) 'near Chislehurst and Sydenham, but not common. End June.'[51] A list of moths captured in London during 1844–5 submitted to *The Zoologist* by George Bedell included the silvery arches (*Polia hepatica*, formerly *Polia tincta*), found in Dulwich Wood in June, *Agrotis suffusa* found there in September, and *Calocampa exoleta*, *Orthosia munda*, *O. sparsa and O. miniosa*, all recorded there in spring. 'I have excluded such species as are considered abundant or common in most places,' Bedell noted.[52]

A few years later, a book aimed at the popular market, Thomas Miller's *Common Wayside Flowers*, with its beautiful illustrations by Birket Foster, included a lyrical celebration of one of the 'signature' plants of Dulwich Woods – the wild bluebell:

There are nooks at the foot of the hill, where they lie like a blue sky between the openings of the underwood, and are as beautiful as ever bloomed, though growing within sight of London, which is seen from the hill-top, like a silent city, – for not an echo of its ceaseless roar reaches the listening bells of those sky-dyed flowers.[53]

On a bright September morning in 1850, Charles Dickens stood on top of Friern Hill, surveying the panorama that surrounded him. He had travelled through Camberwell and Peckham Rye, marvelling at the winding lanes, high hedgerows and green fields populated by cows, all of which looked 'uncommonly like "the country," considering how short a time it is since we left the "old smoke" behind us'. From the hilltop, he could see Shooters Hill, Blackheath and Greenwich, the masts of ships in the Thames, and the trains of the London, Chatham & Dover Railway running along like 'magic toys' in the distance. Looking north, he saw 'the grand sombre dome of St. Paul's', Westminster Abbey and, in the distance, the spire of the church at Harrow-on-the-Hill. To the south, his eye fell on Norwood Hill and the new cemetery there, Dulwich College, Dulwich Wood, and Forest Hill – a vista of 'fields; scrub; patches of furze, lying dark and colourless, with here and there a streak of bright light' that he found astonishing within a few miles of central London.[54]

THE PALACE AND THE RAILWAY

1850–1900

'Then the Crystal Palace came,' John Ruskin recalled. After the closure of the Great Exhibition of 1851, Joseph Paxton's huge glass and iron greenhouse was dismantled and moved from Hyde Park to Penge Place, where it was reconstructed and enlarged between 1852 and 1854. 'The traveller passing along the Brighton Railway,' noted The *Observer* in June 1853, would have seen 'enormous mounds of earthwork and bricks heaped up along the base of the hill', a 'vast extent of sandy-looking soil, denuded of trees or verdure, and towering above like the skeleton remains of some huge antediluvian monster, the . . . gigantic ribs and framework of the building'.

The Palace was opened by Queen Victoria on 10 June 1854, and two water towers, designed by Isambard Kingdom Brunel, were added the following year to feed the many fountains. Standing 280 feet tall – almost half the height of the present Crystal Palace transmitter – they were clearly visible across much of South London. Ruskin was characteristically disparaging, describing the structure as 'possessing no more sublimity than a cucumber frame between two chimneys' and complaining that 'its stupidity of hollow bulk, dwarfs the hills at once; so that now one thinks of them no more but as three long lumps of clay, on lease for building.' The Palace

SKETCH ON THE PROPOSED SITE OF THE CRYSTAL PALACE, SYDENHAM.

Penge Place just before the relocation of the Crystal Palace, from the *Illustrated London News*, 5 June 1852.

The Crystal Palace and the High Level Station, from the *Illustrated London News*, 30 September 1865.

changed the area dramatically, 'for ever spoiling the view,' Ruskin continued,

> and bringing every show-day, from London, a flood of pedestrians down the footpath, who left it filthy with cigar ashes for the rest of the week: then the railroads came, and expatiating roughs by every excursion train, who knocked the palings about, roared at the cows, and tore down what branches of blossom they could reach.[1]

Straddling the Kent–Surrey border, the structure itself covered eighteen acres, and was set in two hundred acres of terraced and landscaped park that completely altered the topography, obliterating Old Cople Lane, Isabel Hill, the shire ditch and what was left of Penge Common. This presented a challenge for the parishioners of Camberwell, who still beat the bounds in the traditional way. On Ascension Day in May 1874, the vicar, constable, beadle – 'gorgeous in the red and gold of ancient Bumbledom' – and vestrymen, accompanied by a number of children, doggedly followed the boundary of their parish through the stately pleasure dome, brandishing willow wands. 'Entering *en masse* through the gate from the High Level Station, the company proceeded through the new dining-room . . . and thence through the intervening courts and elegant saloon, where the diners seemed somewhat astonished at [their] entrance . . .' Afterwards, the parishioners retired to the Greyhound in Dulwich, 'where ample justice was done to a very capital repast'.[2]

The Crystal Palace stamped its name on the area and speeded its development. Between 1854 and 1884, it attracted an average of two million visitors a year. In addition to its orchestra of a thousand musicians, it also required ushers, administrators, ticket clerks, bookkeepers, caterers, maintenance workers, cleaners, gardeners and watchmen, drawing a substantial population to the area. They in turn required homes, boarding houses, shops and pubs. A suburb was born.

For the College of God's Gift at Dulwich, the Crystal Palace was indeed a godsend. The school had limped into the nineteenth century in a sorry state: its academic record mediocre, its buildings damp and dilapidated, and its finances – diminished by the falling demand for woodland produce – precarious. It was, in the words of its historian William Harnett Blanch, a 'sad story of baffled hopes and perverted munificence'. Part of the problem lay in its founder Edward Alleyn's stipulation that the master and warden should be 'of my blood and sirname, and for want of such of my sirname onlie'. Despite a relaxation of the rule in the eighteenth century to admit candidates who spelled their name Allen, this severely restricted the talent pool on which the college could draw, and much of its history was blighted by a lack of effective leadership. In 1857, the college finally obtained an Act of Parliament to dissolve the old corporation and create a new governing body unencumbered by antiquated statutes. In Canon Alfred Carver, it found a resourceful and energetic master in tune with the educational ideals of the Victorian age, while the development spurred by the relocation of the Crystal Palace provided a substantial and much-needed injection of cash.

As early as 1854, the governors had commissioned the Estate's surveyor, Charles Barry, to report on ways to increase revenue while preserving the rural character of the area. Barry in turn asked the landscape gardener William Andrews Nesfield to draw up a detailed plan for the development of the whole estate. Nesfield considered the woods to be 'the grand feature of the entire scenery' and recommended that they be preserved, while new roads and villas were constructed around them. Noting 'the laudable desire of the Governors to preserve the remarkable beauty of the estate', he advised them that 'even an increase of income must be subservient to this object'.

Nesfield and Barry understood that the governors' objective was to rebuild Dulwich College in a setting comparable to those of Eton or Winchester. Within this 'sylvan' landscape, substantial villas would be constructed to attract the sort of families who could afford to send their sons to the school. 'Were it a mere question as to how much rent could be obtained,' Nesfield wrote,

> many other building sites might be pointed out, yet it would he obviously unfair towards tenants who may be induced to spend money liberally on houses of pretension to subject them hereafter to that depreciation of their property which must inevitably ensue, if buildings of an inferior description, more closely packed, were allowed to be introduced. [3]

Although the Estate continued to sell timber and underwood from parts of the wood into the 1860s, the report marked a fundamental shift in perspective: what had formerly been an economic resource was now viewed primarily as an ornament. This would determine the fate of the woods for at least a century to come.

To raise cash for new college buildings, the governors sold plots of land along Sydenham Hill on one-hundred-year leases, and seven very large villas were built between Cox's Walk and the junction with Crescent Wood Road, which was laid out in 1858. The first of these, Lapsewood, was constructed in 1860 as his own residence by Charles Barry Junior, who had succeeded his father as the estate surveyor in April 1858. The younger Barry was a scion of Victorian England's leading architectural dynasty: his father had built the Houses of Parliament, his brother Edward Middleton Barry designed the Royal Opera House in Covent Garden, while a third brother, John Wolfe Barry, would go on to construct Tower Bridge. From the terrace of Lapsewood, Charles could look out over the treetops as the campanile and pinnacles of his new college, built in a style he called 'North

Italian of the Thirteenth Century', rose from the fields. The novelist and poet Lawrence Durrell, whose brother Leslie was a pupil at the school in the 1930s, described it as 'a fair candidate for the wildest Victorian building in the whole of London, with a crazy Dostoevskian gleam in its eye.'[4]

The next house along, built around 1862, was named Singapore by its first occupant, an East India merchant called William Patterson, who lived there until his death in 1898. After a couple of years, he renamed it Beechgrove. Old photographs show it as a grand three-storey villa in the Italian Renaissance style, with a loggia built out over a porticoed entrance, and a steeply sloping lawn, flanked by steps that still survive amid the undergrowth. The garden wall fronting Sydenham Hill also survives, in a crumbling condition. The house was subsequently the home of Lionel Logue, speech therapist to King George VI.

Immediately to the south of Beechgrove stood Fairwood, also built around 1862; its first occupant was Alderman David Henry Stone, a future Lord Mayor of London. In the woodland at the end of his garden, he had a folly constructed in the form of a ruined Gothic chapel by the firm of James Pulham and Son, manufacturers of artificial stone garden ornaments. Beside it, a small stream tumbled over a cascade of Pulhamite rocks. Beyond Fairwood, 'standing on the apex almost of Sydenham Hill,' was the Hoo, praised by the local historian William Harnett Blanch in his 1875 book *Ye Parish of Camerwell* as 'not only substantially built but elegantly designed', its tall, cupola-topped turret 'a recognised boundary mark far and wide . . .' Blanch also drew attention to the survival of part of the woods in its grounds:

A well kept lawn, neat beds, and paths of primness first attract the eye, but a rapid descent suddenly transports the visitor into a wild and woody scene, and an almost endless succession of surprises.

> This woody adjunct – a portion of the once famous Dulwich
> Wood – renders the grounds of 'The Hoo' altogether unique,
> for nowhere else within the hamlet is to be seen in such close
> juxtaposition, the landscape garden and a mazy labyrinth
> of trees.[5]

The steep slope required the gardens of these villas to be butt-
ressed by a series of terraces, supporting lawns, flowerbeds, elaborate
water features and extensive glasshouses, and many of the foot-
ings can still be seen in the woods. A small cedar of Lebanon
pictured in the grounds of the Hoo in Blanch's book survives in
Sydenham Hill Wood as a substantial tree, a gnarled mulberry
still bears fruit in what was once the garden of Lapsewood, stands
of bamboo can be found amid the hazel and hawthorn in the
precincts of Fairwood, while a Chilean pine is hidden deep in
the woodland that has recolonised the grounds of Fernbank.

RAILWAY RIVALRIES

The choice of Sydenham for the relocation of the Crystal Palace
was dictated by the interests of the directors of the company that
ran it. One, Leo Schuster, owned Penge Place, and sold it to the
company, while he and the chairman, Samuel Laing, also served
on the board of the London, Brighton & South Coast Railway.
Since its route already ran through Sydenham, they calculated
that it would not be difficult to create a short branch line to the
Palace to benefit from the additional traffic it would attract.
Parliamentary approval was granted in July 1853, and within
weeks workmen were excavating a cutting through Penge
Woods. By March 1854, the line was complete, terminating at a
station on Anerley Road, below the level of the Palace, in time
for its opening by Queen Victoria that June.

Soon, however, the London, Brighton & South Coast Railway faced competition. Keen for a share of the profit generated

by visitors to the Palace, the London, Chatham & Dover Railway, which was already planning to extend its main line north from Beckenham to Victoria, decided to create a branch line from Nunhead to a new terminus on Crystal Palace Parade, directly in front of the exhibition hall. A subsidiary company, the Crystal Palace & South London Junction Railway, was set up to run the line; the trains would be operated by the London, Chatham & Dover Railway, with the two companies sharing the profits.

The line from Nunhead would enter the Dulwich Estate from the north-east, crossing Cox's Walk near where it joined the woods. From a triangular junction immediately west of Cox's Walk, a branch line would curve through the fields now occupied by the golf course to join the main line to Victoria near the present site of Sydenham Hill Station. From the junction, another branch would snake through the middle of the woods, roughly following the eighty-metre contour to minimise the gradient. It would pass below Low Cross Wood Walk, which would be carried over the line on an archway, before ascending though a series of cuttings to emerge at a new High Level Station directly in front of the Crystal Palace.

Given the steep banks and cuttings required, this plan, had it been carried out, would have almost completely obliterated what was left of Dulwich Wood.[6] At a special meeting on 8 February 1860, the Estate governors resolved that 'with the object of protecting the interests of the Trustees of the College Estate, the Solicitor, with the assistance of the Surveyor, be instructed and authorised . . . to take such steps as may be necessary in order to oppose the Bill for the Metropolitan extension of the London, Chatham and Dover Railway'.[7]

Barry's objections to the line to Victoria were relatively minor, and mainly concerned the size and design of bridges, and the proximity of an embankment to Croxted Road. It was the Crystal Palace spur, and its effect on the landscape, that troubled him and the governors. Their objections succeeded. On 9 June 1860, the Estate's finance committee noted that 'with the exception of the proposed small branch line to Crystal Palace, through the Wood, the Bill for the extension of the London, Chatham and Dover Railway passed the House of Commons last night, Friday.'[8] The Dulwich Estate then sold land to both railways, raising a further £40,000 towards its new buildings.[9]

Work began swiftly on the London, Chatham & Dover extension to Victoria via a 2,290-yard tunnel under Sydenham Hill. The Crystal Palace & South London Junction Railway, meanwhile, was reluctant to abandon its plan for a line to the Palace, and entered into negotiations with Barry. While they attempted, through 1861, to agree on a mutually acceptable route, the London & Brighton Railway re-entered the fray with a new scheme. On 4 January 1862, the Estate governors met to consider the rival proposals. The line projected by the London & Brighton Railway would run from Peckham, and enter the Dulwich Estate near the Plough Inn on Lordship Lane. From there, it would continue to Court Lane, and on through the fields to Dulwich Common, which it would cross on a bridge seventeen feet above ground. It would then curve round to the west to pass beneath College Road (then known as Penge Road) in a cutting before continuing to Gipsy Hill station, where it would join another railway, the West End of London & Crystal Palace Railway. It would cross nearly a mile and three-quarters of the estate, occupy some twenty-five acres of land, require four bridges over the line and three under it, and affect fourteen or fifteen leaseholds. 'The injury to the Estate,' Barry advised the governors, 'would be very great and without any compensating benefit whatever – except that a station to serve Dulwich would probably be placed at Lordship Lane.'

The route put forward by the Crystal Palace & South London Junction Railway was a considerably modified version of the 1860 plan, and appeared much less damaging. Running south from Nunhead, it skirted the western side of the remnant of Oak of Honor Wood, where a station would be built to serve the recently created Camberwell Cemetery (now Camberwell Old Cemetery). From Lordship Lane, it would cut through Lapsewood and Ambrook Hill Wood, and then tunnel under Sydenham Hill to emerge beyond Wells Park Road (where Upper Sydenham Station would be built in 1884). Further south, a second tunnel would lead to the High Level terminus at Crystal Palace.

Knowing that Parliament was unlikely to approve both plans, the Estate governors decided to throw their weight behind the Crystal Palace & South London Junction Railway proposal, which they had already had a considerable hand in reshaping. There would be no branch connecting it to the main line to Victoria, and no messy junction on the estate. It would not 'alter the levels of any public road or path, and will only require one bridge over Lordship Lane, and one at Cox's Walk,' Barry noted approvingly. 'The works will be nearly all in cutting or tunnel, and therefore will not materially affect the appearance of the estate.'[10] The governors' main concern was that the visible infrastructure should be in keeping with their view of the dignity of the area. In the event, the bridge and station at Lordship Lane were designed, at their insistence, by Charles Barry, while the magnificent Gothic High Level Terminus at Crystal Palace was the work of Edward Middleton Barry.

The Crystal Palace High Level Railway, as it became known, received Parliamentary approval in July 1862, and construction began. On Saturday 12 November 1864,

an interesting ceremony took place in the Crescent Wood tunnel, on the South London and Crystal Palace Railway, which was to place the last brick of the tunnel at the entrance to Wells Road, Upper Sydenham. The inside of the entrance was tastefully fitted up with evergreens. A champagne luncheon was provided in the most excellent style by Mr. Collins of the Longton Grove Hotel . . .'[11]

The second tunnel, known as the Paxton Tunnel, was completed in February 1865, and the line opened to passengers on 1 August. Six years later, the French Impressionist painter Camille Pissarro, while living over a dairy in Westow Hill to escape the Franco-Prussian War, painted the view towards Lordship Lane station from the Cox's Walk footbridge; his canvas shows the embankments on both sides of the railway almost devoid of trees, though at his back, on the other side of the bridge, much of the woods survived.

WOODLAND FOR RENT

Even before the exact course of the railway had been determined, the Estate was receiving requests from the occupants of the new villas on Sydenham Hill to rent parts of the woods between their gardens and the embankment, one of whom was 'contemplating clearing the land and adding it to his garden'. Barry advised the governors that 'it could be a desirable arrangement to let the intervening woodland to the tenants of the several plots which abut on the Railway along that line, but very undesirable that the land should be allowed to be cleared for gardens, inasmuch as the Railway itself will of necessity clear a great deal, and the appearance of the woods should not be interfered with more than is necessary.'

The board agreed to rent out plots of woodland on seven-year leases on condition 'that no trees be removed, and only so much of the underwood cleared as may be necessary for paths, which arrangement if made, the land, otherwise inaccessible and value-less to the College, may be productive of rental and the ornamental effect of the Woods from all parts of the Estate may be preserved.'[12] A subsequent agreement included the proviso that the lessee 'covenants not to cut down the underwood, nor to erect any building on said Land'.[13] The decision preserved Blanch's 'mazy labyrinth of trees' in accordance with Nesfield's plan, and allowed the survival of a significant tract of ancient woodland to the east of the railway in what is now Sydenham Hill Wood Nature Reserve.

By 1867, the Dulwich Estate was letting out parcels of woodland behind the villas on College Road and Wood Crescent Road, as it was then called, on the same terms as it had to those on Sydenham Hill,[14] and wedges of privately rented land, of two or three acres apiece, began to jut deep into the wood on the Dulwich side of the railway. It appears that the tenants were allowed to fence off their pockets of woodland, since in 1870 the governors agreed that should they repossess these plots before twenty-one years had elapsed, they would compensate the lessees for the cost of the fencing.[15] By 1876, only twenty-one acres of woodland remained under the direct management of the Estate, consisting of the lower parts of Lapsewood, Ambrook Hill and Peckarmans Wood, and a long panhandle corresponding to the path that still runs through the latter to Low Cross Wood Walk.[16]

FROM COUNTRYSIDE TO SUBURB

The railways spurred the suburban development of the area, and villages once accessible only by carriage were now within a short train ride of the city centre. Instead of the substantial villas of the Georgian period, rows of terraced housing for those of more modest means spread outward from the newly constructed stations at Herne Hill, Honor Oak, Lordship Lane, Norwood Junction, Sydenham and Anerley. At Selhurst Junction, the London, Brighton & South Coast Railway sliced through Dragnel Wood – by then known as Selhurst Wood – in 1862, leaving its southern portion hemmed in within a triangle of tracks.

With the new roads came street lighting, banishing the nocturnal darkness that had shrouded the woods for millennia. As early as 1847, the Croydon Commercial Gas and Coke Company was operating more than three hundred lamp posts across the parish,[17] and in 1855 the Board of Health signed an agreement with the Crystal Palace Gas Company to provide street lighting in Norwood.[18] The following year, the Lambeth Lighting Committee recommended that the parish accept an offer from the Crystal Palace Gas Company to supply street lighting to those areas where its mains pipes ran.[19] Gas lamps were installed along Sydenham Rise and Crescent Wood Road in 1862.[20]

Urbanisation also altered the hydrography of the entire London basin, with far-reaching consequences for the surviving woodland. The River Effra, which had become an open sewer along its lower reaches, was bricked over 'for the convenience of Mr. Biffin, the chemist, and others,' Ruskin lamented, during the first half of the century.[21] In 1858, amid concerns over public health, construction began on Joseph Bazalgette's ambitious network of sewers, designed to channel the effluent polluting the Thames away from the city and out into the estuary. A new pipeline diverted much of the Effra's flow from Westow Hill away to the east, beneath Peckham to New Cross, where it joined the Southern High Level sewer. This in turn combined with the Southern Low Level sewer at Deptford, before discharging into the Thames at Crossness.[22] The new tarmacked streets incorporated drains to carry away surface water, reducing the output of the springs along the Norwood Ridge. And with the construction of the High Level Line, the Ambrook, which had flowed from a spring on the flank of Sydenham Hill though the wood that bore its name to join the Effra at Dulwich, was channelled under the railway and along a ditch beside the western side of the track.

Stanford's 1862 *Library Map of London and its Suburbs* shows the Crystal Palace in its newly created park. Palace Road and Victoria Road – today's A2199 – now bisect King's and Vicar's Oak Woods Alongside Rock Hill, a straight, steep path through Low Cross Wood, the Lambeth Waterworks has been built. Ten years later, on the 1872 edition, the changes are even more apparent. Between Dulwich Road – today's Fountain Drive – and Victoria Road, the trees have given way to houses, separating the northern and southern parts of the woods, while the southern part has been further dissected by Farquhar Road. To cater for the growing population, new churches were constructed, the industrious Barry being responsible for both St Stephen's on College Road (1868) and St Peter's on Lordship Lane (1875). Pissarro captured the newly built St Stephen's in a view looking up College Road, with the trees of Low Cross Wood on the left and the church on the right.

With much of Dulwich Wood leased to private tenants, the Estate governors had to decide what to do about access to the parts they still managed directly. In 1887, the gates into the wood from Cox's Walk and Church Path (as Low Cross Wood Walk was then known), and at each end of those walks – a total of six – were fitted with locks. The secretary had thirty keys cut, of which five were issued to the bailiff and five to the estate surveyor. Two were issued to Mrs Ward, the tenant of Dulwich Wood Farm, which stood at the top of Grange Lane by the edge of the surviving woods; after she asked for more, on the grounds that she supplied the whole neighbourhood with milk and had to employ several delivery men, the governors agreed to let her have another two, as 'damages to the fences may result' if they were not provided.

The tenants of several neighbouring houses had created their own private gates into the wood, which were not shown on their leases. The Estate solicitor was instructed to draw up a short-form agreement allowing them access to the wood on payment of an annual fee of £1, subject to termination at three months' notice.[23] The arrangement did not always go smoothly.

The following year, the solicitor reported that a Mr Bett, the lessee of one of the houses on Crescent Wood Road, refused to sign the agreement. He was informed that unless he did so, his gate into the wood would be blocked off.[24]

This was not the only problem arising from neighbouring householders' access to the woods. In September 1885, the secretary reported that Dulwich Wood 'is in several places disfigured by heaps of garden refuse and other rubbish deposited by the residents of plots abutting thereon'; the governors resolved to send a circular letter to the residents demanding that they remove the rubbish outside their gates. In 1890, the culprit was none other than the farmer Mrs Ward, who had hauled '60 to 70 loads of manure from an adjacent garden through the woods, doing considerable damage', which she was asked to make good.[25] In the spring of 1895, the governors were informed of a number of cases of trespass by boys hunting for birds' eggs and men shooting wood pigeons, 'especially on Sundays'. One of the estate's workmen was employed to keep watch in the woods on Sundays, with the result that several trespassers were turned away. The secretary and general manager were requested 'to make arrangements for the protection and preservation of Dulwich Woods until further notice'.[26] The following September, the *South London Press* reported complaints that 'certain young men, all the more formidable because they are generally found in gangs, resort to Cox's Walk after dark,' where they 'hustle, threaten and otherwise molest' passers-by.[27]

The system of issuing keys to local residents, which would remain in place for almost a century, marked the final transformation of Dulwich Wood from a productive woodland to a private amenity, accessible only to those authorised by the Estate, and its 'protection and preservation' was now a matter of maintaining its tranquillity and scenic attraction for those in a position to enjoy them. What had once generated income

THE WREN.

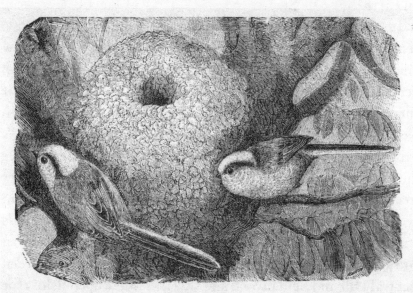

LONG-TAILED TIT.

Wren and long-tailed tit, from W. Aldridge, *Wild Birds of Norwood*, Upper Norwood, 1885.

directly, through the sale of timber and underwood, now did so indirectly, through its enhancement of the value of the adjoining properties.

In 1882, W. Aldridge, a local cabinet maker and upholsterer with premises on Westow Street[28] and a keen amateur ornithologist (he judged the stuffed-bird category at the Crystal Palace Bird Show in 1887), published a series of articles on the birds of the area in the *Norwood Review*; in 1885, they were collected in a small book, *A Gossip on the Wild Birds of Norwood and Crystal Palace District*, illustrated with charming engravings. His book reveals this Norwood tradesman to have been a keen pipe-smoker, angler, painter and amateur taxidermist, well travelled – he had visited Paris, Holland, Switzerland, Norway and Prussia – well read, and a believer in a benign Creator; he quotes approvingly Izaak Walton's remark on birdsong: 'Lord, what psalmody hast Thou provided for Thy saints in heaven when Thou affordest bad men such music on earth?'

In all, he listed fifty-one bird species, which he considered 'a very respectable quantity for a suburb of London within a few miles of St Paul's'. The only raptors he reported were the 'much persecuted' kestrels, occasionally sighted hovering on the air currents between Westow Street and Beulah Spa, and on South Norwood Hill. One evening, smoking his pipe in a friend's garden on Belvedere Road, he saw a barn owl glide silently over the ground. He also reported rooks and jackdaws in the taller trees from Dulwich to Beulah Hill; green woodpeckers in Sydenham Hill Wood; nightingales nesting in Sydenham Woods and at Elmer's End; cuckoos, goldfinches and bullfinches in Grange Wood; redwings and fieldfares in winter between Central Hill and Beulah Spa; and skylarks in the open fields that still existed on either side of Wells Road between Sydenham Hill and Sydenham town. 'The oldest inhabitant,' he reported, recalled that thirty years previously there was 'a small Heronry in the old Norwood woods', the nests 'as large as bushes, at the tops of trees'.

Aldridge took a melancholy view of the future of bird life in the area. 'In a few (very few) years,' he wrote, 'when, by the increase of population, Norwood will be a part of London, undivided by fields and hedges, most of the birds will have retired beyond our district, and be as extinct in Norwood as the Ichthyosaurus and Plesiosaurus – nay, more so, for these monsters, or, rather, their restored figures may still remain in the Palace grounds . . .'

He was perhaps too pessimistic, underestimating the capacity of many species to adapt to urban conditions. While it is true that nightingales and skylarks have long since disappeared from the suburbs of South East London, the swifts and swallows, thrushes, finches and tits have held out, while other species, absent in his day, have reappeared. In addition to kestrels, buzzards and sparrowhawks patrol the skies over Sydenham Hill Wood; magpies, made scarce in Victorian times by persecution from gamekeepers, staged a recovery in post-war years and are now ubiquitous; the green woodpecker has been joined by the great and – more rarely – lesser spotted varieties; and goldcrests and firecrests, absent from his list, are now frequent winter visitors.

THE OPEN SPACE MOVEMENT

Between 1861 and the eve of the First World War, the population of Greater London more than doubled, rising from three million to seven million. The corresponding urbanisation of the surrounding areas created a demand for an elected authority to cover the whole metropolis. The Local Government Act of 1888 brought about sweeping reform, establishing fifty-nine administrative counties, governed by elected councillors instead of the local courts, throughout England and Wales. Among them was a new

County of London. Parts of the adjoining counties into which the metropolis had spread now came under the authority of the London County Council (LCC): the civil parishes of Camberwell and Lambeth were transferred from Surrey, while Lewisham was annexed from Kent. The crest of the Norwood Ridge, which had divided the two counties for a millennium, was now no more than the boundary between two metropolitan parishes.

Local affairs such as road maintenance, however, were still governed by parish vestries; the socialist Sidney Webb argued that the duties they neglected were more significant than those they performed.[29] A further Local Government Act in 1899, which came into effect the following year, stripped the vestries of their remaining civil powers and converted the civil parishes into Metropolitan Boroughs run by elected councillors. Croydon became a self-governing County Borough within Surrey. The hamlet of Penge was removed from Battersea, to which it had belonged since Saxon times, to become an Urban District, with its own council, in Kent.

By now, only a few disconnected fragments of the North Wood remained, and the rural idyll celebrated by Ruskin and Tupper had given way to suburbia. Sydenham Hill Wood was now bisected by the railway, and mostly incorporated into the grounds of the villas on Sydenham Hill, while the remnant of Dulwich Wood curved round in an arc from Cox's Walk to the Crystal Palace. The triangle of woodland between Crystal Palace Parade and Farquhar Road had been mostly given over to housing, with only a few fragments of Vicar's Oak Wood remaining. To the north were Telegraph Hill, One Tree Hill, and Friern Hill; to the south, along Beulah Hill, Biggin Wood, Beulah Heights and White Horse Wood, hitherto surrounded by fields and connected by hedgerows, were now pockets of open space separated by tarmacked streets and suburban villas.

The appearance of the area at this period is captured in a remarkable series of photographs by no less an observer than

Émile Zola. The French novelist fled to Britain in 1898 to escape imprisonment for seditious libel for his defence of Alfred Dreyfus, a Jewish army officer falsely accused of spying. Settling in the Queen's Hotel in Norwood, Zola, a keen photographer, sent for his camera and darkroom equipment and set about recording the life of the suburb, with the great bulk of the Crystal Palace looming over it all. Several of his photographs include parts of the North Wood. He photographed his wife, Alexandrine Zola, at the bottom of Hermitage Road, by one of the surviving oaks of Great Stakepit Coppice. He captured the view up Wharncliffe Road as it ran through White Horse Wood from the junction with Grange Road; the trees on the left side, which is now lined with inter-war semis, survived in the grounds of Falkland Park, an Italianate villa built for the Scottish tea merchant Thomas McMeekin in 1890. Standing exactly where his compatriot Camille Pissarro had stood twenty-eight years earlier, Zola photographed the view up College Road, with Low Cross Wood on the left and St Stephen's Church on the right. The scene had changed little then, and has still changed little today.

As the metropolis expanded, philanthropists and social reformers became increasingly concerned about the disappearance of open space, which they considered essential to human health and happiness, as a result of the Enclosure Acts. Among the founding members of the Commons Preservation Society (later the Open Spaces Society) in 1865 were Octavia Hill (1838–1912) and Robert Hunter (1844–1913), who together saved Hampstead Heath from development and went on to found the National Trust in 1907. A friend and protégée of Ruskin, Hill would walk from her home in Bloomsbury to the Dulwich Picture Gallery to make drawings of the paintings. 'I enjoy Dulwich extremely,' she wrote to her sister in 1859; 'you know it is so nice to see a little country . . . I have such lovely walks home past trees with rooks' nests.'[30]

Hill was passionately concerned about the wellbeing of the urban poor, and with Ruskin's assistance created model housing estates in Lambeth and Walworth. She also saved Brockley's Hilly Fields for the public, and a stretch of the Wandle valley in Merton from development. 'The need of quiet,' she wrote in 1888, 'the need of air, the need of exercise, and, I believe, the sight of sky and of things growing, seem human needs, common to all men and not to be dispensed with without great loss.'[31]

Her concerns were shared by the Rev. James Johnston, vicar of St Margaret's Church in Upper Norwood. In 1885 he published a pamphlet entitled 'Parks and Playgrounds for the People', addressed to the politician and philanthropist Reginald Brabazon (later Earl of Meath), in which he warned of the social consequences of the lack of open space in his parish.

'The present inhabitants,' he wrote,

remember its shady woods, and dwell with fragrant recollections on the happy days spent in its glades and wastes, no man questioning their liberty to wander at their own sweet will . . . Such was Upper Norwood in the past. What is it now? It is either covered with buildings, or, ominous words, it is *laid out* . . .

So rigidly has this commercial principle been carried out, that of all the extensive forest of Norwood . . . there is not a spot of ground which the public, either rich or poor, can call their own, or enjoy by sufferance without paying for it. No man, woman, or child in Upper Norwood can step from the public road, except into his own or a friend's house or grounds, without committing a trespass. Hundreds of young people may be seen on a summer evening sauntering listlessly in the thoroughfares or hanging about the corners of the streets, with temptations of all kinds to draw them into folly and dissipation, and no place of healthful recreation to which they could, and gladly would, resort.[32]

The idea of creating a green belt around London was first proposed by Brabazon in 1889. A social reformer and chairman of the London County Council's Parks and Open Spaces Committee, he was also an ardent imperialist worried about the effects of urbanisation on the moral and physical health of the British populace. During his extensive travels in Europe, Australia and America, he had been impressed by the beltways around Chicago and Boston and the *Ringstraße* in Vienna. In 1901, he requested that the LCC 'furnish London with a green girdle, linking the parks with one continuous chain of verdure'. This would consist of a series of broad, tree-lined boulevards, five to eight miles from Charing Cross, linking 12,696 acres of open parkland including Hampstead Heath, Alexandra Palace, Epping Forest and Wanstead Flats. South of the Thames, it would stretch from Plumstead and Woolwich Commons, through Blackheath to Crystal Palace, before continuing via Streatham and Tooting Commons to Richmond Park.[33]

The same year, William Bull, the Conservative MP for Hammersmith, published a still more ambitious plan for 'a green girdle' half a mile wide, joining the existing open spaces around the edge of built-up London. This 'circle of green sward and trees,' he proposed, would remain 'permanently inviolate'.[34] Although these ideas generated considerable interest, the Green Belt would not become a reality until after the Second World War, by which time inter-war suburban development meant that it had to be located much further out, leaving the relict woodlands of Dulwich and Crystal Palace marooned deep within the built-up area.

The campaigning of people such as Johnston and Hill, however, helped to ensure that, as the remaining farmland around South London was developed, some open space was allowed to remain. One of the last inner London open spaces to be laid out, Dulwich Park opened in 1890 on seventy-two acres donated by the College on what was formerly Dulwich Court

Farm. Like so much else on the Estate, it was designed by Charles Barry Junior. Several ancient oaks that marked field boundaries were incorporated into the park, and survive to this day. To the south, the Corporation of Croydon bought Grangewood Park for the public in 1900, constructing a bowling green, tennis courts and bandstand, while preserving the surviving fragment of White Horse Wood.[35] On the heights of Norwood, thirty acres of hilly common were acquired by London County Council in 1903, and opened as Norwood Park in 1911, retaining many old trees and stretches of hedgerow.

This growing movement achieved legislative recognition in the Open Spaces Act of 1906, which provided for 'any land of which not more than one-twentieth is covered by buildings and which is laid out as a garden or used for the purposes of recreation' to be transferred to a local authority on condition that it be administered for public enjoyment as an open space 'and for no other purpose'.

In the same year that Dulwich Park was inaugurated, the tea merchant and Forest Hill resident Frederick Horniman threw open his former home on London Road to the public as a museum displaying the collection of botanical specimens and musical instruments he had assembled during his travels around the world. In 1897, in recognition, the local historian John Corbet Anderson dedicated his facsimile of the section of Rocque's 1745 map showing the wood 'to Frederick John Horniman, Esq., MP, Fellow of the Royal Geographical Society, etc., who generously founded a Public Free Museum at Forest Hill, within the limits of the ancient North Wood.' Horniman's collection soon outgrew the premises, and in 1898 he commissioned Charles Harrison Townsend, an associate of Octavia Hill and architect of the Whitechapel Gallery, to design a purpose-built museum. With its rounded corners, tapering tower and carved reliefs of trees and other plants, the distinctive Arts and Crafts Horniman Museum that arose at the junction of

London Road and Sydenham Hill over the next three years was designed to reflect the natural world.

After a severe drought led to the failure of his hay crop, the tenant of Dulwich Wood Farm, Albert Cullen, attempted to recoup his losses by sub-letting some of his fields, which covered what was once the Fifty Acre Wood, to local golfers without the knowledge of the Estate governors. One rainy night in November 1893, four golfers met at Hitherwood, a villa on Sydenham Hill. Over whisky and cigars, they decided to formalise the arrangement and establish a Sydenham Hill Golf Club. Unknown to them, however, the Dulwich Estate had its own plans for a golf club, and once the proposal was made public, the governors told Cullen to stop the arrangement immediately and dismantle the shed he had put up for the golfers.

The following year, after protracted negotiations, the Estate relented, and agreed that Cullen could sublet four of his fields, covering some forty-two acres, on condition that the two rival clubs amalgamated to form the Dulwich and Sydenham Hill Golf Club. Over the following years, the club rented more fields in order to enlarge the round from nine to eighteen holes, and by the 1920s, Dulwich Wood Farm had been totally absorbed into the golf course.[36] Superimposing a modern aerial photograph on to a nineteenth-century map shows that many of the old field boundaries survive in the rows of mature oak and other trees that separate the fairways.

What open space remained was prized, and at times fiercely defended. In 1895, the Dulwich Estate proposed to build a parish hall for St Peter's Church across the lower end of Cox's Walk, giving rise, the *South London Press* reported, to 'a prevailing feeling of uneasiness in the locality at the mere suggestion of encroachment upon what is regarded as public land'. In order to preserve the right of way, Camberwell Vestry – the forerunner of the Metropolitan Borough of Camberwell, which in turn was absorbed into the London Borough of Southwark in

1965 – persuaded the Estate to transfer ownership of the walk to the parish 'to preserve it in a rustic condition' for 'the free use of the public'.[37]

An attempt to establish a golf club at Honor Oak proved more controversial than at Dulwich. In 1896, a private company quietly put up a six-foot fence around One Tree Hill with the aim of turning it into a golf course. A series of meetings on Peckham Rye the following year led to the formation of the Enclosure of Honor Hill Protest Committee, which included several councillors from the newly formed boroughs of Camberwell and Lewisham. While the committee gathered evidence that the hill was common land, local people grew impatient with its constitutional methods. On Sunday 10 October 1897, a crowd of around fifteen thousand – according to some reports – pulled down the fence and swarmed the hill. The next Sunday an even larger crowd was met by a detachment of five hundred police, mounted and on foot. When they were unable to demolish the fence, which had been reinforced during the week, protestors climbed over it, threw stones at the green-keeper's cottage and set the undergrowth alight.

While condemning the violence, the protest committee used the prospect of the 1898 London County Council elections to drum up support. By 1899, Councillor John Nisbet, secretary of the Protest Committee, and C. W. Tagg, the Town Clerk, had convinced Camberwell Council to buy the land. After the owner demanded the then excessive sum of £1,000 per acre, the council persuaded the London County Council to insert a clause into its General Powers Bill of 1902 that would permit the compulsory purchase of the site. In December 1904, the case came before the Sheriffs' Court for arbitration. The court found in the council's favour, and on Monday 7 August the following year, Nisbet and Councillor H. R. Taylor officiated as One Tree Hill was opened as a public park, planting an oak in place of the one under which Queen Elizabeth I was said to have rested.

'We can congratulate ourselves,' Nisbet wrote, 'that a beautiful and historic resort has been saved from the hand of the
all-devouring speculative builder, and secured for the use of
the public for ever.'[38]

THE HOME FRONT

1910–1945

By the beginning of the twentieth century, the urbanisation of much of the area once covered by the North Wood was all but complete. The ornithologist F. D. Power, writing in 1910, observed that the district had 'altered very greatly' during the previous thirty years:

> What little waste land existed in 1874 between Brixton and Herne Hill is now covered with houses; in fact, the two suburbs are continuous, and Herne Hill can no longer claim to be in the country. Even Dulwich Hamlet is fast losing its old village appearance, though exhibiting the least change of any of the neighbouring suburbs, and is still notable for its grand old elms.[1]

Sheep still grazed on the slope below Dulwich Wood, and cattle were still kept on the twenty acres of Grange Farm not yet given over to the golf club, while the owner of Belair House maintained a small herd to supply his household with milk into the 1920s.[2] Norwood, according to Kelly's *Surrey Directory* for 1913, was 'finely wooded, very hilly, exceedingly healthy, and is remarkable for its fine views. There are several large hotels; and numerous well-built detached houses, villa residences and mansions are scattered all over the district.' To the south, the surviving portion of Selhurst Wood, to the north of the railway junction, was felled by 1908 to make way for Croydon Common Athletic Ground which, from 1918 to 1924, was the home of Crystal Palace FC before it was replaced in turn by a railway depot.

By now, the woods had been reduced to more or less their present extent, and would face no further significant threat from development until the 1960s. The main challenge to their survival came from the collapse of the woodland economy and the consequent abandonment of traditional management practices. Once coppicing ceased, the woods gradually grew dark and overgrown, and the understorey, deprived of light and rainwater, became impoverished. In 1908, the governors of the Dulwich Estate commissioned the land management company Cluttons to report on the state of the woods. Following an inspection on 11 November, the firm reported that 'nothing appears to have been done for a great many years, and the oak timber, tellars, and undergrowth have been allowed to grow up together to the detriment of each other, and the wood generally has a neglected appearance.' Since neither timber nor underwood was of sufficient quality for commercial purposes, their report recommended that

> the rough and crooked portions of the oak underwood and undergrowth should be cut, especially in those places where there are on the ground a good number of oak standard trees or young oak tellars likely to develop into ornamental trees . . . After many years of neglect any process of thinning should be carefully carried out, especially when the object in view is timber, &c., of an ornamental character.[3]

Around this time, oak woodlands throughout Britain were facing an environmental challenge known as Oak Change.

Previously, acorns falling within existing woods would germi-
nate and grow to maturity, providing a new generation of
trees; now, although young oaks still grew freely on open
ground, woodland saplings struggled to survive. A number of
explanations for this phenomenon have been advanced, including the decline of woodland management, which reduced the
amount of light reaching to the forest floor. The most widely
accepted explanation, however, is the introduction from America of oak mildew (*Microsphaera alphitoides*) around 1908.
This fungus has little effect on oaks growing in the open, but
can fatally weaken a sapling already contending with shady
conditions.[4]

One observation may give some insight into the health of the
wood at this period. Power noticed sparrows and starlings in
the tree canopy, feeding on the larvae of the green oak tortrix
(*Tortrix viridana*), a moth whose caterpillars can rapidly defoli-
ate a mature oak. He also noted a decline in the number of
migrant bird species in the area, which he attributed to suburban
development, adding that 'it is owing to our local parks and
commons and the still existing woods of Dulwich and Sydenham
that so many birds are still attracted, and that the breeding
species are even now fairly numerous.'

A frequent visitor to Dulwich Wood, Power recorded a
number of species there. Sparrows, robins, wrens, great and blue
tits were plentiful; more unusually, marsh tits were seen there in
1904 and 1905 as late as July 'so in all probability it nested in the
immediate neighbourhood'. Ring doves and turtle doves were
fairly common, and a few pheasant could occasionally be found
wandering the woods. Lesser spotted woodpeckers were plentiful, green woodpeckers could be seen occasionally, but the great
spotted woodpecker was a 'great rarity'. Of the corvids, magpies
were rare, and jays 'much diminished over last 15 years', though
he had seen three or four pairs nesting in the woods. A nutcracker
had been seen on the golf course in 1905.

Power saw several pairs of hawfinches in Dulwich and Sydenham Woods every spring and summer, and believed they nested
there, while bramblings – common before the development of
the wider area – could also be seen there from time to time.
Goldcrests, he thought, 'may breed in the Crystal Palace district'.
Wrynecks could be seen every spring on Cox's Walk, and the
keeper at Dulwich Wood reported a landrail in an adjoining
meadow in 1905. He had not seen a nuthatch or tree creeper
in the woods since 1901, and a nightingale was last heard in
Crystal Palace Park in 1897.[5]

ZEPPELINS OVER DULWICH

Once the First World War broke out, the shortage of men and
materials brought suburban development to an abrupt halt. On
4 August 1914, the day Britain declared war on Germany, W. A.
King, the keeper of Dulwich Woods and a reservist in the
Queen's Royal West Surrey Regiment, was ordered to rejoin his
regiment. As he was a married man with a child of nine months
old, the Estate agreed to pay his wife the difference between
his Army pay and the wood-keeper's wages for the duration of
the war.[6] A temporary wood-keeper, E. Major, was taken on in
King's place, but the work recommended by Cluttons on thinning out diseased and damaged trees stopped, and was not
resumed until late in 1918.[7]

The first Zeppelin raids in the spring of 1915 took Britain by
surprise, and a chain of anti-aircraft defences was hastily organised under the command of the Royal Naval Air Service.[8] Gun
emplacements and searchlights were positioned at Croydon and
Dulwich (in the grounds of James Allen's Girls' School, next to
Green Dale), and a 3-inch 20-cwt gun was installed on the
summit of One Tree Hill to counter the threat; its octagonal
base can still be seen today. The site was well chosen, offering
commanding views over the metropolis. On the night of 7–8

September, along with other guns around London, the Honor Oak emplacement opened fire on Zeppelin L13 as it flew over Holborn and the City in a raid that killed twenty-two civilians. A month later, on the night of 13–14 October, it discharged nine rounds at the same airship as it was caught in the Blackheath searchlight while bombing the Royal Arsenal at Woolwich. During the same raid, Zeppelin L14 bombed Croydon, killing nine people, including three children, before passing over Crystal Palace.[9] Over the coming months, Zeppelins killed ten people in Albany Road, Camberwell, six at Ilderton Road in Bermondsey, and fourteen, including nine children, at Hither Green in the final airship raid on London.

By the autumn of 1916, improved anti-aircraft defences had made the Zeppelins increasingly vulnerable, so the German air force switched to using Gotha GVs, heavy twin-engine biplanes, to devastating effect. On 6 December 1917, two incendiary bombs fell on Beechgrove, damaging the house and destroying a greenhouse in the garden. An 'Air Raid Map of the Metropolitan Area and Central London' in the 1920 edition of *Harmsworth's New Atlas* shows a total of four bombs falling on Sydenham Hill along the edge of the wood, and a further two in the wood itself, close to the railway line.

Both Kingswood House and Grangewood Manor were used to billet Canadian troops. In January 1917, passenger services on the Crystal Palace High Level Line were suspended; they did not restart until March 1919.[10] In December 1917, the Dulwich wood-keeper E. Major wrote to the Estate governors that 'owing to air raids and gun-firing, he feels compelled to resign'. His resignation was accepted, and he was granted a bonus of £10 in recognition of additional work he had undertaken making paths and waterways in the woods.[11]

THE NEW SUBURBIA

The suburban expansion put on hold by the First World War resumed energetically after the Armistice as London's population continued to increase, rising from 7.25 million in 1911 to 8.73 million in 1939. The character of the new wave of development was different from what had come before; instead of the terraced housing of the inner suburbs, homebuyers now favoured lower-density detached or semi-detached properties with large gardens and access to green space.

Just as the railways had facilitated the urban expansion of the second half of the nineteenth century, this new wave of development was driven by the growth of car ownership. In 1919, there were just 100,000 cars on the UK's roads; by 1938, the number had grown to two million.[12] The open fields that in 1914 still extended to the south of Streatham, east of Sydenham, and south of Elmer's End were, in the course of the 1920s and 1930s, covered by semi-detached houses, many with garages. In 1922, Charles Hay Walker, a Baptist civil engineer who had bought Falkland House from Thomas McMeekin, gave the estate to Spurgeon's College. The Baptist training centre sold off some of the land, and the houses that now line the western side of Wharncliffe Road were built – but within the grounds of the college, which still occupies the house, part of White Horse Wood survives. As a result of such developments, by the beginning of the Second World War the built-up area extended without a break from London to Croydon.

Between the wars, Dulwich Wood remained closed to the general public, though keys were issued to some two hundred estate residents and golf and tennis club members. There was a hard tennis court in the middle of Peckarmans Wood, near the point where five paths now meet. Walter Johnson, a regular contributor to *The Naturalist* and editor of Gilbert White's *Journals*, described the wood at this period in *The Nature-World of London* (1924):

There still remains to us a remnant of Dulwich Wood, running up to Sydenham, where we can get glimpses of the wild arum, cuckoo pint, or lords-and-ladies, besides the enchanter's nightshade and, best of all, the dainty, fragile wood anemone. Among the grasses, the wood melic, the wood poa, the false brome, and the meadow soft grass, or Yorkshire fog (*Holcus lanatus*), are noticeable. As we walk along the sunny fringe of this woodland and listen to the blue-tit and chaffinch, there arises a wish that we might thoroughly explore the dark recesses at leisure, and ascertain whether any uncommon herbs by chance linger there; but the wood appears to be forbidden ground to casual strollers. The earnest student, however, would be admitted on special application.[13]

To the south, the oak woods of Grangewood Park formed 'a perfect nature sanctuary', according to Edward Martin, a local naturalist and honorary curator of the museum in the mansion there. Noting the park's sizeable population of red squirrels, whose nests the keepers were at pains to protect, he added, 'So far as I know, the American grey squirrel has not yet arrived, and one hopes that he will not do so.'[14] It was, sadly, a vain hope. Introduced from North America in the nineteenth century, the grey squirrel (*Sciurus carolinensis*) was already outcompeting the native red (*Sciurus vulgaris*); furthermore, it carried a disease known as squirrel pox, to which it was itself resistant, but which was fatal to the red. Within a couple of decades, the red squirrel, once common throughout the North Wood, had disappeared from the area.

In the same year that Johnson published his book, Croydon Corporation purchased the fifteen acres of Long Lane Wood in Monk's Orchard for public open space. This remnant of the Eighteen Acre Wood shown on Rocque's 1762 map of Surrey – the name Long Lane Wood first appears on the 1894 Ordnance

Survey map – had been surrounded by fields as recently as 1912; soon it would be hemmed in by housing estates, providing a precious amenity to their residents. Less than half a mile to the south, the council purchased, by public subscription over a period of two years, three acres of ancient woodland that had survived at the bottom of the gardens of nearby houses; Glade Wood, as it became known, would be retained as undeveloped woodland, not open to the public, as more houses sprang up around it.

By the 1920s, Biggin Wood had long been abandoned and overgrown with brambles. In 1928 a local newspaper reported that the Streatham Antiquarian and Natural History Society was campaigning for the sixteen-acre site to be dedicated to public use. Betty Griffin, a local woman who was an active member of the Norwood Society and several other community groups, was four years old when her family moved into one of the newly built semis on Covington Way next to Biggin Wood in 1928. 'In the middle of the wood,' she later recalled,

> stood some very large specimens of oaks which had been left uncut, and were probably quite old. The main part of the wood was composed of oak trees, but there were quite a few tall elms and where there was enough space and light, the elder and hawthorn bushes grew in profusion . . . Many bats also inhabited the trees flying on summer evenings, with stag beetles flying along the edges of the trees.[15]

In 1932, the local historian and naturalist W. C. Cocksedge presented a paper to the London Natural History Society, entitled 'The Great North Wood'. Regrettably, it was not a botanical survey, but a brief history of the wood, drawn largely from local historians such as J. Corbet Anderson and Allan Galer, other secondary sources, and Rocque's 1745 map.[16] Cocksedge had been a pupil at Dulwich College in the latter half of the 1890s

when Anderson's book was published, so his interest may have
dated back to his schooldays. While his paper offers no evidence
of the state of the woods in the 1930s, it did at least draw attention to their existence at a time when, fragmented and hemmed
in by suburban development, they had been largely forgotten.

More informative is E. G. Swayne's 'Birds of the Norwood
District', presented to the Society the following year. Covering
southern Lambeth and north Croydon from Brockwell Park to
Grange Wood, it drew together reported sightings from the
beginning of the century. 'Patches of wood run from the Crystal
Palace grounds to the east to Streatham Common on the west,'
he noted. 'These form a chain only broken by the main roads, so
that a migrant bird may easily pass from one end to the other
un-noticed.'

Swayne recorded seventy-nine species of bird, both resident
and migrant, a significant increase on the fifty-four species
observed by Aldridge half a century earlier. Swayne attributed
this to the greater maturity of trees in the area, many of which
had been planted during the Victorian suburban expansion; a
more likely explanation is that Aldridge included only his own
sightings over a period of seven years, whereas Swayne also drew
on the observations of others dating back some three decades.

Swayne remembered nightingales singing in the woods near
Church Road, but had not heard one himself for thirty years,
though several people had told him that they had heard them
for three or four successive nights as recently as 1932. The night-
jar was last reported in the area in 1902. Kestrels were seen
regularly, and bred locally, though sparrowhawks were only
occasional visitors. Crows were common, though rooks were
seldom seen on the hilltops any more because of the felling of
the trees in which they built their rookeries. Jackdaws, though
relatively scarce, were sometimes seen on Beulah Hill. Jays were
common, with few copses without one or two pairs, though
magpies were rare. Great spotted, lesser spotted and green

woodpeckers were breeding locally, and both nuthatches and tree creepers were resident, often nesting in gardens. Bullfinches were common all year round in the woods on Beulah Hill, while woodcock were occasionally present there. A kingfisher had been seen on Norwood Lake.[17]

Betty Griffin's recollection of the birds in Biggin Wood before the war corroborates Swayne's reports. She remembered 'a small colony of rooks in the elm trees'; two pairs of jays; little and barn owls; sparrowhawks and kestrels; all three native woodpeckers; blue tits, great tits, long-tailed tits, marsh tits and coal tits; chaffinches, bullfinches, goldfinches and greenfinches; mistle thrushes, song thrushes, and blackbirds; robins and wrens; wood warblers, tree creepers, spotted fly-catchers and dunnocks; and swifts and cuckoos in summer.[18]

In 1934, the derelict Biggin Wood House was destroyed by fire, and a battle began over the future of the wood. Croydon Council proposed to connect the two halves of Covington Way, which would bisect the wood, and build houses on the northern part. In 1938 the Streatham Antiquarian and Natural History Society, in conjunction with the Metropolitan Public Gardens Association, renewed its campaign to preserve the wood as public open space, and in 1939 James Epps's granddaughter sold the estate to the council on condition it was maintained as a bird sanctuary. The fields to the east of the wood were turned into allotments, which are still in use today.

On the night of 30 November 1936, a far more catastrophic fire broke out in the Crystal Palace. At around 7.25 pm, a watchman spotted flames at the rear of the staff offices. The Penge Fire Brigade were called out by 7.59 pm, and were soon joined by reinforcements from all over London. High winds fanned the blaze which, according to reports, reached three hundred feet and could be seen from Brighton, while molten glass and debris rained down on the surrounding area. Despite the efforts of more than four hundred firemen using eighty-nine tenders, the building was completely destroyed by midnight, with only the two water towers left standing. For the first time in eighty-five years, this huge edifice no longer dominated the skyline above the woods. Ruskin, had he still been alive, would have rejoiced.

Croydon Council, meanwhile, continued its programme of securing public open space with the purchase in 1938 of two large houses in Upper Norwood, Hazelwood and Beaulieu Lodge, from the Ecclesiastical Commissioners. Their extensive grounds included a surviving remnant of the Archbishop of Canterbury's wood, which the Corporation intended to turn into a public park. The Second World War put the plan on hold, however, and Beaulieu Heights did not open to the public until 1965.

WAR IN THE WOODS

After the declaration of war on 3 September 1939, the Norwood Ridge, with its commanding views over London, made an ideal site for an anti-aircraft battery, so the Army requisitioned the farm that still occupied the land at the top of Grange Lane between the golf course and Cox's Walk. The emplacement was manned by the Royal Artillery's 103 HG 53rd (City of London) Heavy Anti-Aircraft Regiment. One heavy gun and a Bofors light AA gun were supplemented by a rocket battery consisting of sixty iron frames. Two men were assigned to load two rockets on to each frame; they then retired to their shelter and fired all 120 rockets in a block barrage. The emplacement's crescent-shaped rampart can be seen on a post-war aerial photograph and the 1952 Ordnance Survey map.

There was also a searchlight battery on the golf course, and a barrage balloon was moored there, guarded by a detachment of the RAF. The Local Volunteer Force – renamed the Home Guard in July 1940 – had their post in the golf clubhouse, with a direct telephone line to the AA emplacement. They also had a

The Dulwich and Sydenham Hill Golf Club's pavilion on the edge of
Dulwich Woods was destroyed by a V1 flying bomb on 26 June 1944.

dugout, roofed with corrugated iron, which tended to become
waterlogged in wet weather and needed to be pumped out
frequently. By night, from 10 pm to 6 am, the Home Guard kept
watch; by day, the golfers returned and the club's horse pulled a
roller over the fairways.

The ranks of the Home Guard included Dr Guy Bousfield
and several other medical practitioners, local builders and property developers, a wine merchant and an undertaker. Among
them was Lionel Logue, the Australian speech therapist who
treated King George VI's stammer and whose story formed the
basis of the 2010 film *The King's Speech*. Logue had moved into
Beechgrove with his wife Myrtle and younger sons in 1932. The
rambling, twenty-five-room villa was by then somewhat dilapidated, but it had five acres of garden, with avenues of
rhododendrons, a tennis court and, at the bottom of the slope, a
stretch of the original woodland.[19] To reach the Home Guard

post at the golf club, Logue would only have had to cross the railway line over the Cox's Walk footbridge and walk through the woods.

Many of the incidents recorded in the Dulwich Home Guard's surviving logbook, which covers the second half of 1940, have a comic aspect that is inevitably reminiscent of the sitcom *Dad's Army*. Just after 10.30 pm on 11 September, Thomas Clerk, on guard that night, challenged 'a curious figure' moving towards the clubhouse. There was no response, but as it came closer, Clerk realised that it was the golf club's horse. Relations between the Home Guard and the other military units stationed around the course were often tetchy. Each reported the other for breaking the blackout regulations. In August, the Royal Artillery gunners asked the Home Guard 'not to phone up unless necessary as it is causing them some inconvenience.'

On Thursday 3 October, in the midst of an air raid, a Home Guard sentry heard voices in the darkness, and issued a challenge. It was two guards from the anti-aircraft emplacement, who said they were looking for a Sergeant Quinn. Shortly afterwards another person appeared; when challenged, he stated that he was Sergeant Quinn. Since no one on duty knew him, his statement was confirmed on 'phone to Battery – Sgt was a little peeved at being held for identification, but incident ended amicably and in an orderly like way.' In November, one of the volunteers asked in the logbook whether the searchlight personnel had permission to use the clubhouse lavatory: 'They say they have nowhere else to go.' In pencil, another has added, 'No. Outside Lav.'

Often, however, the logbook records far more serious events. From their hilltop post beneath the blazing anti-aircraft battery, the volunteers could look out over all London as the sky was raked by searchlights, planes were shot down and fires raged from Battersea to the docks. Just after midnight on Sunday 15 September 1940, a bomb fell near the clubhouse, causing serious damage but no injuries. On 14 October, a Messerschmitt 109 dived low over the post, and a barrage balloon came down on the 13th fairway. On 25 October a basket of incendiary bombs exploded on the golf course, forcing the unit to extinguish fires over a wide area. Mysterious lights were seen in the woods, and gunfire was heard through the trees. Desperate times required desperate measures, and on 18 September, after repeated complaints about violations of the blackout at the Grange, a large, isolated house halfway up Grange Lane, volunteers Egan and Dean went round and shot out the lights.[20]

Because its position in South East London placed it directly on the flight-path of bombers coming from across the Channel, the area suffered heavy damage during the Blitz of 1940–41. Between October 1940 and June 1941, high-explosive bombs fell on Dulwich Woods, Spa Hill, Beaulieu Heights and Long Lane Wood. In Biggin Wood – where a small brick air raid shelter had been built near the Covington Way entrance – a 100 lb bomb left a crater about fifteen feet across and a few feet deep. It was still visible in 2004, covered in bluebells and brambles. Some nineteen high-explosive bombs and countless incendiaries fell on Dulwich during the nine months of the Blitz. George Brown, a local air raid warden, recalled the 'searchlights glimmering over the Chapel or stabbing the deep dome of the sky like silver swords as it reflected the fires of London that boiled and blazed around us'.[21]

As a result of the Dig for Victory campaign, the area resumed something of its former agricultural character, albeit temporarily. Dulwich Park was dug up for allotments, hay was mown in Dulwich Village, and local people were encouraged to keep pigs and poultry. Dulwich Woods remained closed to the public and the tennis court was abandoned and became overgrown, as ammunition for the anti-aircraft battery was stored in the woods. Ken Round, a local man who served in the Home Guard as a boy, told the Dulwich Society that one of his duties was to guard the dump, which was situated near the junction of Low Cross Wood Lane and College Road.[22]

During the course of 1940, concerns were raised that the two Crystal Palace water towers, which had survived the 1936 blaze, could act as landmarks for enemy aircraft. Because of its proximity to houses, the south tower was carefully dismantled during the winter of 1940–1; the north tower, which did not present such a risk, was blown up the following April. In January 1941, services on the Crystal Palace High Level Line were reduced, and in May 1944 they ceased altogether on account of a lack of manpower. The line did not reopen until March 1946.[23]

As the privations of war began to bite, Logue was finding the upkeep of Beechgrove increasingly challenging. Forbidden to use petrol in his motor mower, he bought a sheep to keep the lawn in trim, but by the end of 1942 the unfortunate animal had been consigned to the abattoir. Much of the garden was turned over to growing vegetables, and in the freezing winter of 1939–40, to supplement their dwindling supply of coal and coke, Myrtle and their gardener felled one of the trees in the grounds. The next day, a bailiff turned up at the house and informed Myrtle that cutting down a tree without permission incurred a fine of £50.

In October 1940, a bomb exploded in a neighbour's woodland, bringing down all the chimneys and several ceilings at Beechgrove. The following January, Logue wrote to the Dulwich Estate, which owned the freehold, asking them to suspend the annual ground rent of £102 8s for the duration of the war, and to repair at least one chimney stack so they could heat the house without filling it with smoke. He also complained that the firing of the anti-aircraft battery was gradually shaking Beechgrove and the neighbouring houses to pieces.[24]

After May 1941, the bombing raids on London became sporadic and less severe. 'The Lull', as it was known, lasted until January 1944, when the Luftwaffe launched Operation Steinbock, which Londoners called the 'Baby Blitz'. Far more serious were the V1 flying bombs, pilotless planes filled with high explosive and known as doodlebugs. On 26 June 1944, one of these projectiles wrecked the Dulwich and Sydenham Hill Golf Club house; a week later, on 3 July, another destroyed Woodhall, a Victorian villa beside the woods on College Road. The ammunition dump was then moved deeper into the woods as it was considered to be in too dangerous a position.

V1s also fell between Biggin Hill and Beulah Hill on 5 July 1944, and on Spa Hill on 15 July. On 10 July, a doodlebug demolished the science block at Dulwich College, and on 21 July, another almost completely destroyed Dulwich Picture Gallery. (The paintings, fortunately, had been moved to Wales for safekeeping.) Even more formidable was the V2, a ballistic missile first launched in September. On 25 November 1944 one landed on a branch of Woolworth's at New Cross, killing 168 people in the worst incident of the campaign; on 15 March 1945, nine were killed in Crystal Palace Road. The last of the V2 rockets to strike London fell in Orpington on 27 March, killing one person. By the time hostilities ended, wrote George Brown, 'parts of the ancient village [of Dulwich], which goes back beyond Domesday Book,' were 'reminiscent of the battlefields of France in the last war.'[25]

What was the impact on the flora and fauna of the woods of the Bofors gun banging away night after night as the sky was raked by searchlights, of jeeps rumbling through the woods loaded with crates of ammunition, and of high explosives on the structure and composition of the soil? The ecological effects of the war were mixed: some species were adversely affected, while others were quick to take advantage of the changed environment. The pulverised brick and mortar of the bomb sites was colonised by lime-loving plants such as buddleia, rosebay willowherb and Canadian goldenrod, while the population of black redstarts, relatively scarce in London before the war, increased significantly.[26] Wood pigeons, on the other hand, declined dramatically after the government organised a series of shoots to eliminate what it regarded as a pest of food crops.[27]

The war left a legacy of unexploded ordnance throughout the area of the North Wood, and disposal experts are still being called in to this day. In 1996, local people were evacuated from their homes after a 50 kg bomb was removed from Norwood Lake and detonated by the Royal Engineers. In 2011, an unexploded 1 kg incendiary device was found by a dog walker in Sydenham Hill Wood near the abandoned railway track, which was presumably its target.[28] In 2016, a Croydon man found an unexploded bomb device in the basement of his house,[29] and as recently as June 2017, Penge High Street was cordoned off and twenty people evacuated after a bomb was discovered on Kingswood Road and detonated in a controlled explosion in Betts Park.[30]

8

A DESIGN FOR LIVING

1945–1970

As the nation emerged from the wreckage of war, two priorities were clear to the newly elected Labour government: food security and the provision of decent housing. Food shortages did not end when the fighting stopped – rationing would continue until 1953 – so increasing production was a matter of urgency. The 1947 Agriculture Act, supported by all political parties, sought to continue and expand the wartime campaign for agricultural self-sufficiency by guaranteeing prices, giving farmers the confidence to invest in the latest agricultural technology. They were also encouraged to maximise crops through the use of higher yielding varieties, pesticides, herbicides and inorganic fertilisers.

The drive for agricultural productivity was an outstanding success, putting cheap, plentiful food on the nation's tables, but it came at the cost of landscape diversity. Farms became larger and more specialised; fields got bigger, and to make way for the new machinery, 50 per cent of the nation's hedgerows were grubbed up. Flower-rich farmland such as hay meadows disappeared, replaced by grass monoculture grown for silage, along with field margins, copses and ponds. In arable fields, few non-crop plants were allowed to survive.

This in turn had a catastrophic effect on animal populations, deprived of habitat and food. By the 1980s, a third of

insects and four-fifths of bird species had undergone serious
decline. Small mammals such as harvest mice and field voles
were also affected, as were reptiles and amphibians.[1] A report
published by the Institute for Public Policy Research in 2019
described the UK as one of the 'most nature-depleted countries
in the world', with its most threatened species having decreased
by two-thirds since 1970.[2] This change mostly took place outside the Greater London area, of course, but it had the effect of
turning the capital's parks, commons and other green spaces,
including the surviving remnants of the North Wood, into a
refuge for plants and animals once more readily associated
with the countryside.

Even before the war was over, plans were being made for the
reconstruction of the blitzed metropolis. The County of London
Plan drawn up by J. H. Forshaw and Patrick Abercrombie in
1943, and Abercrombie's Greater London Plan of 1944, focused
on five main issues: population density, housing, transport,
employment and recreation. Abercrombie, a founder of the
Council for the Preservation of Rural England, attempted to
reconcile two of Octavia Hill's potentially conflicting objectives:
the construction of decent housing at a price affordable to as
many people as possible, and the provision of green space for
social and psychological health:

> We are opposed to a policy involving the development of the
> whole of the green wedges of undeveloped land which are still
> happily to be found between the radiating sprawl of outer
> London. Even though this filling-in were carried out on the
> most approved planning lines, with open spaces and playing
> fields, and even if it were an example of skilful tactics, it
> would be strategically disastrous.[3]

Abercrombie outlined a series of four concentric rings: inner,
suburban, Green Belt and country. In the inner area, new housing

Detail of the Open Space Plan, showing Dulwich and Sydenham, from John Forshaw and Patrick Abercrombie's 1943 County of London Plan.

would be concentrated in bomb-damaged areas. The suburban ring would be developed with a mix of housing and light industry to a lower density, with ample open space. Around it, a Green Belt – an idea first mooted by Hill – would limit sprawl into regional areas by restricting all development outside existing villages. Beyond the Green Belt, a series of new satellite towns would be built to house people from the overcrowded areas of inner London.[4]

The two plans would determine the capital's development for decades to come, and shape the future of the woods. Connecting the County of London and the Greater London area beyond, Forshaw and Abercrombie envisaged a series of 'green wedges leading towards the Green Belt'. The Crystal Palace site, which lay just outside the county boundary, 'might well be considered as being part of a recreation and sports area serving South London. This would include the Dulwich Common area to the north, and its provision would necessitate a restriction on further house building in that district.' In the Development and Zoning map included in the County Plan, however, the area between Sydenham Hill, Crescent Wood Road and the Crystal Palace High Level Railway – much of today's Sydenham Hill Wood reserve – is designated residential, presumably because it had already been built on, and the gardens of these Victorian villas were not considered open space.[5]

Many of Forshaw and Abercrombie's proposals were incorporated into the 1947 Town and Country Planning Act, which made it necessary for developers to secure planning permission from local authorities. The London County Council imposed a compulsory purchase order on the Kingswood estate, acquiring a total of thirty-seven acres near Sydenham Hill Station, of which thirty was allocated to housing and about three and a half reserved for schools. The plans, unveiled in December 1947, provided for 748 flats in three- and four-storey blocks, along with forty-six cottages. The new buildings were widely spaced, with many old trees preserved between them, while the original mansion was retained as a library and community centre, providing a focus for the estate.

FROM AUSTERITY TO PROSPERITY

Just as the reassembly of the Crystal Palace at Sydenham had boosted the local economy, its destruction reduced the area's prosperity and status. Amid the austerity of post-war Britain, few people wanted to buy – and take on the expense of maintaining – an elaborate villa complete with porticoes, turrets, loggias and parterres in an unfashionable South London suburb, especially as they were approaching the end of their leases and thus impossible to sell or mortgage. Some were used by Camberwell Council to house families made homeless by the Blitz; others were divided into flats and bedsits by private landlords.

In April 1947, Lionel Logue sold the remainder of his lease on Beechgrove to the Community of Nursing Sisters of St John the Divine, and moved to a small flat in Knightsbridge. Myrtle had died just as the war was ending, and their sons were now grown; not only was the house too big for him, it also, he wrote sadly to King George, 'held too many memories'. In 1952 Beechgrove became a Red Cross Home for the Aged Sick; after this closed in 1961, the building slowly lapsed into dereliction.[6]

Without the Crystal Palace to attract passengers, the High Level Railway ceased to be viable; the last train ran on 20 September 1954, a century after Queen Victoria had opened the Crystal Palace at Sydenham. The rails were lifted in 1957, and the trackbed sold to the London County Council, which apportioned parts of it to Lewisham and Camberwell councils. The Lordship Lane bridge and station were torn down, and housing was built on the site of the station, and between the Sydenham and Paxton tunnels; the High Level Station was demolished in 1961.[7] The cutting through the woods, meanwhile, began to revert to nature.

The anti-aircraft battery at the top of Grange Lane was dismantled after the war, and the associated huts became a Territorial Army training centre. After the site was returned to the Dulwich Estate in 1960, some of the dilapidated buildings were handed over to the Boy Scouts, while the rest were cleared to make way for the Gun Site allotments, which opened in 1966. This was not the end of military activity around the woods, however. Since the bombing of its pavilion, the golf club had occupied a Victorian house on Dulwich Common. In the mid 1960s, it had a modern clubhouse built on the original site.

Alongside it, a Royal Observer Corps underground monitoring post was dug, one of eight hundred built throughout the country at the height of the Cold War. It was 'a pretty basic affair,' one member of the local ROC recalled,

> housing a complement of two or three operatives. Furniture consisted of two bunk beds, a chemical toilet and storage space for emergency food supplies and a couple of canvas chairs for seating. Lighting was provided by a single dimly lit bulb. Access to the bunker was via a steep ladder – topped off with a heavy metal access cover. Filtered air was produced by a special ventilator shaft. Lining the walls were the specialist instruments for monitoring fall-out. It was not a place that I would wish to stay for any length of time . . . I was sceptical as to whether ROC members would rush to the relative safety of an underground concrete bunker – leaving their loved ones to be incinerated during a nuclear attack.'[8]

The bunker was no secret, and was featured in a 1983 London Weekend Television documentary.[9] In 1991, as the Cold War came to an end, it was decommissioned and converted into a water tank for the golf club's sprinkler system.

One highly visible change to the area was the construction of the BBC's Crystal Palace aerial on the peak of the Norwood Ridge, where Brunel's north tower had stood. It began transmitting in March 1956 when only half complete; on reaching its full height of 708 feet (216 metres) in December 1957, it would be the tallest structure in London until One Canada Square was built in Canary Wharf in 1991. On Beulah Hill, a mile to the south, ITV's Croydon transmitting station had already begun broadcasting from a small tower built in 1955; this was replaced by the present 500-foot (152-metre) antenna in 1962. These two masts still dominate the skyline for many miles.

A SECRET WILDERNESS

Throughout these changes, Dulwich Woods remained closed to the public, and a gamekeeper was employed by the Estate to keep down the numbers of wood pigeons. One close observer of the woods at this period was J. K. Adams, the editor of *Country Life* and a resident of Alleyn Park in West Dulwich. Over the cryptic byline 'JKA', he was a regular contributor to the *Guardian*'s Country Diary from the late 1940s to the early 1960s. Between reports from such majestic landscapes as the South Downs and the Yorkshire Dales, he did not neglect the smaller, semi-secret wilderness on his South London doorstep.

'I never cease to marvel at the variety of birds that are to be seen in the delightfully open stretch of country between Dulwich Village and Sydenham Hill,' he wrote in December 1949. 'Kestrels and sparrow-hawks are a frequent sight at all times of the year, and in spring and summer the fields and gardens echo the calls of the cuckoo and all three British species of woodpecker . . . Last spring I saw hawfinches and wood-wrens in a corner of Dulwich Wood.' In December 1954, he noted that a woodcock had 'frequented the woods below Sydenham Hill for the past two or three winters', and that a pair of snipe could be seen on 'the pond on the outskirts of the wood'. The following February, he reported long-tailed tits in and around the woods.

By the spring of 1957, his tally of birds had almost equalled that of Swayne two decades earlier. 'During the past ten years,' he wrote, 'I have seen or heard nearly seventy species in Dulwich, including hawfinches, wood-warblers, reed-warblers, redstarts, kingfishers, little owls, and partridges. Other people have seen red-backed shrikes, lapwings and even snipe and woodcock' (10 April 1957). In March the following year, he saw a goldcrest – now resident in the woods – in Dulwich for the first time, and in May 1960, he noted that 'At least one cuckoo

can be heard here every summer, calling insistently from early
May' (8 May 1960).

On 23 April 1961, he reported that:

> The resident willow-wrens have arrived and this morning
> there were several singing on the outskirts of Dulwich Wood.
> In a shrubbery near one of them a blackcap was trying out
> its song, and some way inside the wood chiffchaffs were
> repeating their names with monotonous regularity from
> their favourite station: – the tops of the oaks. Ten years ago
> wood-wren used to nest among the brambles and bracken
> under these oaks, but it is some time since I heard their shiv-
> ering notes ring out over the bluebells. White throats, on the
> other hand, which should be here any day now, and garden
> warblers, which are due early in May, remain faithful to the
> outskirts of the wood in spite of the amount of building that
> is going on.

The ornithologist P. J. Oliver was a regular observer of the birds
of Dulwich Woods between March 1959 and May 1960, though
his records were not published until almost half a century later.
He found a substantial population of wood pigeons, despite the
fact that the gamekeeper had shot three hundred in September
1959. The keeper, he noted, was not raising game, and did not
persecute corvids or raptors. A pair of kestrels was resident on
the golf course, sparrowhawks were well known to the keeper,
both tawny and little owls were present, and a pair of magpies
nested in the woods in both years. Both great and lesser-spotted
woodpeckers were resident, and while Oliver had no record of
green woodpeckers, he assumed that was because they were 'too
common to note'. He heard cuckoos calling in both springs, and
recorded a juvenile migrant redstart in August 1959, a pair of
tree creepers nesting in the woods in April 1960, and a few sightings of goldcrests, mostly outside the breeding season. Other

bird species included mistle thrush, whitethroat, blackcap, chiff-chaff, willow warbler, spotted flycatcher, marsh tit, willow tit, starling, tree sparrow, chaffinch, brambling and goldfinch.[10]

While Adams and Oliver were recording the birds of the wood, Edward Lousley, an acclaimed amateur botanist and curator of the South London Botanical Institute, was turning his attention to its plant life. In 1958, he obtained permission to survey the trees and understorey in Dulwich Woods. Accompanied by J. E. Woodhead, a resident of the Dulwich Estate, he made a number of visits over the summer and autumn of that year. Confining himself to the area west of the disused railway, bounded by the golf club, the gun site, Low Cross Wood Walk and the houses on Crescent Wood Road, he noted that the dominant tree throughout was sessile oak. 'The trees have very straight trunks contrasting sharply with the gnarled boles of very occasional common oaks (*Q. robur*), and are mostly some 50 to 60 feet tall . . . While the height of the canopy is fairly uniform, it is evident that there is considerable variation in age.'

In Peckarmans Wood, he also found a few wild cherry, ash, sycamore, beech and hornbeam trees. The shrub level consisted of holly, guelder-rose, hazel, rowan and elder, while the field layer was dominated by bramble and bracken. Bluebells were plentiful, though some appeared to have hybridised with cultivated varieties; dog's mercury, wood dock and enchanter's nightshade were common, but wood anemone was rare. Wood sedge and two species of woodrush occurred in places. The tennis court was 'now so overgrown that it would be almost impossible to recognize its former use'. Despite the presence of invasive garden plants such as rhododendron, Peckarmans Wood, he concluded, was 'probably the most natural example of a sessile oakwood in the London Area – it has been virtually free from the influence of trampling' except around the Territorial Army base.

In Ambrook Hill Wood, Lousley found many hornbeams, but sessile oak remained the dominant tree. In the portion of Lapsewood between the railway and the golf course, he noted that the soil was black, crumbly and acidic. The trees, then as now, were mostly sessile oak, but around the edge of the wood he found rowan, wild cherry, hornbeam, beech, and cut-leaved whitebeam, along with yew seedlings. The rich understorey included sheep's sorrel, wood sage, heath woodrush, sedge and wavy hair-grass. Other species included two types of hawkweed and three species of grass. His report makes sobering reading for anyone familiar with this part of the woods today, where trampling has left the soil so badly compacted that little can be found growing beneath the canopy apart from the occasional patch of holly and bramble.

Along the railway embankments, ash, sycamore and birch were common. The rides were fringed with cow parsley, nipplewort, wall lettuce, wood violet, greater stitchwort and *Hypericum perforatum*. Near the tunnel mouth, he observed large colonies of great horsetail (*Equisetum telmateia*); this primeval, fern-like plant can still be found there, though not in such great quantity. The round pond, he noted, was 'rather shaded', and the only plants it contained were bittersweet, an unusual grass called *Glyceria declinata*, a few clumps of rush (*Juncus effusus*), and the ubiquitous duckweed. Although he did not venture beyond the railway, he noted that the trees in the grounds of the houses on Sydenham Hill were 'relics of woodland before the cutting was excavated'.[11]

The following May, Lousley and Woodhead returned to the woods with Francis Rose and E. C. Wallace. This time, they were able to observe a number of spring-flowering plants including wood anemone, greater stitchwort, wood violet, ramsons and hairy woodrush – all indicators of ancient woodland. 'Thanks to the energy and enthusiasm of Dr Rose on a very rainy day', they were able to cross the disused railway into the grounds of the Hoo, where they found a substantial area of sessile oak, a part of Ambrook Hill Wood cut off from the rest when the track was laid. Among the understorey he observed ramsons, butcher's-broom, *Vinca minor* – recorded by Curtis in 1780 on Lordship Lane – and Solomon's seal; the latter two plants, he observed, 'may be native in Dulwich Woods'. He also found lily-of-the-valley (*Convallaria majalis*) growing there, and had 'no hesitation in accepting the species as relics of the plants which Curtis in 1785 knew as "not uncommon in woods about Dulwich"'.

Lousley also explored several other remnants of the Great North Wood that year. Behind Farquhar Road, where several houses had been destroyed by enemy bombing, he discovered a five-hundred-yard strip of sessile oakwood, once part of Vicar's Oak Wood. Much of it lay within the grounds of private houses, but in the part he was able to investigate he saw bluebells, celandine and great horsetail. At Grangewood Park he found many sessile oaks, but noted that the ground was so trampled that there was little understorey other than holly. He was unable to get into Convent Wood, but from the road was able to observe numerous sessile oaks, with an understorey of holly and bramble. At Biggin Wood he found a similar range of vegetation, with patches of acid grassland, although the northern part had been compromised by invasive garden plants such as laurel and rhododendron.[12]

'By the autumn of 1958,' Lousley noted towards the end of his first report, 'men and tractors were at work clearing paths through the wilderness' that had engulfed the ruins of Wood Hall to make way for the construction of a new housing estate. It was a foretaste of things to come.

MID-CENTURY MODERN

By the late 1950s, London had once again expanded far beyond its administrative bounds. In 1957, a Royal Commission was appointed to 'examine the present system and working of Local Government in the Greater London area' and to suggest improvements. Its report, published in October 1960, recommended the creation of new boroughs under the umbrella of an elected council for the whole metropolitan area. Many of its findings were implemented in the London Government Act of 1963, which came into effect on 1 April 1965, abolished the County of London and created a new, much larger administrative area – 616 square miles compared with the 117 square miles of the County of London – to be run by a Greater London Council (GLC). The Metropolitan Borough of Camberwell was merged with Southwark and Bermondsey to form the London Borough of Southwark, which embraced the northern parts of the woods. Croydon, which covered the surviving fragments of the Archbishop's Woods, was removed from Surrey to become the southernmost of the London boroughs. The Urban District of Penge was abolished, and the area was transferred from Kent to the London Borough of Bromley. Responsibility for town planning, roads, housing and the environment was shared between the GLC and the various London boroughs. For the first time in history, all the remaining parts of the North Wood came under one unitary authority.

The enthusiasm of Harold Wilson's Labour government, elected in 1964, for the 'white heat of technology' often found itself at odds with a growing environmental movement. The publication of Rachel Carson's *Silent Spring* in 1962 had highlighted the devastating effects of pesticide use on wildlife, and in March 1967 the forlorn efforts to save huge numbers of seabirds from oil spilled from the wreck of the tanker *Torrey Canyon* off the Cornish coast were broadcast nightly on the nation's TV screens. In the course of the decade, environmentalism was transformed from a niche concern into a mass movement. The World Wildlife Fund (now the Worldwide Fund for Nature, or WWF) was established in 1961, and both Friends of the Earth (FoE) and Greenpeace were founded in 1971. Towards the end of the 1960s, the Wilson government set about establishing a Department of the Environment, although it did not come into being until October 1970, after Edward Heath's Conservative administration had taken office.

Both Southwark Council and governors of the Dulwich Estate, meanwhile, saw an opportunity to build new housing on the sites of the decaying villas on Sydenham Hill and Crescent Wood Road, and even in the adjoining woods; designated as residential land under the 1947 Town and Country Planning Act, they remained closed to the public and had no protection against development. The Act empowered Southwark Council to require the Estate to prepare a Dulwich Development Plan or face compulsory purchase, so a plan was set up as a joint venture between the Estate's architects, Austin Vernon & Partners, and the building firm Wates.

Charles Edward Barry, the third of his family to serve as the Estate's architect and surveyor, had retired in 1937. His successor Austin Vernon in turn retired in 1959, to be succeeded – true to the dynastic precedent – by his nephew, Russell Vernon. Inspired by the Bauhaus architects Walter Gropius and Mies van der Rohe, the younger Vernon set about creating group housing in communal, park-like grounds of the type pioneered by Modernists in Scandinavia and the United States. The plan took fifteen years to complete, and resulted in the construction of more than two thousand new homes – many of them two- or three-storey terraced houses – in and around the woods.

The work Ted Lousley had observed in progress on the site of the bombed-out villa was the construction of the Woodhall Estate, a development of some forty detached houses in landscaped grounds, ringed by a semi-circular access road giving on to College Road at either end. On its completion in 1965, the new estate was not confined to the former grounds of Wood Hall, but encroached on about three and a half acres of Dulwich Wood, bringing the houses and their gardens right up to College Road and the lower end of Low Cross Wood Walk.

In 1963, the Estate governors submitted an application to develop housing in Peckarmans Wood. The plan was to build on and sell the plots fronting Crescent Wood Road, then those bordering Dulwich Wood, and finally to clear the adjacent woodland for further housing. It was partly in response to this development that the Dulwich Society was established in 1964 'to foster and safeguard the amenities of Dulwich', including its 'trees, gardens, verges, wildlife and other natural endowments'.

Just outside the estate, on Friern Hill, the young Scottish architect Kate Macintosh created a strikingly original housing scheme for Southwark Council in 1964. Determined to avoid the impersonality of much public housing, she designed two ziggurat-like blocks of varying height, rising step-like from two storeys at their perimeters to twelve in the centre. The varied height ensured that every one of the 296 one- to four-bedroom split-level maisonettes had views and received sunlight even in winter. Crowning the ridge like an Italian hill town, the Dawson's Heights estate is a prominent local landmark, and a monument to the egalitarian ideals of the 1960s. Later, in the 1990s, encouraged by London Wildlife Trust volunteers, a resident set up a nature reserve in the grounds, converting part of the hill back into meadow, planting trees and shrubs, but mostly allowing natural regeneration to take its course.

To the south, in Norwood, Convent Wood was being encroached upon by building at either end. In the mid-1950s, nearby St Joseph's College built a new infants' and junior school on the western end of the wood, and in 1967 Rockmount Junior School was built on its eastern end, beside Hermitage Road.

Between them, the two schools replaced some two acres of ancient woodland that had survived the enclosures and the suburban development of the Victorian period.

In 1966, to avoid a compulsory purchase order on the remaining thirty acres of woodland, the governors of the Dulwich Estate offered Southwark Council the Lapsewood site and other parcels of land in West Dulwich and Herne Hill. They also applied for permission to build a further 115 houses, maisonettes and flats between Low Cross Wood Walk and Rock Hill.[13] The new estate, known as Great Brownings, was reached by a private access road and set back from College Road behind a surviving strip of woodland. Like Peckarmans Wood, the estate was designed by Malcolm Pringle of Vernon & Partners, and once again built by Wates. The dense woodland setting restricted access for heavy materials, so the houses were timber-framed – the first, it was claimed, to be built in London since the Great Fire of 1666.

Both Peckarmans Wood and Great Brownings are well-planned and well-built ensembles of attractive houses, much admired by enthusiasts of Mid-Century Modern architecture. Their appeal is enhanced by the woodland into which they encroached and so, ironically, the residents of these new estates – articulate, professional people, many of whom worked in the media – were soon to form the vanguard of resistance to any further development in the woods.

9

SAVE THE WOODS!

1970–1997

In the spring of 1971, the Dulwich Society spent several weeks surveying hundreds of trees on the closed site then known as Fernbank – in effect the whole of the area that now forms the Sydenham Hill Wood reserve, including the grounds of Beechgrove. The results were plotted on to a detailed 1:1250-scale map by John Westwood. Across the thirty-acre (twelve-hectare) site, the Society counted 523 mature forest trees, of which they considered 130, including oaks, beeches and yews, to be outstanding. The mature trees included 310 oaks, forty-seven beeches, fifty-one yews, twenty-one hornbeams and fourteen chestnuts, in addition to ash, elm and silver birch. There were 2,200 smaller trees, totalling more than forty species, including invasive garden shrubs such as rhododendron and laurel.

Oak lined the western edge of the trackbed, on the border with Dulwich Wood. To the east was a deep band of oak interspersed with hornbeam, holly and yew. Along the trackbed just to the north of the footbridge, the wood was composed largely of ash, creating a more open canopy; to the south of the bridge was a line of beeches, of which there were also several large specimens in the grounds of Beechgrove. On the upper slope towards Sydenham Hill the tree cover was generally sparser, though there were still a significant number of

mature oaks on the Fernbank site. Cherry laurel and rhododendron had advanced downhill from the old gardens into the
denser woodland below.

The Society concluded that 66 per cent of the area was hill
forest of first-class importance, although thinning and forestry
work were required, 22 per cent of the area was in a 'natural
state' and could easily be improved, while only 14 per cent could
be classified as derelict land. Its findings were to be significant
evidence in the planning battles to come.

DULWICH UPPER WOOD

Meanwhile, on Farquhar Road, a number of Victorian houses
had been destroyed by bombing, and several others had become
derelict and were demolished in the years after the war. By 1960,
much of the site had reverted to nature, with only one house still
occupied. The result was the six-acre (2.4-hectare) triangle that
Lousley had investigated the previous year, incorporating both
regenerated woodland and fragments of the ancient Further
King's Wood and East and West Vicar's Oak woods, including
two old coppice boundaries – a line of ancient coppiced and
pollarded trees and a ditch.

In 1973, local residents learnt that the Greater London Council planned to build eight blocks of flats on the plot. They could
not understand why so many fine trees had to be destroyed to
provide homes when the adjacent site of the Crystal Palace High
Level station, torn down in 1961 after the line was closed, was
larger, flatter and far easier to develop. With advice from the
Dulwich Society, they formed the Farquhar Road Area Residents'
Association, and commissioned John Westwood to survey the
wood; he found 387 trees of various species, including a veteran
oak well over 120 inches in girth, and a variety of wildlife.

After submitting numerous reports and engaging in lengthy
discussion with the GLC and Southwark's planning committee,

the Residents' Association, supported by the Dulwich Society, succeeded in persuading the authorities not to encroach on the woodland, but to confine development to the High Level Station site – a decision announced at a crowded meeting of the Crystal Palace Forum on 17 March 1975.[1] On 4 November 1980, the Ecological Parks Trust and Southwark Council confirmed that approval had been given to the establishment of the Farquhar Road woodland as an ecological or city nature park by the EPT. The station site was sold to the Abbey National building society, which constructed the Abbey Estate of houses aimed at first-time buyers. After four years of negotiations with Southwark, the Ecological Parks Trust (now Urban Ecology, an arm of The Conservation Volunteers) finally obtained a seven-year lease on Dulwich Upper Wood from the Dulwich Estate in 1985, with the prospect that it could be extended to twenty-five years. A warden, Andrew Loan, was appointed.

On Saturday 11 May, more than 160 people attended the official opening of the reserve by the Deputy Mayor of Southwark, Sam King. The rusty corrugated iron fencing was replaced with iron railings, and around them a hedge of hawthorn, blackthorn, dog rose, hazel and field maple was planted to enhance the appearance of the wood, increase habitat and species diversity, and discourage the dumping of rubbish, of which twelve skip-loads had been removed. A hut was obtained from the recently closed William Curtis Ecological Park near Tower Bridge to provide office space for the warden, teaching facilities for school visits, and an area for displays. Hazels were coppiced, and a tree nursery established. The basements of the demolished houses were retained, and remain an important feature of the wood.

These efforts rapidly attracted a range of wildlife. Lesser and great spotted woodpeckers, woodcock, nuthatches, redpolls, and tree creepers were reported to have returned. A fungi survey added five new species to the existing list of seventy. Seven species of spider were recorded, along with three types of butterfly – red admiral, small tortoiseshell and large skipper – more commonly found in gardens and grassy areas. A bat detector recorded pipistrelles flying round the treetops.

AN AMENITY FOR THE FEW?

In 1976, after repeated enquiries from the Dulwich Society to know what plans were in place for the care and use of Dulwich Woods, the Estate governors commissioned a forestry expert, Professor Lindsay, to survey the woods. Listing the trees and reporting on their condition, he recommended the removal of dead and dying specimens and their replacement with, in some cases, species new to the woods. The Estate also asked Lindsay whether the woods could be revenue-producing, since the cost of maintenance far exceeded the income from the rental of keys, which could be hired from the Estate office for £3 per annum, but in his opinion a twelve-acre woodland would have no commercial value. Unfortunately, the Society reported, some keyholders did not behave responsibly, neglecting to report gates that would not close, while some were in the habit of leaving gates unlocked so their children and pets could have access to the woods.[2]

Early in 1978, the Dulwich Estate sold the fifteen-acre (six-hectare) Fernbank site (at this period confusingly referred to as Lapsewood, although the actual site of Lapsewood House lay to the north of Beechgrove, at the top of Cox's Walk) to the London Borough of Southwark. The council, which now owned or leased the whole of Sydenham Hill Wood except for Beechgrove, announced plans to build forty houses with gardens and garages along the top of the site, from the boundary with Beechgrove on Sydenham Hill and along Crescent Wood Road to Peckarmans Wood. An access road would run around the back of the development, cutting deep into the wood.

On 9 January 1979, a deputation from the Dulwich Society, the Dulwich Residents' Association and the Peckarmans Wood

Residents' Association met the Joint Housing and Planning
Committee at Southwark Town Hall to put forward their views
on the future development of the site. Towards the end of a sharp
'but not unfriendly' discussion, the delegation encountered
fierce opposition from two councillors who accused them of
selfishly trying to safeguard the amenities of the few at the
expense of council tenants. 'However,' the Dulwich Society
reported, 'their opposition was expressed in such extreme terms
that it proved counter-productive, and we did in fact receive a
good deal of support from a number of councillors.'[3]

By the end of 1979, Southwark's plans had stalled, not as a result
of environmental objections but because of the difficulty and cost
of building on the steeply sloping, unstable site. In 1981, the housing committee agreed to dispose of the top part of the wood on
the open market. The lower part, around the old railway
trackbed, was transferred to the Library and Amenities Committee as an open space. The committee reported that Sydenham Hill
Wood was an 'extremely rare and important resource', one of the
only major areas of woodland in the borough that could be made
available for unrestricted use by the public.

The following year, Bob Smyth, a journalist and local councillor who would go on to write a guidebook to Britain's urban
wild spaces, founded the Southwark Wildlife Group to manage
the wood as an unofficial reserve, and to campaign for its preservation. At this point, a major new player entered the scene.
Chris Rose, a field officer with the Herts & Middlesex Wildlife
Trust, approached Smyth and other environmental activists
across the capital to discuss the possibility of setting up a London
body. Following a meeting at a pub in Fulham, they organised a
conference, 'Nature in London', which was held in May 1981 at
a school in Stoke Newington and attracted four hundred people.
The following November, the London Wildlife Trust (LWT)
was formally incorporated with Smyth as its chair; it opened
its first office under the Westway flyover a year later.[4] The

Southwark Wildlife Group merged with the new city-wide organisation, which was in turn affiliated to the Royal Society for Nature Conservation (RSNC); this subsequently evolved into The Wildlife Trusts. The first president of the LWT was the writer and broadcaster Richard Mabey, and its aim was to protect the capital's wild spaces and support the right of its inhabitants 'to share our environment with nature and wildlife'.

'A century ago,' read the LWT's founding Primrose Hill Declaration,

> London people pioneered the use of common land for public amenity at Epping Forest and Wimbledon Common: now is the time for conservationists to take up the common ground throughout London. In the inner city and around the suburbs, our natural heritage is still enclosed within corrugated iron, despoiled or locked behind chain-link fencing. This has been the expropriation of London's natural heritage by industry, development, greed, waste and misconception.

Southwark Council then decided to transfer the lower part of Sydenham Hill Wood to the new organisation, with a mandate to develop it 'sympathetically along natural lines', and in 1982 it became the London Wildlife Trust's first nature reserve; today, the LWT manages thirty-seven reserves across Greater London. The Trust began to restore the wood, with volunteers clearing the fly-tipping that had accumulated over decades, formalising paths, combatting soil erosion, excavating a small pond to the east of the railway trackbed, controlling invasive shrubs, and undertaking surveys of plant, bird and insect life. The new reserve was separated from Dulwich Wood to the west, and the sites of the old villas to the east, by chain-link fencing. Along Sydenham Hill and Crescent Wood Road, the derelict sites were fenced off with corrugated iron, which was soon adorned by graffiti reading 'Save the Woods'.

THE LONDON WILDLIFE TRUST

c/o Peckham Settlement, Staffordshire Street, SE15

SAVE THE WOOD!

Southwark Council want to build on part of Sydenham Hill Wood

DON'T LET THEM!

A London Wildlife Trust campaign leaflet from the 1980s.

In 1984, having failed to find a buyer for Fernbank, South-wark Council revived its plan to build housing there, and on the site of Lapsewood House. Under its Mid-South Southwark Local Plan (MSSLP), the council proposed to develop up to two hundred dwellings on twelve acres (five hectares) of woodland. The Trust's 'Save the Woods' campaign was spear-headed by Bob Smyth, now chairman of the LWT, and two local residents, Lucy Neville and Amrit Row. It soon attracted the support of politicians from all three main parties. John Maples, Conservative MP for West Lewisham, was a promi-nent backer. Gerald Bowden, Conservative MP for Dulwich, pointed out the unsuitability of the site and asked Patrick Jenkin, then Secretary of State for the Environment, to inter-vene in the matter.[5] Kate Hoey, the Labour candidate who contested the seat in 1983 and 1987, was also a vociferous sup-porter. 'I resent the implication that you have to be an owner-occupier to appreciate natural beauty,' she declared, echoing the sentiments of Octavia Hill a century earlier.[6] Simon Hughes, the Liberal MP for Southwark and Bermond-sey, told the House of Commons that 'Sydenham Hill Wood, one of the remaining very old woodlands in the south of Eng-land, is under threat. There is a very strong lobby against its destruction by the London Wildlife Trust. But it is primarily the local people who are fighting by means of a public inquiry to protect that wood.'[7]

A public inquiry in January 1985 heard evidence from a dozen ecologists on the wood's wildlife diversity, while other witnesses described its educational and amenity value.[8] After visiting the site and listening to the views of several hundred local residents at a public meeting at Kingswood House, the inspector found that 'All parties accept that notwithstanding the one-time pres-ence of the railway in the valley and the houses fronting Sydenham Hill Wood, the Wood is now a valuable ecological, educational and local amenity.'[9]

While he believed that the 1.4-acre Lapsewood site was not of sufficient wildlife value to be retained as part of the woodland, the inspector concluded that 'The development of the two Fernbank sites however would be very different. Today, they form a prime part of the remaining woodland . . . I am in no doubt any development of the two Fernbank sites must seriously damage the existing quality of Sydenham Hill Wood'. He went on to recommend that no housing should be built on the site during the ten-year life of the MSSLP.[10]

In June 1985, recognising that it was unlikely ever to receive planning permission for the Fernbank site, Southwark Council agreed to lease it to the London Wildlife Trust for a peppercorn rent, and the area was incorporated into the reserve. The nature trail that still winds through the reserve today was marked out by numbered posts running from the Crescent Wood Road entrance via the cedar of Lebanon and the folly to the old foot-bridge over the railway trackbed. In July 1985 a delegation from the Dulwich Society was conducted on a tree walk through the woods by two members of the LWT. 'Everyone's feelings,' they reported, 'seemed to be of delight and astonishment at the intense greenness and seclusion there. It would be tragic if this was destroyed, and we must continue to hope that no development will take place in any part of the Wood.'[11] That September, the whole Dulwich Wood area, including the reserve, was designated a Conservation Area in the Southwark Local Plan, for both its architectural and landscape value.

The Trust had meanwhile persuaded the Greater London Council to fund an ecological survey of the whole metropolis, with eight people working for two years to identify and cata-logue green spaces of more than 0.5 hectares (1.2 acres) that were worth preserving for their value as wildlife habitats. The GLC was living on borrowed time, however. After years of animosity between the Labour-led London authority and Margaret Thatcher's Conservative administration, the Local

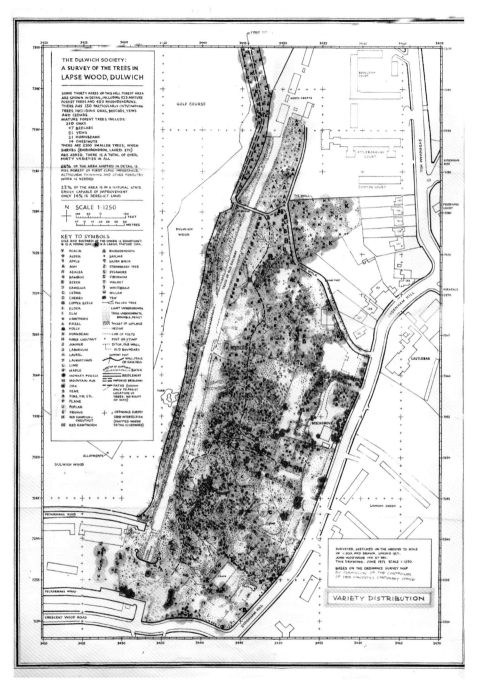

John Westwood's 1971 survey of the trees in Sydenham Hill Wood. Courtesy of the Dulwich Society.

Oak and hornbeam, the two main trees of the North Wood, have fused together at the root in Sydenham Hill Wood.

The circular pond in Dulwich Wood.

The former railway trackbed runs past the open glade in Sydenham Hill Wood (photo: Daniel Greenwood).

Cox's Walk footbridge at Sydenham Hill Wood today.

A kestrel (*Falco tinnunculus*) coasts on a thermal as it scans the ground for prey.

A tawny owl (*Strix aluco*) roosts amid oak and ivy in Sydenham Hill Wood.

The Eurasian nuthatch (*Sitta europaea*) is a common sight in the woods, running up and down tree trunks in pursuit of insects (photo: Daniel Greenwood).

The green woodpecker (*Picus viridis*) is the largest of the three woodpeckers native to the British Isles, and its eerie 'yaffle' is part of the soundscape of the woods (photo: Daniel Greenwood).

The purple hairstreak (*Favonius quercus*) is one of the 'flagship species' of the woods, though it is rarely seen on account of its preferred habitat high in the oak canopy (photo: Daniel Greenwood).

The speckled wood (*Pararge aegeria*) is one of the commonest butterfly species found in the Great North Wood today (photo: Daniel Greenwood).

Southern hawkers (*Aeshna cyanea*) are among the dragonflies that hunt over the ponds in Sydenham Hill Wood (photo: Daniel Greenwood).

The European stag beetle (*Lucanus cervus*) spends up to seven years as a larva living in rotting wood before the adult emerges for one brief summer to seek a mate (photo: Daniel Greenwood).

Blackthorn (*Prunus spinosa*) is one of the first wild shrubs to flower in spring.

Flowering in March and April, the wood anemone (*Anemone nemorosa*) is a characteristic plant of ancient woodland (photo: Brian Whittle).

The seed-bearing samaras of the hornbeam (*Carpinus betulus*), photographed in Sydenham Hill Wood in June.

The grassy glades in Long Lane Wood are carpeted with native English bluebells in spring.

Fungi in Sydenham Hill Wood.

Angel's bonnet (*Mycena arcangeliana*) is often found on fallen trunks or branches in broadleaved woodland.

The caps of these newly emerged shaggy parasols (*Chlorophyllum rhacodes*) will open to form umbrella-like mushrooms.

The glistening inkcap (*Coprinellus micaceus*) is often found growing in clumps on or around decaying wood.

Trooping funnel (*Clitocybe geotropa*) is so-called because it can often be found growing in lines or fairy rings.

This veteran oak in Spa Wood is estimated to be between 300 and 600 years old.

The oaks of Grangewood Park in South Norwood, a survival of the ancient Whitehorse Wood.

The Oak of Honor, One Tree Hill.

Sydenham Hill Wood in winter (photo: Daniel Greenwood).

Biggin Wood, in Upper Norwood, is a surviving parcel of the Archbishop of Canterbury's woods.

Laid out in the early eighteenth century, Cox's Walk is still lined with oaks today.

The view over the City of London from One Tree Hill.

The River Pool in Lower Sydenham.

Rays of sunlight penetrate the canopy at Sydenham Hill Wood.

Government Act of 1985 abolished the GLC and divided its functions between the London borough councils and central government. For the next fourteen years, there would be no elected body directing policy throughout the metropolitan area, so the various parcels of the North Wood now came under the remit of the Department of the Environment and the borough councils of Southwark, Lambeth, Lewisham and Croydon. The work of the Trust's habitat survey, fortunately, lived on in the form of the London Ecology Unit, set up in 1986 to provide ecological advice to all thirty-two London boroughs, conduct Environmental Impact Assessments, assist in developing nature reserves and ecology parks, designate of Sites of Importance for Nature Conservation (SINCs), and identify Areas of Deficiency (AoDs) that were one kilometre or more from an accessible SINC. These policies remain in effect today, and the Unit's legacy also includes thirty Ecology Handbooks, among them *Nature Conservation in Croydon* (1988), *Southwark* (1989), *Lambeth* (1994) and *Lewisham* (1985, 1999).

In the mid-1980s, funding from the Manpower Services Commission's Community Programme enabled the LWT to expand its staff to more than sixty at one point, including, from 1986, a full-time warden for Sydenham Hill Wood, Bob Young, based at Kingswood House. The LWT embarked on an ambitious scheme of woodland management, positioning a shipping container near the entrance to the tunnel to provide a base for an MSC team and storage for tools and tea things. Maintenance work was undertaken by community service teams, school parties and LWT volunteers on Sunday work sessions. A drained gravel path was laid along half a mile of the muddy nature trail, areas compacted by trampling were fenced off to allow the understorey to regenerate, and trees were planted. A pair of sparrowhawks, a species absent from the woods for a decade, was spotted.

After the Manpower Services Commission was wound up in 1987, the post of warden was reduced to a part-time one, but in 1989, new funding from Southwark Council and other sources allowed it to become full-time again, based at the Horniman Museum.

STRANGE WEATHER

The Industrial Revolution was only a few decades old when a handful of prescient observers began to notice its effects on the Earth's climate. 'Through the destruction of forests,' warned the German naturalist Alexander von Humboldt in 1844, 'through the distribution of water, and through the production of great masses of steam and gas at the industrial centres', human activity was having far-reaching effects.[12] Forty years later, John Ruskin, who had lamented the despoliation of the woods by the relocation of the Crystal Palace, noted in a lecture to the London Institution a 'plague-wind of the eighth decade of years in the nineteenth century; a period which will assuredly be recognized in future meteorological history as one of phenomena hitherto unrecorded in the courses of nature . . . It looks partly as if it were made of poisonous smoke; very possibly it may be: there are at least two hundred furnace chimneys in a square of two miles on every side of me.'[13]

It was not until the 1970s, however, that scientists became increasingly aware that changes to the world's weather patterns were generated by human activity. Humboldt and Ruskin's warnings came to seem startlingly prophetic, and the term 'climate change' entered the vocabulary.[14] In Britain, the summer of 1976 was one of the hottest on record, with temperatures reaching 30° C for eighteen days running, following a lengthy period of drought. That August, fire broke out at Beaulieu Heights, destroying an acre (0.4 hectares) of oak woodland. Local volunteers cleared and replanted the burnt-out area, which was soon recolonised by woodland flora and fauna.[15]

Climate change manifested itself not only in higher temperatures, but also in extreme weather events. During the night of
15–16 October 1987, a powerful extratropical cyclone – the
worst since 1703 – smashed into the UK, killing eighteen people
and blowing down some fifteen million trees. The south east of
England was the most severely affected, with gales of up to one
hundred miles per hour. In the Borough of Croydon alone,
some 75,000 trees were uprooted. The older standard oaks in
Biggin Wood were severely affected, with 'branches flung
about like so much wood, and landing on all the younger trees
around, causing much damage.'[16] In Dulwich Wood, the
damage was also extensive, with many trees down and others
left in a dangerous condition. Tree surgeons were brought in by
the Estate, and by the following April most of the fallen timber
had been cleared.[17]

In Sydenham Hill Wood, more than fifty mature trees were
blown down, including many oaks and hornbeams; a massive
poplar lay in the pond, while numerous heavy branches were left
hanging precariously from trees. LWT staff and volunteers
managed to clear the paths within a week of the storm, but tree
work continued throughout the winter. Removing some of the
larger trunks proved problematic, as the steep slopes made the
use of motorised vehicles difficult, and it was likely to damage
plants and the soil structure. In February 1988, the National
Working Horses Trust in Etchingham, Sussex, supplied two
heavy Ardennes mares, Logique and Mateus, to haul out the
remaining trunks. 'The use of these traditional working horses,'
said Gary Grant, the Trust's Southwark field officer, 'probably
not seen in London since World War II, other than for dray or
carthorse work, is entirely compatible with the wildlife interests
of the woods.'[18]

The event received extensive coverage in the press, including
The Times, the *Independent* and the *Guardian*, and the timber,
mostly oak, was sold to raise funds for the London Wildlife

Trust. The impact of the storm was not entirely negative. As Bob Andrews, the reserve warden, reported, it also created 'the opportunity to open up glades, widen ridges and diversify the age structure of the trees, while increasing the amount of deadwood, so important for fungi, insects and birds'.

Another positive outcome of the storm was the LWT's decision to set up a nursery to replace some of the lost trees. In December 1988, with support from Southwark Council, the World Wildlife Fund and Lloyds Bank, the Trust took over a disused council depot on Marsden Road, Peckham. Under the stewardship of Dawn Eckhart and Jill Goddard, the project developed into the London Wildlife Garden Centre (now the Centre for Wildlife Gardening), which opened in June 1989 as an educational and communal resource for local people, with raised beds, a pond and, since 1991, a handsome, eco-friendly visitor centre.

Extreme weather events struck the United Kingdom with increasing frequency in the decades that followed: Cyclone Daria, also known as the Burns' Day storm, hit Northwest Europe on the night of 25 January 1990, bringing down some three million trees and causing widespread damage; a further storm later that year caused trees to collapse into the Cox's Walk footbridge; and there were heatwaves in July 2000 and August 2003, when the UK's highest temperature, 38.5° C, was recorded in Kent, and two thousand more deaths than average were reported. Between December 2013 and February 2014, six major storms occurred, leading to severe flooding in many parts of England.

The increasing frequency of such events has only served to underline the importance of woodlands, especially in urban areas: trees act as windbreaks, they have a cooling effect in hot weather, they help to cleanse air pollution, and they alleviate flooding by absorbing water run-off.

THE BATTLE OF BEECHGROVE

Beechgrove had finally been demolished in 1983, and the fate of the site hung in the balance. In 1986, the Estate governors applied for planning permission to build thirty-six flats with parking spaces, an access road and pavements in two blocks on the two-acre (0.8-hectare) plot of land. Southwark Council, the London Wildlife Trust, the Dulwich Society, the Sydenham Society, the Peckarmans Wood Residents' Association, and the Dulwich Residents' Association were united in opposition to the scheme. 'Sometimes,' said Lucy Neville, 'it seems as if most valuable wildlife habitat is regarded as a blank space on a map that needs to be filled in.'

A public inquiry at Southwark Town Hall from 25 to 27 November 1986 became a tense battle, with both sides repre-sented by effective lawyers. Opponents of the plan argued that Lapsewood, Beechgrove and Fernbank should be amalgamated with Sydenham Hill Wood to form a nature reserve managed by an ecological organisation such as the London Wildlife Trust. In its advocate's closing speech, Southwark Council stated that it considered a small development of houses with gardens to be appropriate. In February 1987, however, the inquiry's inspector found that 'the proposed development would create significant detriment to the character and appearance of this locality and cause an erosion of the setting of Sydenham Hill and Dulwich Woods in terms of visual detriment as well as detriment to ecological and nature conservation values,' and rejected the Estate's plans.

Undeterred, the Dulwich Estate submitted yet another proposal to develop the Beechgrove site in March 1988. The LWT, the Dulwich Society, local amenity groups and residents turned out in strength at a meeting of Southwark Council's plan-ning sub-committee on Wednesday 21 September to oppose the plans, and the committee rejected the application. John Archer, the Trust's Southwark field officer, said: 'Southwark Council is to be congratulated on standing firm over Beechgrove. We are particularly pleased that the sub-committee also made a firm commitment to seeking designation of the whole of the Sydenham Hill Wood complex as a statutory local nature reserve. Any development on Beechgrove would cause irreparable damage to the rest of the wood.'

The Estate governors pressed on regardless. 'Each successive defeat merely appears to whet their appetite to do further damage,' an editorial in the *Dulwich Society Newsletter* noted in a fierce denunciation of the governors' 'bone-headed intransigence'. Sydenham Hill Wood, it continued,

> is a marvellous, prized, precious place which should be left as it is. Dulwich needs it – all of it – because it is like nowhere else for miles around; and because without it, and places like it, cities would scarcely be worth living in. It is, of course, much more than a wood. It is a park, a playground, a classroom, a wilderness. It is a reserve and a refuge – for both people and wildlife. It is somewhere to go sledging, berrying, exploring, walking the dog. It is somewhere to remind oneself, and teach one's children, what autumn and winter and spring are like. It is a unique asset, an invaluable resource. Yet it is treated by the governors like real estate.[19]

The following year, the Estate appealed to the Department of the Environment against the planning committee's ruling, and a public inquiry was set for 5 September.[20] For the third time in as many years, the proposal was rejected. The DoE inspector, M. J. Croft, ruled that 'the broad generality of the objectors' concerns' was well founded and carried 'considerable weight'. He noted that Sydenham Hill Wood was the nearest ancient wood to central London, that the shade cast on to the proposed houses by the surrounding trees would create pressure for more to be felled, and that the 'once a housing site, always a housing site' argument did not apply as the environment now had a higher priority than when Beechgrove was last occupied.[21]

Meanwhile, in Dulwich Woods, which the Estate managed directly, improvements were taking place. In 1985, the governors obtained the help of the Flora and Fauna Preservation Society in restoring the round pond and clearing it of silt. The following year, the scheme whereby residents could rent keys to the wood was discontinued because it did not defray the cost of maintaining the fences, and Dulwich Wood was finally opened to the general public. A woodsman was employed three days a week, metal railings replaced a rickety wooden fence along Low Cross Wood Lane in 1988, paths were improved, and kissing gates were installed at the Grange Lane and Cox's Walk entrances to stop people riding motorbikes into the woods. Perhaps most significantly, the unsightly chain-link fencing that separated Dulwich and Sydenham Hill Woods was replaced in 1991 by a less obtrusive row of wooden posts, reuniting what were, historically and environmentally if not in terms of legal ownership, two adjoining parts of the same woodland.[22]

In Sydenham Hill Wood, the steep steps leading down from Crescent Wood Road were replaced by a gentle incline, and the path was re-routed over the top of the tunnel mouth in 1993. The Trust also printed maps for visitors, and leaflets about the birds and mammals to be found in the reserve. By 1992, Mathew Frith, the warden at Sydenham Hill Wood, was able to report that

Spring saw carpets of coltsfoot, wood anemone, lesser celandine, bluebell, ramsons, dog violet, bugle and stitchwort. A botanical survey in May recorded almost 180 species, including some which had never been previously recorded; barren strawberry, tutsan and slender St John's wort (all ancient woodland indicators). Birds thronged into the trees, and fluttered in the low shrubbery. The first recording of a little owl in the Wood was noted on a Dawn Chorus walk in April, and a little later a visit of recipients of the Lambeth Talking Newspaper (for the visually handicapped) were given a guided walk, with bird-song pinpointing the different habitats – chiffchaff, blackcap, long-tailed tit, tree creeper, great spotted woodpecker, dunnock, nuthatch and wren were just some that painted the picture. Other birds noted through the year included kestrel, sparrowhawk, hawfinch, bullfinch, goldcrest and lesser spotted woodpecker.[23]

The biological importance of Sydenham Hill Wood was receiving growing recognition. In 1986 the Nature Conservancy Council (now English Nature) included the reserve in its Inventory of London's Ancient Woodlands; it was designated a Site of Metropolitan Importance for Nature Conservation by the London Ecology Unit in 1989, declared a statutory Local Nature Reserve by Southwark Council in 1990, and given the UK-MAB Urban Wildlife Award for Excellence in 1997.

The publicity around the planning battles also fostered interest in the North Wood as a whole, and the preservation and integrated management of its surviving fragments. In the summer of 1987, the London Wildlife Trust's Southwark Group had published a thirty-two-page history of the Great North Wood by Lucy Neville, with photographs by Amrit Row and a well-researched map showing the extent of the wood in 1600. The Friends of the Great North Wood was founded in 1992 at the instigation of Mathew Frith, and with LWT support, 'to revive the Great North Wood in the minds of local people and the wider public', 'to ensure more consistent management of the woods for the benefit of wildlife', and to create a 'Living Landscape' that would enable it 'to utilise the whole array of woodlands and interconnecting green spaces'. Publicly launched in March 1993 by Tessa Jowell and Jim Dowd, MPs for Dulwich

and Lewisham West, and Sinna Mani, Deputy Mayor of Lewisham, the group soon attracted some one hundred members. A
newsletter, *The Wood Warbler*, was published and ran for
twenty-six issues, illustrated talks and walks were held, and
exhibitions were displayed at various events. In August that
year, the LWT joined forces with the Friends of the Great North
Wood and Southwark Council to hold a Southwark Woodland
Festival in Sydenham Hill Wood, at which a Young's brewery
waggon was hauled up Cox's Walk by a dray horse; the event
attracted around a thousand people. Two leaflets, 'The Great
North Wood' and 'From the Nun's Head to the Screaming Alice'
(rhyming slang for the Crystal Palace) were printed, and an
exhibition entitled 'The Great North Wood: The Story of a
South London Landscape' opened at the Horniman Museum in
December 1995, using photographs, dioramas and maps to
demonstrate the former extent of the woods and the effect of the
city's expansion upon their wildlife.

The fauna of the woods came under increasingly systematic
observation at this period. In 1994 the Trust surveyed most of
the Great North Wood sites for the purple hairstreak (*Quer-
cusia quercus*), first recorded in the area by Moses Harris back
in the eighteenth century. This elusive butterfly, which lives
high in the oak canopy, was found at Long Lane Wood, Biggin
Wood, Dulwich Wood and on the Dulwich College playing fields.

In 1997 the Trust launched a survey of another of the woods'
'flagship' species, the magnificent greater stag beetle (*Lucanus
cervus*), in partnership with Bromley Council. Britain's largest
terrestrial insect spends five years as a finger-sized maggot
burrowing through dead wood before it pupates, to emerge as an
adult in May or June. The male flies off in search of a mate, who
then lays her eggs. By the onset of autumn – if the beetle hasn't
already become a handy, protein-rich snack for magpies or
foxes – it dies. Listed as 'near threatened' by the International
Union for the Conservation of Nature, stag beetles are a victim

of our practice of tidying away rotting wood, the use of grinders to remove tree stumps, and pesticides. Counter-intuitively, they seem to fare better in London suburbs, especially south of the river, than in the countryside, perhaps because of the absence of agricultural chemicals and the number of compost heaps, rotting fences and decaying sheds.

Unlike earlier surveys, which were largely carried out by entomologists, this one was designed to involve the general public, in order to promote awareness of stag beetles and their habitat as well as generating new records. London Wildlife Trust members in Bromley and Southwark, and – through local papers – the wider public, were asked to record any stag beetles they had seen. Of the 600 forms sent out, more than 200 were returned, recording more than 400 sightings. These were combined with findings from separate surveys in Bromley, Wandsworth and Croydon, and mapped on the Trust's GIS/MapInfo system. The results revealed a swath of sightings across South London, with particular concentrations in Beckenham and the Dulwich-Camberwell area. Since then, annual surveys have confirmed this pattern, while the interest generated by the Trust and other wildlife groups has led to the creation of stag beetle loggeries in gardens, parks and green spaces.[24]

The growing awareness that South London's scattered oak woodlands were in fact parts of an ancient whole, with distinctive resident species, encouraged the formation of local pressure groups to preserve them. In 1994, Honor Oak residents set up the Friends of One Tree Hill (FrOTH), and in 1997 Action for Biggin Wood was formed which, with the British Trust for Conservation Volunteers (now The Conservation Volunteers), undertook work to manage the wood, restore paths and repair steps.

In 1998, Southwark Council, which had owned Cox's Walk since 1965, placed it under London Wildlife Trust management.

The oak-lined walk, a rare surviving example of an eighteenth-century formal avenue, is officially a public square. Though surfaced with gravel and lined with street lamps, it was designated a Site of Local Importance for Nature Conservation, and the Trust embarked on a programme to enhance its wildlife value by allowing patches of woodland pasture and native shrubs to grow, laying a hedge along the border with a neighbouring allotment, and scalloping the verges to promote biodiversity. At last, a holistic approach to the preservation and management of the disparate parts of the old North Wood seemed possible.

10

A NEW MILLENNIUM

1997–2021

Following its landslide election victory in 1997, Tony Blair's Labour government merged the Department of the Environment with the Department of Transport to form the Department of the Environment, Transport and the Regions. After criticism of its handling of the 2001 foot and mouth epidemic, the department's environmental responsibilities were detached and merged with the Ministry of Agriculture, Fisheries and Food to form a new Department for Environment, Food and Rural Affairs (Defra). On 7 May 1998, the new government held a referendum in Greater London to gauge support for its plan to reinstate a centralised administration for the whole metropolitan area, led by an elected mayor. Just over 72 per cent voted in favour, and the following year the Greater London Authority Act was passed. This set up the Greater London Authority, with responsibility for public transport, policing, emergency services and, working with local councils, the environment. A statutory duty was imposed on the Mayor to publish a Biodiversity Strategy, which appeared in 2002.

The London Ecology Unit, set up to advise borough councils on ecological planning and designation, was absorbed into the new GLA's environment team in 2000. The London Wildlife Trust's London Biological Recording Project, which had been gathering data on the capital's wild flora and fauna since 1996, became a semi-autonomous body called Greenspace Information for Greater London (GiGL) in 2003, and since 2013 has been registered as a Community Interest Company.

One Tree Hill was declared a Local Nature Reserve in 2007. In September 2010, the Green Chain Walk through South East London was extended from Nunhead Cemetery to Crystal Palace, following the route set out in the Friends of the Great North Wood's 'Screaming Alice' leaflet through One Tree Hill, Camberwell New Cemetery, Horniman Gardens Nature Trail and Sydenham Hill Wood, with a spur leading along Cox's Walk to Dulwich Park. That year, the Friends of Grangewood Park was established to carry out practical work directed towards conservation and biodiversity, and to promote social inclusion, good health and wellbeing in the local community.

There is a story, possibly apocryphal, that the biologist J. B. S. Haldane once remarked that if there were such a being as a Creator, he must be 'inordinately fond of beetles' for having made so many. In 1997 and 2000, the London Wildlife Trust commissioned the entomologist Richard Jones to undertake surveys of the invertebrates in Sydenham Hill Wood. The first of these, which also drew on records held by the Horniman Museum and the LWT, noted 687 species of invertebrate, including ninety-eight types of beetle. There were eighteen species of butterfly (mostly recorded by the reserve officers Mathew Frith and John White), including purple hairstreak, silver-washed fritillary (*Argynnis paphia*), which breeds on wood violets, red admiral (*Vanessa atalanta*), comma (*Polygonia c-album*), speckled wood (*Pararge aegeria*), holly and common blue, and five species of whites. In addition, thirty-one species of moth were identified. Despite Jones's qualification that 'woodlands are not ideal habitats for dragonflies', four species were recorded: southern hawker (*Aeshna cyanea*), common darter (*Sympetrum striolatum*), broad-bodied chaser (*Libellula depressa*) and four-spotted chaser (*L. quadrimaculata*). Among the arachnids were forty-seven species of spider and two common harvestmen, though few were woodland specialists.

The second survey focused exclusively on beetles classified as 'saproxylic', those that live in dead wood. Because they require an uninterrupted supply of rotting timber to feed and breed, their presence is regarded as evidence that an area has been continuously wooded for a considerable time. Throughout Sydenham Hill and Dulwich Woods, Jones recorded a total of 164 species of beetle, of which seventeen were ancient woodland specialists. In addition to the greater stag beetle (*Lucanus cervus*), he found several other less spectacular but equally important saproxylic insects, including the lesser stag beetle (*Dorcus parallelipipedus*), various rove beetles, bark beetles, woodworm beetles, ground beetles, click beetles, weevils, minute beetles that breed in fungus, and three species of long-horn beetle associated with dead wood. This 'very respectable' count placed the woods high in the national league table of ecological continuity,[1] and together, his surveys confirmed the biological diversity and ecological importance of this area of woodland so near to the centre of London.

Further evidence of the antiquity of parts of Sydenham Hill Wood was provided when, in 2002, Jon Riley undertook a vascular plant survey for the London Wildlife Trust, finding no less than thirty-three Ancient Woodland Indicators. This was followed up in 2005, when Sarah Graham-Brown of the Friends of Queen's Wood in Highgate undertook a comparative survey of AWIs in that surviving enclave of the old Forest of Middlesex, and those of Sydenham Hill Wood. Among the plants she considered were the sessile oak and hornbeam of the wood itself; shrubs such as wild holly (*Ilex aquifolium*), Midland hawthorn (*Crataegus laevigata*) and butcher's-broom (*Ruscus aculeatus*); and, in the herb layer, ramsons (*Allium ursinum*), wood anemone (*Anemone nemorosa*), wild bluebell (*Hyacinthoides non-scripta*), lily-of-the-valley (*Convallaria majulis*), wood sorrel (*Oxalis acetosella*), Solomon's seal (*Polygonatum multiflorum*) and hairy wood-rush (*Luzula pilosa*).

The majority of the latter were spring-flowering plants that appeared before the tree canopy closed over. In Sydenham Hill Wood as a whole, 60 per cent of the areas surveyed contained AWIs; for the ancient woodland, the figure was 73 per cent, while in secondary woodland the figure was 48 per cent. Noting the ability of some AWIs to colonise secondary woodland within a few decades, Graham-Brown focused on those species that were slowest to spread and could therefore be considered 'strong' AWIs. These included ramsons, wood anemone and bluebell, which were predominantly found deep within the areas of ancient woodland.

Despite the presence of invasive species such as cherry laurel, spotted laurel and Highclere holly (a bird-sown cultivar that can hybridise with wild holly), Graham-Brown was able to look back over the botanical records from Curtis in 1785 to Lousley in 1958–59 and conclude that 'Historical research . . . showed considerable continuity in the species found over several hundred years, with only a few losses.'[2] Given the changes the wood had undergone and the pressures it had faced over the previous two centuries, this was remarkable testimony to the resilience of this ecosystem.

A significant if often overlooked part of the woodland ecology are lichens, the coral-like micro-organisms that encrust wood and stone, especially in moist conditions. A lichen is a symbiotic combination of a fungus and an alga or cyanobacterium (a bacterium that can photosynthesise); the species that form lichens have evolved together, and rarely exist independently. The alga or cyanobacterium produces carbohydrates by photosynthesis and supplies them to the fungus, which cannot do this; in return, the fungus provides shelter by anchoring to a tree or rock, forms a resilient structure, and absorbs water vapour from the air to keep its partner moist. Lichens are a vital component of the biosphere, adding organic material to the soil, increasing the nutrients available to plants, and providing shelter, concealment and food for many insects, as well as nest-building material for birds.

Because they contain two or more life-forms from different kingdoms, lichens are notoriously hard to classify: their taxonomy is based on the species of fungus present, but since the same fungus may team up with different algae, quite distinct lichens end up classified as the same species. There are, broadly, three forms of lichen: crustose or crusty, which form a thin coating on a rock or branch; foliose, or leafy; and fruticose, bush-like lichens that grow out from the surface to which they adhere. Under a magnifying glass, they are often extraordinarily beautiful, displaying a kaleidoscopic array of colour and form. Some lichens are more sensitive than others to air pollution – especially sulphur dioxide – so the presence or absence of certain species is a useful indicator of air quality.

In August 2005 Feliciano Cirimele, an Environmental Protection Officer (EPA), and Breda Gallagher carried out a lichen survey in Sydenham Hill Wood. They recorded a total of thirty-two species. Around the outer fringes of the reserve, near roads, the allotments and the golf course, they found, unsurprisingly, a narrow range of hardy, nitrate- and sulphur-dioxide-tolerant lichens; the sheltered inner parts of the wood had a more diverse lichen population, including sensitive, locally scarce species that favour acidic woodland, on oak and hornbeam branches – a transition that could clearly be seen along Cox's Walk.[3] The survival of these vulnerable organisms within the reserve provided further evidence, if any were needed, of the importance of woodland in maintaining air quality in a polluted city.

THE WOODS AND THE WATER

Watercourses flow oblivious to property ownership, and the circular pond, which lies on the Dulwich Wood side of the green posts, is fed by the Ambrook, which runs through Sydenham Hill Wood. In wet weather, the overflow from the pond is channelled through drainage ditches on the golf course to feed the ornamental lake in Dulwich Park. As the planning battles of the 1980s and 1990s receded into the past, relations between the LWT and the Dulwich Estate improved, and in 2011 the Estate governors invited the Trust to manage the pond in Dulwich Wood, which was once more in need of restoration.

By this time, both the Ambrook and the pond had become choked with fallen branches and silt, and the pond, completely overhung by trees, was anaerobic and devoid of life. Aided by funding from the recycling company SITA, LWT volunteers cleared the stream and pond of deadwood before contractors brought in a small mechanical digger to dredge and deepen them. A shallow scrape was dug to allow water to filter from the brook to the pond; volunteers built a railway sleeper bridge over the stream; and the whole area was fenced off with chestnut palings to allow the vegetation to recover, helped along by volunteers planting marginal species such as flag iris, marsh-marigold, brooklime, meadowsweet, ragged-robin and hemp-agrimony to offer invertebrates a greater range of nectar sources and habitat alongside this ancient stream. The project was completed with the construction of a pond-dipping platform on the bank of the pond.

'At our feet they lie low,' wrote the poet U. A. Fanthorpe in 'Rising Damp': 'The little fervent underground/ Rivers of London/ Effra, Graveney, Falcon, Quaggy/ Wandle, Walbrook, Tyburn, Fleet . . .' The Effra, of which the Ambrook is a tributary, had long since disappeared underground, but it could still make its presence felt. Along its course, its waters took up much

of the capacity of the storm drains, leaving them unable to cope
with additional demand; the road junction at Herne Hill was
badly flooded after heavy rainfall in 2004 and 2006, and again
after a water main burst in 2013. As Thames Water and Southwark Council undertook a £4.28 million flood alleviation
project, building earth bunds in Belair and Dulwich Parks and
underground geocellular block storage in the Dulwich sports
grounds to contain up to 51,000 square metres of water during
storms, the LWT launched its Lost Effra Project to develop a
sustainable water management strategy at the community level.

The scheme was seed-funded by Defra, with additional
funding from the Carnegie Trust, and supported by Thames
Water, the Greater London Authority and the London Boroughs
of Lambeth and Southwark. In January 2014 the project co-
ordinator Lucy Townsend began holding workshops with local
people to create a range of small-scale landscape features known
as Sustainable Urban Drainage Systems (SuDS) within the
catchment of the River Effra. These reduce local flood risk by
holding rainwater where it falls, create green spaces, and spread
understanding of the relationship between water and the built
environment.

Working with more than a thousand volunteers, Lucy and her
successors Helen Spring and Rachel Dowse created six green
roofs on houses, sheds and public buildings to absorb rainwater
and allow it to evaporate back into the atmosphere, while also
providing habitats for bees and other insects; replaced seven
areas of hard paving in local streets and estates with free-
draining gardens; created three rain gardens irrigated from
downpipes and one to capture run-off from roads; installed rain
butts to provide water for use in gardens during dry periods; and
replaced tarmac and concrete with permeable paving to allow
water to soak into the ground.

THE GREAT NORTH WOOD PROJECT

In October 2014, the Dulwich Estate, finally accepting that it was unlikely ever to receive planning permission to build on the Beechgrove plot, offered the LWT a twenty-five-year lease on the site, which was to be managed as a nature reserve on the understanding that no building would take place. In April 2016, after negotiations with the Trust's solicitors, the lease was approved, filling in the final piece of the reserve's jigsaw. In 2017, after positive feedback from residents about the LWT's management of Sydenham Hill Wood, a four-year partnership between the Trust and the Dulwich Estate was agreed to facilitate conservation work in Dulwich Wood, Low Cross Wood (long closed to the public), and Hitherwood.

The Friends of the Great North Wood having long since dissolved, there was a pressing need to consider how to manage the scattered remnants of the woods as a whole. While both Sydenham Hill Wood and Dulwich Upper Wood had full-time project managers and dedicated teams of volunteers supported by grants from Southwark Council, less well known parts of the North Wood such as Hillcrest Wood and Long Lane Wood were suffering from serious neglect and fly-tipping. Large areas had become overgrown by non-native invasive species such as cherry laurel and speckled laurel as well as native evergreens, particularly holly; the dense shade they cast deprived other plants of light to the extent that ground flora was entirely absent in places. It also discouraged oaks, which are very light-demanding as seedlings, from regenerating. This problem was compounded by the number of visitors to many sites, where the volume of foot traffic resulted in soil compaction, leaving barren areas where plants could not establish themselves.

In February 2016 the London Wildlife Trust launched its Great North Wood Living Landscape Project to conserve, revive and enhance the remaining fragments of this historic woodland

and promote a holistic approach to their management. With Heritage Lottery funding of just under £100,000, and an additional £9,400 from the Mayor of London's Tree and Woodland Community Grant Scheme, the initial nine-month pilot was launched in Brockwell Park, Herne Hill, on 19 February 2016, where members of the public were encouraged to plant native trees such as oak, hornbeam and hazel.

Over the following months, the project's development officer, Sam Bentley-Toon, worked with the Trust's ecologist Tony Wileman to survey some twenty-four woodland sites to assess their condition and note the species they sheltered in order to inform decisions on what work was required. Representatives of local interest groups were invited to meetings to hear an outline of the scheme, and responded with enthusiasm, keen to explore ways in which they could participate.

In June 2017, the Trust announced that it had succeeded in its bid for a grant from the Heritage Lottery Fund, and would receive almost £700,000, as part of the Living Landscapes initiative, to finance the Great North Wood project. Further support came from the Mayor of London, Veolia Environmental Trust, the Dulwich Estate and the Dulwich Society. This ambitious project – launched on 16 October, the 30th anniversary of the 1987 storm – would run for four years to raise awareness of the woodland and work with volunteers, community groups, landowners and five London borough councils (Bromley, Croydon, Lambeth, Lewisham and Southwark) to manage all its surviving parts in a way that fostered their environmental health and biodiversity, and improved public access.

The project identified five 'flagship species' – oak, hornbeam, great spotted woodpecker, purple hairstreak and stag beetle – to be monitored through regular transects. A pool of a hundred volunteers, including local schoolchildren, was assembled, and four thousand volunteer hours were logged in the first year. The team constructed or repaired paths and steps in Dulwich Wood,

London Wildlife Trust leaflet promoting the
Festival of the Great North Wood, 2018.

Biggin Wood and elsewhere, cleared litter, and removed invasive species such as cherry laurel. The project even recreated a lost portion of the North Wood when, in December 2018, volunteers planted more than a thousand trees in Norwood Park, along with a forty-metre hedge of hazel, hawthorn, blackthorn, spindle, dog rose and guelder-rose – all native hedgerow plants.

Guided walks, education sessions and talks helped to spread the word about the Great North Wood and its wildlife, and inspired people to develop a closer connection to the landscape. Electronic gate counters were installed on four of the entrances to Sydenham Hill and Dulwich Woods, allowing the Trust to monitor visitor numbers. In September 2018 the London Wildlife Trust held a one-day Festival of the Great North Wood in Sydenham Hill Wood to encourage people to explore the natural places on their doorstep. LWT staff guided visitors on bird, fungi and tree identification walks; the entomologist Richard Jones held an insect identification workshop for children; the local artist and writer Tim Bird discussed his graphic novel *The Great North Wood*, an innovative retelling of the story of the area; one of the regular volunteers gave a demonstration of wood-turning using a traditional pole lathe; and there was live folk and acoustic music and stalls selling street food.

The following year, in September 2019, the festival was held at Spa Wood. In addition to most of the previous year's attractions, it featured archery, axe throwing, storytelling, juggling, a camera obscura, and animals from the Mudchute Park and Farm on the Isle of Dogs. In 2020, as a result of the Covid-19 pandemic, the festival took place online over a week in December, and included talks and film screenings, craft workshops, yoga, a virtual woodland walk, and nature writing, spoken word and baking workshops.

By the time the project came to an end in June 2021, it had mitigated decades of neglect, brought all the surviving fragments of the North Wood back into active management and taught

thousands of people about the importance of this largely forgotten environment. Local community groups had been established
to continue maintaining the woods beyond the end of the
project, and a Great North Wood management plan provided
guidance for them and councils on how to care for the woods in
the future. Interpretation boards were set up at thirteen key sites
to help people to navigate between the surviving pockets of the
wood, and to provide information about each place and how it
fitted into the broader landscape.

HEARTS OF OAK

The remaining parcels of the North Wood had survived into the
new millennium with the most serious threats from development
held at bay, and their status as Local Nature Reserves, SINCs,
Conservation Areas and/or Metropolitan Open Land assured.
There was no ground for complacency, however, as events were
to demonstrate. In July 2012, Croydon Council granted planning permission for the demolition of Rockmount School, which
stood within Convent Wood by Hermitage Road, and the
construction of a new Priory School for children with special
educational needs. Although most of the development would
take place on the existing built area, some of the outbuildings
and the construction of a path required the felling of eighteen
trees, including six mature oaks, along with ash, willow, field
maple, sycamore and lime trees.[4]

Worse was to come. The following October, the adjoining
Virgo Fidelis Convent School in Norwood applied for planning
permission to build seven terraced houses and a block of thirty-
two flats, with parking facilities and an access road, on a
0.44-hectare site on the western edge of the wood, necessitating
the removal of fifty-four trees. Despite the fact that Convent
Wood has been recognised to be ancient woodland, and its
designation as a Site of Nature Conservation Importance, the

council considered that 'their removal would not detract from the overall tree cover and none of significant amenity value would be lost'. Despite objections from the Norwood Society and Councillor Alisa Flemming, the plan was approved, and residents watched in dismay as scores of veteran oaks were felled and hauled away.[5]

Croydon's community groups and environmental bodies were further alarmed when, in 2016, the council gave notice that it planned to sell the Victorian Heath Lodge and its garden on the edge of Grangewood Park for redevelopment, having allowed the building to fall into disrepair. Under pressure from local people, the council backed down, but in December 2019, it once again announced that it planned to sell the lodge, along with a further 195 square metres of open space adjoining it to allow an access road to be built. Notice was published between Christmas and New Year, and was open for comments only until 13 January 2020 – 'shoddy tactics', according to the Environmental Law Foundation, 'employed sadly all too frequently by councils' to evade public scrutiny. After a furious backlash, with three thousand people signing a petition organised by the Friends of Grangewood Park, the council backed down, and agreed to work with local groups to find a use for the building.[6]

Meanwhile in Southwark, by 2019 the brick retaining wall along the Farquhar Road side of Dulwich Upper Wood was in danger of collapse, forcing Southwark Council to close the footpath on that side of the road. In order to repair it, Southwark proposed to fell up to thirty-four mature trees. After a public campaign and the intervention of the Dulwich and West Norwood MP Helen Hayes and Councillor Andy Simmons, the council came up with two alternative proposals, both of which involved moving the line of the wall forward to the kerb edge and narrowing the road to allow for a pavement and cycle path, thus retaining the trees. Work was due to begin in 2021.

At nearby Sydenham Hill Wood, however, Southwark Council proved less responsive to public opinion. The footbridge over the railway trackbed, from which Pissarro had painted the railway almost 150 years earlier, was falling into disrepair, with the wooden superstructure that supported the parapet badly rotted. Southwark Council, which owned the bridge, believed that the brick abutments at either end also needed replacing. This would require two oaks, thought to be 150 and 120 years old, that grew at either side of the western end of the bridge, to be felled to allow access, and because their roots were allegedly damaging the brickwork. Like Croydon, Southwark advertised its public consultation for the legal minimum of two weeks between 17 and 31 December 2018 (despite government guidelines in the 2008 Code of Practice stating that consultations should run for a minimum of twelve weeks), clearly hoping to push the plan through with as little public involvement as possible.

On 8 January 2019, the London Wildlife Trust wrote to Southwark's planning division objecting to the proposal, pointing out that the roots in question were those of ivy, not oak, and that repairs to the bridge had been made in 2005 without any need for felling. The Trust also demanded clarification on how other trees would be protected from damage, how vegetation and soil within the reserve would be protected from compaction and digging, and how the works would be timed to avoid disturbance to nesting birds. It also drew attention to Southwark's Core Strategy, which committed the council to 'protect important open spaces from inappropriate development' and to conserve woodland and trees.

At the same time, independently of the LWT, a group of local people began to mobilise in opposition to the plan, and in August a Save the Footbridge Oaks Campaign was launched. At the end of that month, two officers from the council's Highways Department had a meeting with representatives of the London Wildlife

Trust, and appear to have persuaded the Trust that minor works would only last a few years whereas the rebuild would last for sixty. The campaigners, however, were unconvinced, and in September they formally requested Southwark Council to commission a second structural assessment from a specialist engineer with expertise in restoring historic structures in sensitive environments. In October, two officers from the council's Highways Department, Dale Foden and Tony Coppock, met more than twenty-five campaigners at the bridge. 'Feelings ran high,' the campaigners reported, 'and we had a lengthy discussion with a question-and-answer session which was responded to by Dale and Tony, who were patient and thorough in addressing many technical aspects, despite considerable pressure.'

On 30 October, however, the council posted notices that the oaks would be felled after 2 November. In December, Helen Hayes was instrumental in persuading Southwark Council to rescind the felling orders 'so that further options can be explored and community engagement take place'. A petition with 2,700 signatures calling for the oaks to be saved was handed in. Recognising the strength of public opinion, the council obtained two design proposals from its consultants that would retain the trees, but concluded that they were too expensive and risky, and in January 2020 put up metal barriers to close the footbridge.

The outbreak of the Covid-19 pandemic in March 2020 put the works on hold, giving the campaigners time to plan their next move. In June the campaign launched a crowdfund to pay for a design proposal from an independent structural engineer, backed up by a registered conservation architect; with the support of more than seventy people, it exceeded its target of £2,500 by the end of the month. The design proposed replacing the western abutment with two reinforced concrete ground beams supported by screw piles, located within the footprint of the existing abutment. This was approved by an independent arboriculturist and submitted to Southwark Council, which again rejected the proposal.

On Friday 6 November, Southwark posted a removal notice on the oaks, stating that the work was scheduled for the week beginning Monday 16 November. In scenes that recalled the passion, commitment and camaraderie of the planning battles of the 1970s and 1980s, the campaigners, mostly women, mounted a round-the-clock vigil, camping under the trees at night, organising a rota by day, engaging with members of the public and encouraging them to sign the petition, which quickly swelled to more than 6,500 signatures. When contractors arrived with chainsaws on the 16th, the campaigners refused to move. The contractors then left. Meanwhile the campaign was reported in the *South London Press* and other local media, and was the lead item on BBC1's *London News*.

A week later, on 23 November, the council posted a notice that it had applied to the High Court for an interim injunction 'to prevent obstruction of the felling of the oak trees'. If granted, this would leave the campaigners liable to fines or imprisonment. On 30 November the case came before Mrs Justice Cutts on the Queen's Bench, who ordered an adjournment so that all parties might be present. When the application was heard the next day, two campaigners, sisters Susan and Colette Haseldine, were represented by the barrister Paul Powlesland, founder of Lawyers for Nature, an organisation dedicated to representing nature and those protecting it in the courts. The judge rejected the application, observing that the urgency claimed by Southwark Council stemmed not from the state of the bridge, but from the fact that permission to fell the trees was due to expire at one minute past midnight on Thursday 3 December.

The campaigners' relief was short lived, for the Highways Department immediately submitted a new application to fell the trees. After it received 177 objections from the public and just three comments in support, however, the planning officers rejected it, and imposed an interim Tree Preservation Order on the whole reserve, to take effect for six months from 19 January 2021, or until the council decided to make it permanent.

'We are accountable to the public and working on their behalf to make the woods accessible to all, via the bridge,' said Councillor Catherine Rose, cabinet member for leisure, environment and roads. 'The public interest in this means that we have a provisional Tree Preservation Order in place, halting the required works, while we look at the next steps forward.'[7]

As this book goes to press, the fate of these oaks remains in the balance. Unfortunately, as these disputes make clear, we still need stalwart campaigners, willing to risk their physical safety, their livelihoods and even their liberty, to hold local and national government to their environmental commitments, to ensure that these are more than just rhetoric, and that ecological thinking permeates every department and informs every planning decision.

As the London Wildlife Trust approached its 40th anniversary in 2021, much had been achieved, but significant challenges remained for those entrusted with the care and management of the woods, not least the perpetual struggle to obtain funding. Woodlands are not static; they require continuing maintenance to conserve and enhance their biodiversity. There is a widespread perception that, left to their own devices, woods will take care of themselves. This is not the case anywhere in an intensively developed nation such as the United Kingdom, and especially not in built-up areas, where woods are generally small, fragmented and exposed to urban pressures. Management is therefore required to ameliorate these influences. Once, herbivores such as deer and wild boar would have cropped the undergrowth, dislodging dead branches and opening up clearings, letting sunlight and rain reach the woodland floor. In later centuries, the livestock that commoners were permitted to graze in the woods, and the activities of the woodmen, played a similar role. Since unleashing large mammals on an unsuspecting South London populace would be a rewilding too far, the LWT's staff and volunteers must recreate their effects by judicious thinning, coppicing and brushcutting, or the woods would become dark and impenetrable, and brambles, ivy and bracken fern would suppress the wildflowers in the herb layer.

Achieving a balance between public access and conservation demands constant monitoring and responsiveness. The woods survive because of their amenity value; local people who love these places have been at the forefront of the campaigns to save them. But any relatively small urban reserve in the middle of a large conurbation will inevitably come under pressure from public access. Even the best-intentioned visitors, through sheer numbers, will cause compaction and erosion of the soil, while their dogs may disturb ground-nesting birds. Unless precautionary measures are taken, there is a real danger that we may simply love the woods to death.

Preventing this requires tact, diplomacy and common sense. Visitors should be encouraged to keep to paths by the least obtrusive means possible. Where there are several possible routes through an area of open woodland, the preferred path should be clearly indicated. Coppice poles or branches laid along the ground and wired to short stakes can provide natural-looking path edging. Without being overly coercive, this can often be quite effective in keeping visitors from trampling the surrounding understorey, but it only works if the paths are kept in good repair; if a stretch of path is allowed to degenerate into a quagmire, people can hardly be blamed for creating a diversion around it.

Where a barrier is required to prevent dogs scampering off to either side – and their owners from following – dead hedges can be effective. These consist of rows of vertical stakes about three to four feet high, filled in with brash and other cuttings. Dead hedges blend in with the woods and provide a habitat for insects and small vertebrates as they decompose, though they must be replenished every few years. More attractive and longer lasting are live hedges, which can be created by pleaching appropriately situated saplings of hazel, hawthorn or holly and laying them to form a horizontal barrier.

Places where the topsoil is severely eroded and compacted may need to be fenced off with a more substantial barrier such as chestnut palings for several years to allow the understorey to recover and saplings to establish themselves. A notice should always be attached to the fence to explain the need for the restriction. Where this has been done, the reactions that staff and volunteers have received from the public have been over-whelmingly supportive.

Nor have the woods entirely shaken off their lawless past. In recent years, Sydenham Hill Wood has seen murders, suicides and attempted suicides; in 2011 a volunteer found a handgun, wrapped in polythene sheeting, in one of the ponds. Vandalism, though not as serious as when the reserve was first established, remains an intermittent problem. On three occasions in the spring of 2013, stolen mopeds were burned out in Sydenham Hill Wood; in August 2014, there were two arson attacks on the tunnel mouth, damaging fencing, posts and other materials stored there. The London Fire Service was called to put out both fires. To prevent any further incidents, Southwark Council covered the tunnel entrance with steel sheeting.

Nature, too, throws out its challenges. One night in May 2013, high winds brought a giant oak on the upper slope of Sydenham Hill Wood crashing to the ground. Its shattered limbs were strewn across the path, blocking it completely. Volunteers were quickly mobilised to cut up the branches with axes and handsaws. Much as we may mourn the death of a majestic old tree, it is part of the natural woodland cycle. Its fall opened up a clearing in which wildflowers now grow, and its prone trunk, as it decomposes, harbours many species of fungi and wood-boring insects. Throughout the woods, such skeletal remains, bleached grey and deeply grooved by the elements, are gradually returning to the soil that nourished them, to bring forth new life.

A TOUR OF THE WOODS TODAY

The surviving fragments of ancient and secondary woodland cared for by the London Wildlife Trust's Great North Wood project cover about one hundred hectares in total, and are scattered over a distance of almost five miles across five London boroughs. They range from revenant woodland that has sprung up along railway cuttings to substantial stands of oak that, either by chance or through the determined efforts of conservationists, have survived the expansion of the metropolis. A number of veteran oaks that were once part of the North Wood also live on in parks, cemeteries, gardens and even as street trees.

NEW CROSS TO FOREST HILL

In the northern part of the Borough of Lewisham, a four-kilometre railway cutting forms a green corridor through Brockley and Forest Hill. Although severely encroached upon by the construction of the Croydon Canal in 1801 and the railway in 1838, the landscape still preserves some traces of Honor Oak Wood and Gorne Wood, and has been designated a Site of Metropolitan Importance for Nature Conservation, known as the M112 Nature Corridor. An ecological survey conducted for the Greater London Authority in February 2006 described

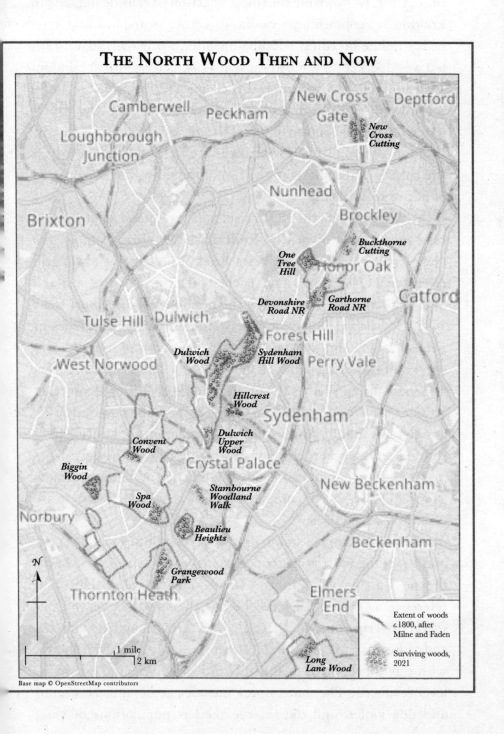

THE NORTH WOOD THEN AND NOW

Camberwell
Peckham
New Cross Gate
Deptford
New Cross Cutting
Loughborough Junction
Nunhead
Brixton
Brockley
Buckthorne Cutting
One Tree Hill
Honor Oak
Catford
Devonshire Road NR
Garthorne Road NR
Tulse Hill
Dulwich
Forest Hill
Dulwich Wood
Sydenham Hill Wood
Perry Vale
West Norwood
Hillcrest Wood
Sydenham
Convent Wood
Dulwich Upper Wood
Biggin Wood
Crystal Palace
New Beckenham
Spa Wood
Stambourne Woodland Walk
Norbury
Beaulieu Heights
Beckenham
Grangewood Park
Thornton Heath
Elmers End
Long Lane Wood

N

1 mile
2 km

Extent of woods c.1800, after Milne and Faden

Surviving woods, 2021

Base map © OpenStreetMap contributors

the cutting as 'Probably the finest selection of railside habitats in London . . . containing woodland, scrub, grassland and reed beds . . . The breeding avifauna includes tawny owl, lesser spotted woodpecker [now mostly absent as a breeding bird in London] and bullfinch. A surprisingly diverse invertebrate fauna includes several nationally scarce species, amongst which is the white-letter hairstreak butterfly.' A SINC review conducted for the London Borough of Lewisham in 2015 found that much of the cutting, particularly to the east of the railway line, consisted of native woodland.[1]

At the time of writing, four sections are managed as nature reserves on land owned by Railtrack. The northernmost, the New Cross Gate Cutting (Vesta Road, London SE4 2NT, grid reference TQ363762) can be reached by buses 171, 172, 343 and 484, and has been managed by the London Wildlife Trust since 1987. Consisting mostly of oak woodland with open glades of neutral and acid grassland, the three-hectare site supports 170 species of flowering plants, including some that are locally rare, and many fungi such as fly agaric, stinkhorn – first recorded in Honor Oak Wood by William Curtis in the eighteenth century – and dryad's saddle. Among its bird population are kestrel, great spotted woodpecker, chiffchaff, song thrush and jay, while its invertebrate inhabitants include stag beetle and butterflies such as speckled wood and comma. Access is restricted, but there are occasional open days.

About a mile to the south, on the routes of buses 122, 171, 172 and P4, is the most recently designated of these reserves, Buckthorne Cutting (Buckthorne Road, London SE4 2DB, grid reference TQ362747). Established by the Fourth Reserve Conservation Trust in 2016, these 2.28 hectares encompass wooded embankments of oak, birch, sweet chestnut and wild cherry, with veteran coppiced field maple and hawthorn, and rare high-level reedbeds. The understorey includes gorse, great horsetail and dog violet, and the reserve shelters populations of bats,

cuckoos, tawny owl, great spotted woodpecker, and locally vulnerable species such as slow-worm and hedgehog. The nearby
Garthorne Road (1.5 hectares) and Devonshire Road (2.5 hectares) Nature Reserves occupy opposite banks of the same
railway cutting, and are run by Lewisham Council. Although
most of the woodland in these reserves post-dates the construction of the railway, a number of plants associated with ancient
woods survive, including bitter vetch, wood avens, garlic mustard and hedge woundwort.

Rising to the west of these reserves in Honor Oak, the steeply
sloping, seven-hectare One Tree Hill (Honor Oak Rise, London
SE23 3RA, TQ352742) can be reached by buses P4 and P12, and
offers spectacular views over London. Writing in *The Spectator* in
1957, John Betjeman described it as 'the nearest and strangest
piece of country surviving in London', offering a view 'better than
that from Parliament Hill'. Clear-felled by the late nineteenth century and subsequently planted with London plane, hybrid black
poplar and other park standards, it cannot be considered ancient
woodland, although a patch of wood at its eastern end, adjoining
the allotments, and the western strip adjacent to Brenchley Gardens contain wild service-tree, Midland hawthorn and some old
oak pollards, and may be ancient. The slopes are covered with
sessile oak, beneath which bluebells thrive, while the open
meadow at the top has retained some of its original acid grassland
flora, including heath-grass and compact rush, alongside bents
and fescue. Owned and managed by Southwark Council, the site
was declared a Local Nature Reserve in 2007, and is maintained
largely through the efforts of the Friends of One Tree Hill.[2]

DULWICH AND SYDENHAM

Beyond the busy South Circular Road, Dulwich and Sydenham
Hill Woods cover some twenty-eight hectares in total, making
them the largest surviving portion of the North Wood. The

dominant trees are sessile oak and hornbeam, interspersed with yew, ash, beech, hazel, goat willow and a few wych elms, with a shrub layer of holly, hawthorn, wild cherry, guelder-rose and field maple. Though separately owned and administered by the Dulwich Estate and the London Borough of Southwark respectively, they comprise one contiguous woodland, which is open at all times, and many visitors are unaware that they are passing from one to the other. Their value to wildlife is enhanced by the fact that they are buffered by a further seventy-five hectares of green space comprising three allotments, a golf course, and several playing fields; across the South Circular, Dulwich and Belair parks continue the open terrain. Modern aerial photographs reveal that the lines of trees on the golf course and the hedgerows around the sports pitches correspond to the field boundaries on Thomas Milne's map of 1800. They must therefore date back to the clearance of the Fifty Acre Wood in 1792; since it was common practice to retain existing trees and shrubs to delineate new fields, these 'ghost hedges' may well be a survival of the North Wood itself.

Both woods can be reached via Cox's Walk (TQ344730), a steeply ascending avenue of oaks that rises from the busy junction of Lordship Lane and Dulwich Common; the P4 and P13 buses stop nearby. Laid out in the early eighteenth century, this is one of the oldest such walks in public ownership in England, and is now designated a Protected London Square and part of the London Green Chain Walk. Voted one of the top thirty wild places in the whole of the UK by *The Times* in 2016,[3] Sydenham Hill Wood (there is another entrance on Crescent Wood Road, London SE26 6LS, TQ344725) is a Local Nature Reserve managed on behalf of Southwark Council by the London Wildlife Trust. It contains a mix of ancient and secondary woodland; its upper slopes were once occupied by Victorian villas and their gardens and are thus secondary woodland, with a few exotic nineteenth-century plantings including a cedar of Lebanon and a monkey-puzzle tree. So too are the embankments on either side of the old railway trackbed, although a band of sessile oak and hornbeam runs along its eastern side. This is Blanch's 'mazy labyrinth of trees' that was left standing after the villas were built, and can therefore be considered ancient.

Beyond the trackbed, the long arc of Dulwich Woods is mostly ancient woodland of oak and hornbeam, bounded by housing on one side and allotments on the other. Several oaks, and one huge ash, have three or more trunks growing from one root, suggesting that they are old coppices that have been left to grow out. Dulwich Wood can also be reached from the opposite direction, from Sydenham Hill Station via Low Cross Wood Walk (College Road, London SE21 7ND, TQ335721). Alongside College Road, a further area, Low Cross Wood, remains closed to the public, although the Great North Wood team, granted access by the Dulwich Estate, have cleared invasive cherry laurel from parts of it.

Both Dulwich and Sydenham Hill Woods, though compromised by non-native garden plants, contain AWIs, including wood anemone, English bluebell, ransoms, sweet woodruff, wood avens, wood dock and stitchwort. Among the many fungi are jelly ear, turkey tail, hairy curtain crust, artist's bracket, chicken of the woods, beefsteak fungus, sulphur tuft, brittlestem, glistening inkcap, fairy inkcap, trooping funnel, parachutes, oysterling, Alfred's cakes and dead man's fingers. A significant bat population includes common and soprano pipistrelle, noctule, Leisler's and brown long-eared bat. Buzzards, sparrowhawks, kestrels and hobbies patrol the skies overhead, tawny owls roost in the great oaks, resident birds include green and great spotted woodpeckers, jackdaw, nuthatch, tree creeper, chiffchaff and stock dove, while winter brings migratory redwings, fieldfares and firecrests. In May 2014, for the first time in forty years, a male cuckoo was heard in the woods, and it has been heard several times again in the years since.

Three other fragments of the North Wood can be found in the vicinity. The largest, at 2.4 hectares, is Dulwich Upper Wood (Farquhar Road, London SE19 1SS, TQ337711), managed by The Conservation Volunteers as an educational reserve with grant aid from the London Borough of Southwark. Open at all times, the wood is staffed by a full-time warden, and has an interpretative hut on site. The basements of the houses that once stood on the site are still visible amid revenant woodland, although there is also a small area of ancient oak wood, a surviving fragment of Vicar's Oak Coppice, which includes several veteran boundary trees. The ground flora includes wood anemone, bluebell, ramsons, yellow pimpernel and dense colonies of ivy broomrape (*Orobanche hederae*), a regionally scarce parasite that, lacking the ability to manufacture chlorophyll, attaches itself to the roots of ivy. The reserve is particularly rich in fungi, with more than two hundred species, and shelters a wide variety of breeding birds, including green and great spotted woodpeckers, nuthatch and tree creeper.

Hillcrest Wood is a belt of sessile oak and hornbeam, partly ancient, interspersed with Victorian plantings, fringing the Hillcrest Estate and the southern entrance to the old railway tunnel, off Westwood Road. Although the wood is designated as a SINC, an application was made to Lewisham Council in 2018 to redevelop parts of it. Concerted action by local residents, the London Wildlife Trust and the Woodland Trust eventually resulted in the application being withdrawn. Just west of College Road, Hither Wood is a small, square fragment of Hither King's Wood covering about half a hectare, that survived behind the gardens of Victorian villas, and is now hemmed in by the postwar housing that replaced them.

UPPER NORWOOD

Further south, we leave the Dulwich Estate and come to the remnants of the Archbishop of Canterbury's woods, ranged along Beulah Hill and all within easy reach of the 468 bus route. To the north, off Hermitage Road, is Convent Wood, a surviving fragment of Great Stakepit Coppice. Privately owned by the Virgo Fidelis Convent, this impressive three-hectare stand of sessile oak and hornbeam is not open to the public, although it can be seen from the nearby streets.

South of Beulah Hill, Biggin Wood (Covington Way, London SW16 3RX, TQ316702) is a 5.4-hectare wood adjoining an allotment and tennis courts. The tree cover is mostly sessile oak, with evidence of past coppicing, and the understorey includes woodland species such as English bluebell, ramsons, wood millet, lords-and-ladies and several clumps of wood anemone. Biggin Wood also supports a rich bird population: a 1979–81 study recorded forty different species feeding or breeding in the wood, and in recent years tawny owls, green and great spotted woodpeckers, chiffchaffs, blackcaps, long-tailed tits, goldcrests and nuthatches have all been observed there. In October 2017, Friends of Biggin Wood was formed with some funding from Croydon Council and the London Wildlife Trust. During the winter of 2017–18, the LWT's Great North Wood project team undertook work in Biggin Wood to clear rubbish, remove invasive shrubs such as cherry laurel, spotted laurel and snowberry, and improve the paths.

Just under a mile to the east is Spa Wood, also known as The Lawns (Spa Hill, London SE19 3TW, TQ327698), a 6.3-hectare park on the site of the former Beulah Spa. This crescent of ancient woodland embracing a grassy meadow was once part of Bewley Coppice, and contains one of the largest and oldest oaks in the surviving North Wood. The understorey includes the Ancient Woodland Indicator species ramsons, wood anemone and wild bluebell. After a considerable period of neglect, the wood has been managed by the LWT's Great North Wood Project, in conjunction with the Friends of Spa Wood and The Conservation Volunteers.

Half a mile further along Beulah Hill, under the TV mast, is Beaulieu Heights (Wilkinson Gardens, London SE25 6BN, TQ334695). The area around the entrance to the seven-hectare site is laid out as a municipal park, but further back is a substantial tract of dense oak woodland that once formed part of Windall's Coppice. Some relict hazel coppices can be found amid the oaks, and the herb layer includes cow parsley, wood anemone and bluebell. The Friends of Beaulieu Heights, set up in 2009, have worked in partnership with Croydon Council and The Conservation Volunteers with the approval of the Forestry Commission to enhance the biodiversity of the wood and improve public access.

Covering just two hectares on the southern slope of Beulah Hill, Stambourne Woodland Walk (Church Road, London SE19 2PY, TQ336701) is one of the lesser-known relics of the North Wood. A narrow strip of the Archbishop of Canterbury's woods that survived by being incorporated into the gardens of Victorian villas, it was purchased from the Church Commissioners by Croydon Council in 1962, and opened as a linear park in 1984. The relict woodland is the classic North Wood mix of oak – mostly pedunculate, including one huge, 350-year-old specimen, with some sessile on the upper slopes – and hornbeam, interspersed with yew and holly. At the Church Road end are a couple of wych elms, and at the Auckland Road end a large old goat willow. Horse chestnut and sycamore are also present, along with some startling exotics: a tree of heaven, an oriental beech, and a soaring dawn redwood from China. A less welcome legacy of Victorian planting is the ubiquitous cherry laurel, darkening the wood and suppressing the understorey. The Friends of Stambourne Woods are making valiant efforts to hack it back, but they have a gargantuan task on their hands. Founded in June 2016, the Friends run monthly weekend activity days, with conservation work for adults and forestry school lessons for children. At ground level, despite the invasive cherry laurel, the herb layer includes garlic mustard, wood dock, celandine, herb-Robert, bluebell (both Spanish cultivars and native wild), and sweet woodruff, while comfrey has recently made a comeback. In spring and early summer, the wood rings with birdsong, and tawny owls have been reported.

SOUTHERN OUTLIERS

Located on Grange Road between Thornton Heath and Upper Norwood, Grangewood Park (Ross Road, London SE25 6TW, TQ330687) is an 11.2-hectare survival of White Horse Wood. It is a public park, with the usual amenities such as ornamental gardens, sports facilities and a children's playground, but also includes extensive stands of mature oak. Much of the area beneath the trees is mown regularly, so there is little understorey, but in one fenced-off area bramble, bracken and furze have been left to grow, along with butcher's-broom, wood anemone, dog's mercury and English bluebell, while the steep bank beside Grange Road is carpeted with daffodils in spring.

About a mile south-west of Elmer's End, near South Norwood Country Park and the Croydon Tramlink Arena station, is Long Lane Wood (Bywood Avenue, Croydon CR0 7RA, TQ356675), the farthest-flung North Wood survivor. At six hectares it is the largest remaining fragment of the Eighteen Acre Wood shown on John Rocque's 1762 map of Surrey, and is composed mostly of sessile oak, wild cherry, field maple, whitebeam, rowan and hawthorn. Although the area under the trees is mown several times during summer, there is a healthy understorey of English bluebell, cow parsley, bramble, wood anemone, pignut, greater stitchwort, field woodrush and wood forget-me-not. Within the wood is the Bywood Avenue Bird Sanctuary, a small fenced-off area closed to the public, which shelters chaffinches along with great spotted and green woodpeckers.

Owned by the London Borough of Croydon, Long Lane Wood has been maintained by the LWT's Great North Wood project team since 2017. With the assistance of local volunteers, the team has cut back bramble that was swamping the herb layer, removed litter and fly-tipping, compiled a plant list and run wildlife walks for the public. A couple of streets away on Lorne Gardens is Glade Wood, a small (1.2-hectare) wedge of the old Eighteen Acre Wood. Also a bird sanctuary, it is closed to the public.

Together, these parcels of woodland provide a large, semi-continuous habitat for wildlife. Just 1.6 kilometres – as the bat flies – separate One Tree Hill and Sydenham Hill Wood; Dulwich Upper Wood is only 1.2 kilometres from Convent Wood; while the greatest distance is the three kilometres from Grangewood Park to Long Lane Wood. To put this in perspective, a common pipistrelle can range up to five kilometres from its roost when hunting; a newly fledged kestrel may fly up to 150 kilometres from the nest; while some migratory butterfly species can travel thousands of miles in a year.

The situation for flightless mammals and amphibians is less rosy: for them, busy roads such as the South Circular are either insuperable obstacles or death traps, leading to habitat fragmentation, which results in a loss of genetic diversity that leaves them less resistant to disease. Professor Sir John Lawton's report on England's wildlife sites, *Making Space for Nature* (known as the Lawton Report), presented to the Department for Environment, Food and Rural Affairs in 2010, noted that 'Surviving in small, isolated sites is, however, difficult for many species, and

often impossible in the longer term, because they rarely contain
the level of resources or the diversity of habitats needed to
support sustainable populations.' It recommended the creation
of 'ecological networks' to 'enhance connections between, or
join up, sites, either through physical corridors, or through
"stepping stones".'[4]

There are measures that can be taken to alleviate the problem
of habitat fragmentation. The preservation of vegetation on
road verges and railway embankments can create green corridors that allow wildlife to move from one island of greenery to
another, and the planting of hedges made up of native deciduous
shrubs such as hawthorn, dog rose and field maple can also help
to join up fragments of woodland. Perhaps most important,
however, are private gardens, which cover almost a quarter of
the surface area of Greater London.[5] By leaving part of their
lawns unmown, allowing seed heads to remain on plants over
winter, building small logpiles and cutting holes at the bottom
of fences for hedgehogs, gardeners can create a safe environment
in which animals can find food and shelter, and a highway along
which they can move from one area to another.

12
WAYS THROUGH THE WOODS

2021–?

A crisp, sunny day in March. Around the elephantine trunks of the hornbeams, new leaves unfurl, creating a pale green shimmer like, as Philip Larkin wrote, 'something almost being said'. As we crunch along the rubble of the former railway track, a small, catkin-festooned hazel is transformed into a burning bush by a glancing ray of sunlight. The machine-gun rattle of a great spotted woodpecker echoes from the depths of Sydenham Hill Wood. Along the slope between the railway embankment and the golf course, tawny mining bees have excavated little mounds of friable earth, like miniature volcanoes.

We make our way down the steep incline of Cox's Walk, between the gnarled oaks, some of which have died or been felled by the wind, sculpted by the elements into weird, twisted shapes. One, seen from the path, appears entirely dead, its white, crumbling heartwood exposed; but on the other side, a thick layer of healthy bark supports a living branch, its buds swelling with leaves about to open. Above us, a kestrel circles the church spire on the hunt for prey; these small falcons have nested and bred in the steeple, right beside the busy South Circular, for the past four or five years. Then I realise that I have become detached from the group; while I was watching the kestrel, they have moved back uphill. When I look up again, the kestrel has gone.

Then, high up, I see a raptor leisurely circling on a thermal. It can't be the kestrel – at that altitude, it would be a mere speck. At that moment, one of my fellow volunteers approaches with a pair of binoculars. We aim them skyward, and recognise the broad, white-arced wingspan of a buzzard. Little wonder the kestrel has disappeared.

A WORLD IN THE BALANCE

On this local level, the prospects for the Great North Wood look brighter than they have done for more than a century. Nationally and globally, however, the challenges facing the ecosphere are terrifying, with melting polar ice, wildfires raging from Amazonia to the Arctic, species loss, topsoil erosion, deforestation and acidifying oceans 'driving a complex, dynamic process of environmental destabilisation' that threatens to undermine not just the natural world but the global economy and human society itself.[1] Meanwhile, a review of seventy-three historical reports around the world, from Germany to Puerto Rico, has revealed that more than 40 per cent of insect species are threatened with extinction as a result of intensive agriculture, pesticide use, urbanisation and habitat loss.[2]

In May 2019, a global assessment published by the United Nations Intergovernmental Science-Policy Platform on Biodiversity and Ecosystem Services (IPBES) issued a stark warning that loss of biodiversity was as great a threat to life on earth as climate change. Compiled by 145 experts from fifty countries, it drew on fifteen thousand scientific and government sources as well as indigenous peoples and local communities to show how land conversion, deforestation, climate change, pollution, overfishing, poaching, and the introduction of invasive species were 'eroding the very foundations of our economies, livelihoods, food security, health and quality of life worldwide.' To avert ecological and societal catastrophe, the report concluded, nations must shift from the pursuit of economic growth at any cost to an understanding that nature is the necessary precondition for all human development.[3]

The school strike of February 2019, in which some fifteen thousand pupils across the UK demonstrated against government inaction on climate change, and the Extinction Rebellion protests in London the following month, proved that many young people are more aware of the gravity of the situation than their elders. In April 2019, after a speech by the then sixteen-year-old Swedish activist Greta Thunberg, the UK Parliament approved an Opposition motion to declare a formal climate and environment emergency.

What difference can a few small urban reserves and green spaces make in the face of such an overwhelming assault on the environment? Both directly and indirectly, they have a contribution to make, however small in the overall scheme of things. Woods help to resist global warming by absorbing CO_2 from the atmosphere through photosynthesis. According to the Woodland Trust, the entire woodland ecosystem – trees and other vegetation, deadwood, roots, leaves and soil – plays its part. A young wood composed of mixed native species can lock up more than four hundred tonnes of carbon per hectare, and carbon sequestration continues in woodland that is centuries old. Urban trees can also reduce air pollution, lower city temperatures and, by absorbing water, reduce the risk of flooding.[4]

The surviving fragments of the North Wood represent a dwindling and irreplaceable resource. According to the inventory compiled by the then Nature Conservancy Council, ancient woodland covers just 2.6 per cent of the land area of England and Wales. Some 7 per cent of the ancient woodland that was present in 1930 has been grubbed up for farming or other uses, and 38 per cent has been replaced with plantations, usually of non-native species.[5] And that was before HS2 threatened at least 108 ancient woods up and down the country with damage or

total destruction. An ecosystem is just that: a system. Remove
one component part and its functioning is impaired, and others
feel the strain. When they in turn start to fail, the whole thing
breaks down altogether, leading to soil erosion, desertification,
flooding and drought.

As pesticides, herbicides, chemical fertilisers and the destruction of hedgerows have driven many species from the countryside
with far more lethal efficiency than any Tudor Vermin Act, the
suburbs of our cities have become a haven for birds and insects,
sheltering species that have been lost elsewhere. Along with
other open spaces and railway linesides, the reserves of the
North Wood provide a habitat for many such species, as well as
a green corridor for terrestrial animals such as hedgehogs that
are threatened by habitat fragmentation.

The reserves also lead the way in the environmental management of urban green spaces, setting an example and emphasising
the importance of leaving dead wood to rot, providing food and
shelter for saproxylic insects. A misplaced concern for tidiness
on the part of councils, contractors and a minority of the public
has created environmental deserts where planting is restricted to
low-maintenance evergreens such as the invasive, biodiversity-
suppressing cherry laurel, long grass is considered a sign of
neglect, weeds – which are simply wildflowers growing where
someone thinks they shouldn't – are zapped with herbicides,
dead wood is assiduously cleared away, and the remnants of
fallen trees are pulverised by stump grinders.

An unfortunate manifestation of this approach took place a
few years ago at Sydenham Hill Wood. Back in the late 1990s,
the London Wildlife Trust had planted a mixed hedge of hornbeam, field maple, hazel and hawthorn along the upper part of
Cox's Walk. By August 2013, the saplings had reached a sufficient size to be laid into a pleached hedge. Volunteers undertook
the work, cutting most of the way through each stem, bending it
almost horizontal and interweaving it with its neighbour. Just a

month after the work was completed, they were alarmed to hear chainsaws on upper Cox's Walk. Apparently a resident had complained to Southwark Council that the hedge was untidy, and they – without consultation or any attempt to discover whether this person's views were representative of local opinion – had sent in contractors, who cut it to the ground and chipped the cuttings. The council subsequently apologised, offered £200 towards new saplings to replace the lost hedge, and agreed to work with the Trust to ensure such mistakes did not occur again.

Wildlife-friendly horticulture ought to be the rule, not the exception, in public spaces. Every park could contain at least one area of wildflower meadow. Road verges should be mown, and trees and hedges pruned, only in the appropriate season. The LWT's Wildlife Garden Centre in Peckham encourages the promotion of biodiversity in private gardens; nature is not just located somewhere 'out there', which we visit by car, but is all around us, including our own back yards. If we are going to live in harmony with the natural world – and our very survival depends upon it – we, as individuals, businesses and local authorities, need to liberate ourselves from the impulse to impose order on every aspect of our surroundings, and let the 'weeds' flourish in our lawns and pavements, road verges and roundabouts. They are not a sign of neglect or decay, but of vigorous life.

In addition to their value as urban green spaces, Sydenham Hill Wood and other London reserves have provided a springboard for the careers of young ecologists, who have gone on to work for other Wildlife Trusts across the country, for Friends of the Earth, National Parks, English Nature, the Royal Parks, and as local authority ecologists and ecological consultants, so that their influence extends far beyond the immediate area.

Perhaps above all, the woods play a crucial role in raising environmental awareness in one of the largest and most

populous cities on the planet. Around 80 per cent of the UK population lives in towns or cities, so it is in urban reserves such as
those which make up the Great North Wood that the battle for
hearts and minds will be won or lost. As the Senegalese environ-
mentalist Baba Dioum wrote in an address to the International
Union for the Conservation of Nature and Natural Resources in
1968, 'In the end we will conserve only what we love, we will
love only what we understand, and we will understand only
what we are taught.'

Through visiting the woods, by joining the LWT's bird, tree
and other nature walks, and above all through volunteering,
people living miles from open countryside come to learn about,
to understand, and to love the natural world. In *The Wild Places*
(2007), Robert Macfarlane describes how he gradually became
'refocused' from seeking nature in the wild grandeur of places
such as the Cairngorms into understanding wildness 'not as
something which was hived off from human life, but which
existed unexpectedly around and within it: in cities, backyards,
roadsides, hedges, field boundaries or spinnies', in what his
mentor Roger Deakin called 'the undiscovered country of the
nearby'. Even in the most urban of environments, nature will
spring back amid the shopping streets and business parks, as tree
roots lift granite kerbstones, hart's tongue fern sprouts from the
mortar of old brick walls, chickweed and ground-elder find
purchase in cement and tarmac.

People actively involved in the environmental stewardship of
a specific site are also more likely to engage with the wider environmental issues: making changes to their own way of life such
as reducing their carbon footprint, cutting down on plastic
waste and making their gardens more wildlife friendly; exerting
pressure on supermarkets, through consumer choice, to cut food
waste and excess packaging; campaigning against environmentally damaging developments; and lobbying politicians at both
the local and national levels.

There is a delicate balance to be struck. Funding bodies and planning authorities tend to favour public engagement over 'pure' ecology – but without the ecology, there would be nothing with which to engage the public. This dilemma is a microcosm of that facing the planet as a whole: how do we cater for the everyday needs and wellbeing of an ever-increasing number of people without wrecking the ecosystem on which their – our – very survival depends?

HUMAN NATURE

Nature is for everyone, and in our attempts to conserve it, we must resist the urge to recreate some pre-human Arcadia, or appear to regard human beings as the enemy. The great, elemental wildernesses of mountain and moorland are beyond the reach of many city dwellers with busy lives and limited budgets, and a purist disdain for the way most people live is not going to save the planet. If the battle for hearts and minds is to be won, we will have to engage not as specialists but as ordinary people, sharing the everyday concerns of our fellow citizens.

We need to involve city dwellers from ethnic minorities, many of whom do not feel welcome in the countryside and, by extension, within the environmental sphere as a whole, which remains overwhelmingly white and middle class. A 2017 report by Dr Richard Norrie of the think-tank Policy Exchange found that the environmental sector was one of the least diverse in the UK, with just 0.6 per cent of the workforce identifying as non-white.[6] Julian Glover's 2019 *Landscapes Review* for Defra reported that '18% of children living in the most deprived areas never visit the natural environment,' that '20% fewer Visibly Minority Ethnic (VME) children go out into green spaces weekly compared to white, middle-class children,' and that 'Black, Asian and minority ethnic board members are extremely rare. Across National

Parks and AONBs, together only 0.8% are from black, Asian or ethnic minorities.'[7]

The following June, the Scout movement ambassador Dwayne Fields presented an item on the popular BBC television programme *Countryfile* that focused on the report. 'When I talk to people from the Black and Minority Ethnic community,' he said, 'It's clear that they don't view the UK countryside as somewhere that's for them.'[7] The responses to that programme on social media from sections of the white community expressed resentment at what they saw as an attempt to politicise an innocuous theatre of recreation. But nature – and especially the right of access to it – is political and, as I hope this history of the North Wood has made clear, always has been.

In part, the environmental movement is itself to blame for this. There has long been a disturbing strain of rural nostalgia within British environmentalism, dramatised by Melissa Harrison in her thought-provoking 2018 novel *All Among the Barley*. A hatred of modern industrial civilisation that originated in the Romantic Movement and the writings of William Cobbett curdled, in the early decades of the twentieth century, into a mindset now identified as ecofascism. Henry Williamson (1895–1977), author of the much loved *Tarka the Otter* (1927), became a fervent admirer of 'the great man across the Rhine'; Rolf Gardiner (1902–1971), a pioneering organic farmer, Morris dance revivalist and friend of D. H. Lawrence, wrote admiringly to Joseph Goebbels in 1933 about the 'new order' he sought to establish in England; while his friend and fellow founder of the Soil Association Jorian Jenks (1899–1963) acted as agricultural adviser to Oswald Mosley's British Union of Fascists.[8]

What links these men's environmentalism with their fascist leanings is a desire to preserve some mythical English 'root stock'. While very few modern environmentalists would endorse their views, their legacy lingers in public perceptions of the environment, and until recently in the predominantly white, male leadership of environmental organisations.

It has also framed the debate about 'invasive species'. For how many centuries must a species such as the sycamore, first recorded in England in the fifteenth century, have to have been present before it is accorded the right to exist here? Such judgements are often subjective, and selective. The brown hare and the fallow deer are seen as characteristic and cherished denizens of the English countryside, yet both were introduced in Roman times or later, and are no more native than the grey squirrel or the ring-necked parakeet. It is not hard to make the imaginative leap from ecological to political nativism, and to see how such attitudes can be seen as exclusionary.

Scattered across one of the most ethnically diverse areas in the country, the woods and green spaces of South London have a role to play in redressing this situation. In fact, the term 'ethnic minority' simply isn't applicable in parts of twenty-first-century South London, where Black and Asian people actually form the *majority*. In Lambeth, three out of five people describe their ethnicity as other than white British;[10] 50.7 per cent of Croydon's population identify as 'Black, Asian and Minority Ethnic';[11] while a quarter of Southwark's population are Black and a third are Asian or of other minority ethnicities.[12]

This huge section of the population is not reflected in the city's wild spaces. The London Wildlife Trust acknowledges that 'there is work to be done on improving representation . . . particularly with regards to ethnic and racial diversity across our volunteer base, staff body and board of trustees.'[13] The imbalance in representation is not just a matter of perception; there are economic factors at play. Environmentalism, like other industries that draw on people's interest and enthusiasm such as publishing and the arts, has become reliant on volunteers and unpaid internships, discouraging those from less well-off backgrounds for whom financial security cannot be taken for granted. To help to redress this situation, the LWT's Heritage Lottery-funded Keeping It Wild Traineeships offer young people aged between sixteen and twenty-five, from backgrounds under-represented in natural heritage, full-time, paid, three-month vocational traineeships at one of the Trust's reserves; several trainees have subsequently found permanent jobs with the Trust.

The Lambeth-based charity Nature Vibezzz provides a forest school, environmental education, practical nature conservation sessions, events and community projects. Wild in the City, a Community Interest Company based in Croydon, offers bushcraft and ecotherapy, with an emphasis on 'supporting people of colour in finding their place in UK natural settings and [creating] opportunities for the representation of black leadership in nature'. Between them, such initiatives are doing a great deal of outreach work with local schools and community groups to ensure that engagement with nature goes beyond the predominantly white, middle-class demographic with which it has been associated for too long.

COVID'S METAMORPHOSES

The effects of the Covid-19 pandemic of 2020 on the reserves of the North Wood were varied, according to their status and local conditions. In March of that year, the London Wildlife Trust cancelled all volunteer workdays and events, including school and family learning sessions, although some of its reserves remained open to the public, and its rangers continued to undertake maintenance work. As restrictions began to ease over the summer, the Trust conducted a few trial workdays, with no more than six volunteers maintaining social distancing and safety measures, including sanitising tools before and after each session. By August, volunteer workdays had resumed at Sydenham Hill Wood with these conditions in place, but after infection rates began to rise again through the autumn, a second lock-down was imposed in early November, and workdays had to be suspended once more.

With many leisure activities off-limits, the public flocked to local parks and reserves for fresh air and exercise. The gate counters at Sydenham Hill Wood recorded 343,000 visits in the course of 2020, an 81 per cent increase on 189,000 in 2019. In the absence of work sessions, this inevitably put pressure on the reserves, leaving paths, gates and fences in poor repair. The need for social distancing led to the informal widening of paths and the creation of new desire lines to the detriment of the under-storey, a situation exacerbated at Sydenham Hill by the closure of the Cox's Walk footbridge.

On smaller reserves such as Garthorne Road and Buckthorne Cutting, which are not open to the public on a regular basis, the situation was different: without the pressure of footfall, small, socially distanced volunteer groups were able to achieve a great deal, clearing invasive species, cutting back bramble and bracken and laying new paths.

At a national level, there was much talk during the early months of the pandemic about how the necessary precautions might encourage us to rethink the way we conduct our lives, and what we really value. Traffic noise subsided, birdsong rang out in cities, wild goats roamed the streets of Llandudno, fallow deer grazed in the East London suburb of Harold Hill, and ecosystems began to heal. Aircraft noise all but disappeared, the sky was no longer criss-crossed with contrails – something unseen since the eruption of the Eyjafjallajökull volcano in Iceland grounded air traffic in 2010 – and atmospheric pollution was significantly reduced. Having learned that meetings and conferences could take place online, we would travel less. We would walk or cycle to work. We would consume less. We would realise that public health must sometimes take priority over profit.

Several premature relaxations and renewed lockdowns later, such optimism seemed misplaced. As early as June, the streets were as busy with traffic as ever, and planes were roaring overhead. That month the Prime Minister, Boris Johnson, announced his 'New Deal for Britain' to aid economic recovery under the slogan 'Build, build, build'. Much of it was old-school, pre-Covid, pre-climate crisis thinking. A pledge to protect the landscape with flood defences, plant thirty thousand hectares of trees every year by 2025, and set aside £40 million for local conservation projects and three thousand new jobs in the environmental sector[14] sat uncomfortably alongside a promise 'to scythe through red tape' by relaxing planning laws, and a jibe at 'newt-counting delays' to development.[15]

Meanwhile, a report published by the Institute for Public Policy Research (IPPR) in July warned that a historic disregard for the destruction of nature had left Britain 'acutely vulnerable' to the effects of climate change and 'woefully unprepared' to meet the challenge. 'Nothing less than the overall transformation of society and the economy,' it concluded, 'is required . . . to bring human activity within sustainable limits and prepare us for the consequences of the damage already caused to nature.'[16] Of course people need jobs, but we need to think hard about what sort of jobs we should be creating. In the autumn of 2019, New Zealand's Prime Minister Jacinda Ardern challenged the tendency to measure success by economic growth and GDP. 'Economic growth accompanied by worsening social outcomes is not success,' she told the Bill & Melinda Gates Foundation. 'It is failure.'[17]

In some respects, the Covid-19 pandemic can be seen as a dress rehearsal for the ecological crisis that will all too soon engulf us. We cannot get back to 'normal'. Like the pandemic, the climate emergency will not be solved by science alone; it will require significant change in all our lifestyles. 'Green' expedients such as carbon offsetting and 'mitigation' planting will not be enough. We must fundamentally reshape our economy, industry, agriculture and urban planning, or face catastrophe. When the UK really begins to feel the effects of the climate crisis – and all the evidence suggests that it will happen much sooner, and much faster, than people think – it will be far more devastating than the pandemic, in both loss of life and damage to the economy. Unless we act now, it is only a matter of decades – and a very few decades at that – before rising sea levels, desertification, food and water shortages, financial instability and wars over dwindling resources will bring about the collapse of our infrastructure and, for most people, of everything that makes life tolerable. It is no longer a matter of saving the birds and the bees, or even the trees; it's about saving human society. Nature will survive in some form, despite mass extinctions. We won't.

WOODLAND THERAPY

We live in an age when our lives are increasingly sedentary and much of our experience is mediated through electronic communication, so that direct, physical contact with the natural world is increasingly rare. In his 2005 bestseller *Last Child in the Woods*, the American commentator Richard Louv coined the term Nature Deficit Disorder to describe the absence of nature from the lives of young people today, and identified it as a contributing factor to conditions such as obesity, depression and attention problems. 'In nature,' he wrote, 'a child finds freedom, fantasy and privacy: a place distant from the adult world, a separate peace.'

In 2015, twenty-eight leading authors including Margaret Atwood, Andrew Motion, Michael Morpurgo, Sara Maitland, Robert Macfarlane, Helen Macdonald and Ruth Padel protested that the latest edition of the *Oxford Junior Dictionary* – aimed at seven-year-olds starting Key Stage Two – had dropped some fifty words related to nature, including acorn, buttercup, conker, heron, kingfisher, lark, magpie, minnow, newt and otter to make way for terms such as analogue, broadband and chatroom.

The same year, The Wildlife Trusts launched their first 30 Days Wild campaign, encouraging people to do 'something wild' every day for a month. Participants were asked to take part in a survey by the University of Derby, which asked how they felt about their health and happiness before the challenge, at the end of it, and two months after it finished. Of the 269 people who took part in both the pre- and post-participation surveys, the number reporting their health as 'excellent' increased by 30 per cent.

Other studies have shown that direct experience of nature has a beneficial effect on human health and happiness, reducing respiratory and cardiovascular disease, hypertension, anxiety and mental fatigue, and restoring attention capacity. The 2010 Lawton Report noted that:

People who live within 500 m of accessible green space are 24 per cent more likely to meet recommended levels of physical activity, while reducing the numbers of sedentary individuals in the population by just 1 per cent could reduce morbidity and mortality rates valued at £1.44 billion for the UK.[18]

Feeling a connection with nature has been shown to correlate significantly with a sense of satisfaction, meaning and purpose in life. A 2019 survey by the University of Exeter Medical School found that spending just two hours a week in natural surroundings significantly improved health and wellbeing. Of the twenty thousand people interviewed, a quarter of those who spent little or no time in nature reported poor health, and almost half felt dissatisfied with their lives. In contrast, only one in seven of those who spent at least two hours in nature said their health was poor, while just a third felt unsatisfied by life. Furthermore, the benefits appeared to be the same for both young and old, poor and rich, and those living in urban and rural areas.[19]

'A culture,' wrote W. H. Auden, 'is no better than its woods.' The surviving parts of the North Wood are not only a natural asset but a historical and cultural one. Between Lambeth Palace on the bank of the Thames and Whitgift's Hospital in central Croydon, there are no buildings more than four hundred years old except for the chapel of Alleyn's college in Dulwich, which dates from 1619, though it was much altered by the Victorians. Sculpted by human activity over more than a thousand years, the woods are the oldest fixed artefact we have in this part of South London. From the Norman Conquest to the climate crisis, they have been shaped by, and have played a part in shaping, the events of local, national and world history. They have been a material and economic resource that powered the expansion of the city into a global metropolis, and a bone of contention between monarchs and churchmen, lords and commoners. They have attracted poets and painters, ornithologists and butterfly collectors; and, in the course of the centuries, they have reflected our changing attitudes to the way we treat the land and interact with the natural environment.

They are also the city's lungs, and thanks to their survival, generations of Londoners young and old have the opportunity to reconnect with the natural world within five miles of the West End, with all the benefits – physical, mental and cultural – that brings. Step into any of these woods and, as the traffic noise gives way to the chaffinch's warble, the staccato drumming of the great spotted woodpecker and the eerie yaffle of its green cousin, you leave the city behind, breathe cleaner air, forget your everyday concerns, and feel your spirit lift. Volunteer, and you will find camaraderie, undertake invigorating physical work, acquire satisfying new skills, learn to identify many species, and come to notice and understand the complex and interconnected life forms around you. Over the course of a year, you will observe the cycle of the seasons, muted to a meteorological inconvenience in our urban lives, but nowhere more richly evident than in a wood.

In the green haze of early spring, the wood anemone, ramsons and sweet woodruff flower before the tree canopy can close out light and rainfall, and bluebells swathe the woodland floor like a ground-hugging mist. The hazels are bedecked with catkins. The first butterflies, overwintering species such as comma and brimstone, emerge from hibernation and open their wings to the thin sunlight. By late April or May, the hawthorns are effervescent with creamy, champagne-foam blossom.

In the heat of summer, more shade-tolerant flowers such as enchanter's nightshade, herb-Robert and lesser celandine line the woodland rides, while the sunlit glades and clearings hum with bumblebees and flicker with butterflies: speckled wood, large, small and green-veined white, orange tip, gatekeeper, ringlet, silver-washed fritillary . . . Dragonflies dart above the ponds in Sydenham Hill Wood – southern hawkers, their long, slim abdomens a zigzag mosaic of Day-Glo blue and green, oxblood-red darters, and huge, cobalt-blue emperors – while hobbies sweep overhead to catch them on the wing.

In the rustling autumn, the hornbeam leaves turn lemon-yellow, the oaks russet-brown, while falling acorns patter like hailstones on the woodland floor. The fruit of the hawthorn and guelder-rose splash bright drops of scarlet against this sepia backdrop, plump sloes hang on the blackthorn, and the damp air grows rich with the musty scent of decaying wood and the fruiting bodies of fungi: puffballs, earthstars, trooping funnel, shaggy inkcaps, brittlestem, oysterlings, sulphur tufts, turkeytail, hairy curtain crust, chicken of the woods, beefsteak fungus, jelly ear, Alfred's cakes, candlesnuff, dead man's fingers . . .

Then comes the equinox, which Edward Alleyn's father-in-law John Donne called 'the year's midnight, and . . . the day's'. In the monochrome of winter, branches stand out black against silver frost, revealing the architecture of the trees, except where yew and holly cast dark green shade, and here and there a cluster of brown, marcescent leaves clings to an oak. The frozen ground is iron-hard and icy puddles crackle underfoot. Tiny, scarlet-quiffed firecrests dart in and out of the yew and ivy, while redwings and fieldfares, winter migrants from Scandinavia, forage for berries. Then, in February, as the yews dust the ground with yellow pollen, snowdrops push their way up through the hoar frost, white blossom bursts from the spiny twigs of the blackthorn – and the cycle of life begins anew.

A fallen oak returns to the soil that nourished
it in Sydenham Hill Wood.

ACKNOWLEDGEMENTS

First, thanks to my wife, Geraldine Beattie, my first and most perceptive reader, for her literary insight and research skills; to my agent, Tom Cull, for his energy and belief in the project; to Robert Davidson, my editor at Sandstone Press, and to all of his superb team; to Daniel Benneworth-Gray for the beautiful cover art, to Georgina Coles for proofreading, and to Roger Smith for the index. Special thanks are due to Rachel Lichtenstein for her richly evocative preface to this book.

A work of this nature inevitably draws on a wide range of expertise and experience, from the muddy boots of practical ecologists to the acid-free storage boxes of historical archivists.

At the London Wildlife Trust, I would like to thank Daniel Greenwood, Reserve Officer at Sydenham Hill Wood from 2012 to 2018, who has also contributed some fine photographs to this book, and his successors Rachel Dowse and Sam Taylor; Mathew Frith, the Trust's Ecological Director; Edwin Malins, its Nature Reserves Manager; Sam Bentley-Toon, Chantelle Lindsay and Andrew Wright of the Great North Wood Project; and Sylvia Myers and Jo Wright at the Centre for Wildlife Gardening in Peckham.

Thanks also to Amanda Tuke, of the Sydenham Hill Wood Steering Group, and to Tiffany Francis Baker, Ruth Bradshaw,

Ann Daniels, Richard Grimshaw, Daniel Harwood, Pennie Hedge, Kate Lake, Philip Melville, Emma Pooley, Christina Sharp, Ernest Thomason, Brian Whittle and all the other volunteers with whom I have shared many happy and restorative days in the woods.

Across the other Great North Wood reserves, I would like to thank Anna-Maria Cahalane and Nicholas MacGuinness at the Fourth Reserve Foundation; Vicky Bruce of the Friends of Biggin Wood; and Sandy Pepperell of the Friends of One Tree Hill.

I am particularly grateful for the generous assistance of Calista Lucy, Keeper of the Archive, and Sharon O'Connor, Archivist, at Dulwich College; to Lindsay Ould and Rosie Vizor at the Museum of Croydon; Judy Aitken at Southwark Archives; the staff of Lambeth Palace Library, the National Archives at Kew, London Metropolitan Archives, the British Library, the Bodleian Library, Oxford, Wandsworth Heritage Service, Minet Library, Lambeth, and, as always, the London Library, where the Topography stacks are a marvel of serendipitous discovery.

I have been fortunate that this corner of south London can boast an unusual wealth of talented local historians, and I am indebted to the work and advice of Bernard Nurse, Brian Green and Patrick Darby of the Dulwich Society, while Steve Grindlay's local history blog for the Sydenham Society (http://sydenhamforesthillhistory.blogspot.com) is a mine of well-researched information.

Any remaining errors are of course my own.

A WOODLAND GLOSSARY

Agistment: the right to graze livestock in a forest or woodland.

Ancient woodland: a site that has been continuously wooded since before 1600.

Assart: a former wood that has been grubbed *(qv)* to create arable fields or pasture.

Bavin, babbin: a bundle of brushwood used for fuel. The produce of the North Wood included bakers' bavins and potters' bavins. 'A bavin giveth a goodly blaze . . . but is soone out.' (Henry Crosse, *Vertues Common-wealth*, 1603)

Billhook, bill or handbill: A heavy, curved blade with a wooden handle, used for lopping branches and cutting underwood. Each area had its own pattern. 'When afternoon came he returned, took a billhook from the woodman's shed, and with a ladder climbed into the lower

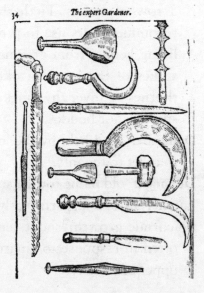

A selection of billhooks and other pruning tools, from the anonymous book *The Expert Gardener*, London, 1640.

part of the tree, where he began lopping off – "shrouding," as they called it at Hintock – the lowest boughs.' (Thomas Hardy, *The Woodlanders*, 1887)

Bolling (pronounced 'bowling'): the permanent stump of a pollarded tree.

Brash (verb): to remove the side branches of a tree.

Brash (noun): material so removed.

Brush, brushwood: small growth cleared before planting trees.

Cambium: the outermost ring of a tree's sapwood; the growing layer, replaced each year by a new ring.

Canhoop: a split sapling of hazel, chestnut or ash for use as a barrel-hoop; usually prepared in the woods.

Coppice (verb): to cut a tree just above ground level to encourage multiple shoots to grow from the stump, or coppice stool. These poles are then harvested at intervals of five to twenty years.

Coppice, copse (noun): an area, often marked off by hedges or ditches, of coppiced trees to be cut at the same time. Coppices are generally harvested in rotation.

Covert: a wood with both thickets and closed canopy.

Dead hedge: barrier created by placing cut brushwood between a row of stakes. Fitzherbert's *Boke of Husbandry* (1534) recommends its use to protect a newly planted quickset, or living hedge, from grazing animals: 'Thou muste gette the stakes of the harte of oke . . . and lay thy small trouse or thornes . . . over thy quickesettes, that shepe do not eate the sprynge nor buddes.'

Demesne: land held by the lord of a manor for himself, rather than let to tenants.

Durmast: old name for the sessile oak, *Quercus petraea*.

Earther: a sapling, particularly for hedging. Also known as a whip.

Epicormic growth: shoots emerging from the trunk of a tree, often in response to environmental stress or damage to the upper branches.

Estover: the right to gather firewood in a forest or woodland. 'Both he and his father and divers others did here fell and fetche their fuell as tenantes to the Archbishop of Canterbury.' (Testimony of Nicholas Jackson, yeoman of Croydon, in *Ridon v. Gouldwell, Snowe and Dawes*, 1578)

Faggot: a bundle of sticks tied together, usually for firewood. 'Faggots, ought to be a full yard in length, and two foot in circumference, made round, and not flat; for so they contain less fuel . . .' (John Evelyn, *Sylva*, 1664)

Farm, farmer: for much of the period covered in this book, 'to farm' did not mean to cultivate the land, but to lease out, or hold on a lease. A King's or Queen's farmer leased land directly from the Crown, and was responsible for collecting rents on its behalf. They had no landlord above them except the monarch, and could bequeath the tenancy to their descendants. The usage survives in the modern expression to 'farm out'.

Ghost hedge: a hedge created by leaving pre-existing trees and bushes standing to mark a boundary after an area of woodland is cleared for arable or pasture (*see* assart).

Grub, grub up: to clear-fell a wood and dig out the roots to prepare the land for arable or pasture use.

Herbage, herb layer: low-growing, non-woody plants, including wildflowers, grasses and ferns.

Hethers, heathers: stems of wood woven together at the top of a hedge to hold the pleachers in place.

Marcescence: the retention of dead, dry leaves by a tree during winter, often occurring in oak or beech.

Mastage: *see* pannage.

Pannage: the practice of releasing pigs into the woods in autumn to forage for acorns or beech mast. 'Go gather up mast/ er time be past/ Mast fats up swine/ mast kils up kine.' (Thomas Tusser, *Five Hundred Pointes of Good Husbandrie*, 1580)

Perch: one 40th of a rood, or one 160th of an acre.

Pimp: similar to a bavin, but made up of smaller twigs. 'Those small light Bavins, which are used in Taverns in London to light their Faggots, and are called in the Taverns a Brush, and by the Wood-men Pimps.' (Daniel Defoe, *A Tour Thro' the Whole Island of Great Britain*, 1724–27)

Pleach, plash: to cut most of the way through a sapling, leaving the cambium intact, in order to bend it to a more horizontal position and weave it together with other pleached saplings to form a living hedge. 'When your hedge is now of near six years stature, plash it about February or October; but this is the work of a very dextrous and skilful husbandman.' (John Evelyn, *Sylva*, 1664)

Pleachers: stems treated in the above way to form a hedge.

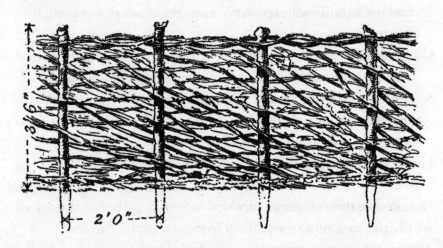

A pleached hedge, using stakes for reinforcement,
from A. Vernon, *Estate Fences*, London, 1899.

Pollard (verb): to cut a tree in a manner similar to coppicing, but at a height of eight to ten feet to prevent the young shoots being eaten by grazing animals.

Pollard (noun): a tree that has been thus treated.

Primary woodland: woods of natural origin that have never been cleared.

Quickset: a hedge created by planting live whips or cuttings directly into the soil. 'The rows of beech look very well indeed, and so does the young quickset hedge in the garden.' (Jane Austen, in a letter to her sister Cassandra, May 1811)

Ride: a track through the woods.

Rood: one quarter of an acre.

Runt: a small tree left standing as seed stock after the larger ones in a wood are felled for timber.

Samara: the green, papery winged case that carries the seeds of a hornbeam, ash, maple or elm.

Saproxylic (adj.): species, especially insects, dependent on decaying wood for their habitat and food.

Secondary woodland: woods of recent growth on a site that was previously unwooded, or had been cleared of trees.

Shred (noun): a tree that has had its lower branches lopped off for firewood or browse.

Sned (verb): to trim off the side branches and twigs from a tree or coppice pole, usually with a billhook. The material removed is known as brash *(see above)*.

Spring (noun): synonym for coppice.

Standard, stadle: an uncoppiced tree, allowed to grow to its full height to provide larger timber.

Stool: the base of a tree felled to produce coppice poles.

Tellar: a sapling or selected coppice shoot left to grow into a timber tree when the underwood is cleared.

Terrier: a survey or register of landed property, from the French *registre terrier* (the breed of dog, incidentally, gets its name from *chien terrier*, or land dog).

Underwood: coppice poles, harvested at intervals of around ten years. 'The low trees that grow among the timber.' (Samuel Johnson, *A Dictionary of the English Language*, 1755)

Veteran tree: an old tree with significant dead wood, loose bark, scars, holes and/or a hollow trunk, providing a habitat for bats, birds, saproxylic insects and fungi.

Waver: a young tree left standing when the rest of a wood is felled.

Whip: a transplanted sapling under about three foot high.

Withe, withy: a strong, flexible shoot, especially of willow, used for binding.

Woodreeve: the manager of an area of woodland. Also known as a woodward, woodman or wood-keeper.

Yeoman: a free person cultivating their own land, either freehold or leasehold.

NOTES

INTRODUCTION

1. Simard, 1997; Wohlleben, 2016
2. *London Review of Books* 29 (23), 29 November 2007

CHAPTER 1: TAMING THE WILDWOOD

1. Rackham, 1976
2. Anderson, 1898
3. Newman, 2016
4. *Fell Road, Croydon: Archaeological desk-based assessment.* MOL Archaeology 2009.
5. Blair, 1991
6. Rackham, 2010
7. Scragg, 2008
8. Gover et al., 1934
9. Meekings & Crook, 1979
10. Dulwich College Archive, MS XVIII, f.16
11. Dulwich College Archive, MUN 315
12. Gover et al., 1934
13. Birch, 1885
14. Lysons, 1811; Maldon 1912

15. Lysons, 1811; Hasted, 1797

16. 'Brixton: The manor of Heathrow, Milkwood and Wickwood', in *Survey of London: Volume 26, Lambeth: Southern Area*, ed. F. H. W. Sheppard (London, 1956), pp. 136-139. *British History Online* http://www.british-history.ac.uk/survey-london/vol26/pp136-139 [accessed 28 July 2018]

17. Gover et al., 1934

18. Rochester Cathedral Library, MS A.3.5 'Textus Roffensis'

19. 'Close Rolls, Edward III: September 1359', in *Calendar of Close Rolls, Edward III: Volume 10, 1354-1360*, ed. H. C. Maxwell Lyte (London, 1908), pp. 641-645. *British History Online* http://www.british-history.ac.uk/cal-close-rolls/edw3/vol10/pp641-645 [accessed 27 October 2018]

20. 'Close Rolls, Edward III: November 1367', in *Calendar of Close Rolls, Edward III: Volume 12, 1364-1369*, ed. H. C. Maxwell Lyte (London, 1910), pp. 396–402. *British History Online* http://www.british-history.ac.uk/cal-close-rolls/edw3/vol12/pp396–402 [accessed 27 October 2018]

21. Thomson, 1829; Magraw & Thomure, 2017; 'The Forest Charter of 1225' https://www.bl.uk/collection-items/the-forest-charter-of-1225#:~:text=On%2011%20February%20 1225%2C%20at,one%20of%20three%20surviving%20originals. [accessed 17 September 2020]; Carpenter, David, 'Revival and Survival: Reissuing Magna Carta https://www.bl.uk/magna-carta/articles/revival-and-survival-reissuing-magna-carta [accessed 17 September 2020]

22. Paget, 1929

23. Dolley, 1953

24. https://www.getsurrey.co.uk/news/local-news/coin-find-is-treasure-4833094 [accessed 8 September 2019]

25. Coles & Coles, 1986

26. Knight, 2009

27. Brigham et al., 2000

28. Rackham, 1976

29. Pryor, 2019

30. Collis, 1983

31. Brooks & Agate, 1998

32. 'Memorials: 1368', in *Memorials of London and London Life in the 13th, 14th and 15th Centuries,* ed. H. T. Riley (London, 1868), pp. 335–336. British History Online http://www.british-history.ac.uk/no-series/memorials-london-life/pp335–336 [accessed 26 October 2018]

33. Croydon Museum, F570(333)PAG, f.68

34. Steinman, 1833

35. Ducarel, 1783

36. Lambeth Palace Library, MSS 275

37. Rackham, 1976

CHAPTER 2: SHIPS, SURVEYS AND STATUTES

1. Museum of Croydon, FS570(333)PAG, f.11–14

2. Museum of Croydon, FS570(333)PAG, f.117

3. National Archives, E 134/20Eliz/East7

4. Bodleian Library, MS Tanner 127, f.60

5. Foxe, 1583

6. 35 Henry VIII, c.17

7. Young, 1889

8. Bickley, 1889

9. Blanch, 1875

10. 'Myatt's Fields, Denmark Hill and Herne Hill: Introduction and Myatt's Fields area', in *Survey of London: Volume 26, Lambeth: Southern Area,* ed. F. H. W. Sheppard (London, 1956), pp. 141-145. British History Online http://www.british-history.ac.uk/survey-london/vol26/pp141-145 [accessed 28 July 2018]

11. National Archives, E 134/20Eliz/East9

12. Royden, 1923

13. 'Lambeth: The parish', in *A History of the County of Surrey: Volume 4,* ed. H. E. Malden (London, 1912), pp. 50-64. British

History Online http://www.british-history.ac.uk/vch/surrey/vol4/pp50-64 [accessed 2 June 2018]

14. National Archives, STAC 4/7/6
15. Drew, 1940
16. National Archives, E133/3/464B
17. National Archives, PROB-11-50-335
18. National Archives, E 133/1/132
19. Exch. K. R., Bills E: Answers, Eliz., Surrey, 5.
20. https://www.historyofparliamentonline.org/volume/1558-1603/member/holcroft-thomas-i-1591 [accessed 14 August 2020]
21. National Archives, PROB-11-50-335
22. National Archives, E123/6 f. 230.
23. National Archives, E123/6, f. 275
24. Bodleian Library, MS Tanner 127, f.60
25. Drew, 1941
26. Bickley, 1903
27. Leman, 1856
28. 1 Elizabeth I, c.15
29. 27 Elizabeth I, c.19
30. *By the King. A Proclamation for Preservation of Woods.* [14 Feb. 1609.] British Library, General Reference Collection C.112.h.1 (99)
31. Standish, 1513
32. 24 Henry VIII, c.10
33. 8 Elizabeth I, c.15
34. London Metropolitan Archives, P73/GIS/057
35. Standish, 1613
36. National Archives, MPB 1/18
37. Rackham, 1976
38. Coulter, 1999
39. Curnow et al., 1905; Wilson, 2016; Neville, 1987

CHAPTER 3: THE WORLD TURNED UPSIDE DOWN

1. Norden, 1607

2. Weston, 1742

3. Estienne, 1616

4. Pluymers, 2011

5. Lyne, R. (2004, September 23). 'Googe, Barnabe (1540–1594), poet and translastor'. *Oxford Dictionary of National Biography.* https://www-oxforddnb-com.ezproxy2.londonlibrary.co.uk/view/10.1093/ref:odnb/9780198614128.001.0001/odnb-9780198614128-e-11004 [accessed 23 November 2019]

6. National Archives, LR2/197 f.116v

7. British Library, Maps 188.k.3.(4.). This copy was made in 1768, but appears to be an exact reproduction of a lost original.

8. Lambeth Palace Library, T1

9. Mar, 1678, Bainbridge, 1800

10. Aubrey, 1982

11. Young, 1889

12. Dulwich College Archive, MS IX, 32r

13. Blanch, 1877

14. Young, 1889

15. Dulwich College Archive, MS VI, f.86

16. Dulwich College Archive, Second Series, LXVI

17. Blanch, 1877

18. Dulwich College Archive, MS XXI

19. Dulwich College Archive, MUN 273

20. Dulwich College Archive, MUN 38

21. Dulwich College Archive, MUN 592, 593

22. Dulwich College Archive, MUN 276

23. Dulwich College Archive, MUN 277

24. Dulwich College Archive, MUN 278

25. Dulwich College Archive, MUN 273–321

26. Close Roll, 12 James I., part 1, n° 2

27. London Metropolitan Archives, CLC/L/HA/H/003

28. Edward Walford, 'Peckham and Dulwich', in *Old and New London: Volume 6* (London, 1878), pp. 286–303. British History Online http://www.british-history.ac.uk/old-new-london/vol6/pp286-303 [accessed 28 July 2018]

29. Paget, 1929

30. O'Riordan, 1993; Coates, 2016

31. Young, 1889; Bickley, 1903.

32. https://www.british-history.ac.uk/no-series/acts-ordinances-interregnum [accessed 21 August 2020]

33. Dulwich College Archives, MUN 27

34. Blanch, 1877

35. Dulwich College Archive, MUN 279

36. Dulwich College Archive, MUN 282

37. Dulwich College Archive, MUN 285

38. Boyd's *Inhabitants of London;* National Archives, PROB 11/255/32

39. Dulwich College Archive, MUN 287–291

40. Dulwich College Archive, MUN 292– 294

41. Dulwich College Archive, MUN 297 et seq.

42. Steinman, 1833

43. Lambeth Palace Library, Comm. XIIa 23 f.66

44. Brereton, 1844

45. Steinman, 1833; Neville, 1987

46. Lambeth Palace Library, T1

47. Defoe, 2003

48. Steinman, 1833

49. Dulwich College Archive, MS VI, f.86

50. Dulwich College Archive, MUN 11

51. Dulwich College Archive, MUN 11

52. Dulwich College Archive, MUN 17

53. Dulwich College Archive, MS VI, f. 125-126

54. Eden, 1975–6

55. British Library, Maps. Crace I

56. Museum of Croydon, GB-352-ar68

57. Shower, 1735
58. Dulwich College Archive, Second Series, LXVIII
59. Aubrey, 1719

CHAPTER 4: FAITH OR SCIENCE?

1. Defoe, 1704
2. Evelyn, 1908
3. Evelyn, 1706. This fourth edition alters the spelling of the title from *Sylva* to *Silva*.
4. Evelyn, 1908
5. Defoe, 1986
6. http://londongardensonline.org.uk/gardens-online-record.php?ID=SOU019 [accessed 28 July 2018]
7. Lysons, 1811
8. Martyn, 1763
9. Martyn, 1763
10. Curtis, 1777–98
11. Martyn, 1792
12. Lambeth Palace Library, TS12, ff. 22–23, 29–30, 36, 42, 56, 65–66, 71–72, 80–81, 89–90, 98–99, 107
13. Lambeth Palace Library, TA638/1

CHAPTER 5: INDUSTRY AND ENCLOSURE

1. Darby, 1966
2. Dulwich College Archive, Second Series, LXV
3. Neville, 1987
4. Dulwich College Archive, Second Series, LXVI
5. Roy, 1790
6. Harley, 1966
7. Lindley & Crosley, 1793
8. Adams, 1979
9. Adams, 1797

10. Coulter, 1999
11. Bull, 1956
12. Dulwich College Archive, Second Series, LXVI
13. Dulwich College Archive, Second Series, XXIX
14. Coulson, 1999
15. Anderson, 1898
16. *The Times*, 26 October 1792
17. Coulter, 1996
18. http://www.grangewoodpark.co.uk/history-of-the-park [accessed 12 March 2018]
19. Young, 1889
20. Anderson, 1898
21. Adeane, 1889
22. Mill, 1982
23. Anderson, 1898
24. Griffin, 2004
25. *Friends of West Norwood Cemetery Newsletter*, September 2005
26. Hughson, 1805
27. Rennie, 1833
28. *Morning Post*, 16 February 1831
29. Gilchrist, 1906
30. Butlin, 2005
31. Bell, 1870
32. Beattie, 1855
33. Sharp, 1897
34. Ruskin, 1886
35. Snow, 1842
36. Anderson, 1898
37. *The Times*, 31 December 1802
38. *Literary Chronicle*, 1824
39. *The Times*, 25 February 1803
40. *The Times*, 22 August 1817
41. *The Times*, 4 November 1836

42. Phillips, 1912
43. Saward, 1907
44. *Sunday Times*, 14 October 1849
45. https://www.oldbaileyonline.org/browse.jsp?id=t18491029-2044-punishment-177&div=t18491029-2044&terms=Stephen_Alfred_jordan#highlight [accessed 2 February 2018]
46. Dulwich College Archive, Second Series LXXI
47. *Morning Advertiser*, 23 March 1857
48. *The Times*, 22 October 1859
49. Cooper, 1836
50. Stephens, 1828–32
51. Wood, 1839
52. *The Zoologist*, Vol. 4, 1845
53. Miller, 1860
54. *Household Words*, Vol II, 1850/1, p. 148

CHAPTER 6: THE PALACE AND THE RAILWAY

1. Ruskin, 1886
2. *Norwood News and Crystal Palace Chronicle*, 16 May 1874
3. Dulwich College Archive, box 482
4. McNiven, 1988
5. Blanch, 1875
6. Plan of the Manor & Estates of Alleyn's College, Dulwich, 1860
7. Dulwich College Archive, Governors' Minutes, Vol. 2, 1860
8. Dulwich College Archive, Governors' Minutes, Vol. 2, 1860
9. Gale, 2011
10. Dulwich College Archive, Governors' Minutes, Vol. 4, 1862
11. *Croydon Times*, 26 November 1864
12. Dulwich College Archive, Governors' Minutes, Vol. 4, 1862
13. Dulwich College Archive, Governors' Minutes, Vol. 11, 1868
14. Dulwich College Archive, Governors' Minutes, Vol. 10, 1867
15. Dulwich College Archive, Governors' Minutes, Vol. 13, 1870

16. Plan of the Manor & Estates of Alleyn's College, 1876

17. *South Eastern Gazette*, 23 February 1847

18. *Croydon Chronicle and East Surrey Advertiser*, 8 December 1855

19. *Lambeth and Southwark Advertiser*, 20 September 1856

20. Dulwich College Archive, Governors' Minutes, Vol. 4, 1862

21. Ruskin, 1871

22. Newman, 2016

23. Dulwich College Archive, Governors' Minutes, 9 June 1887

24. Dulwich College Archive, Governors' Minutes, 8 March 1888

25. Dulwich College Archive, Governors' Minutes, 10 April 1890

26. Dulwich College Archive, Governors' Minutes, 14 & 28 March & 9 May 1895

27. *South London Press*, 28 September 1895

28. Advertisement in the *Croydon Guardian,* 30 October 1886

29. Webb, 1891

30. Maurice, 1913

31. Hill, 'More Air For London'. *The Nineteenth Century*, February 1888

32. Johnston, 1885

33. Brabazon, 1901; Sturzaker & Mell, 2017

34. Thomas, 1964

35. http://www.grangewoodpark.co.uk/history-of-the-park/ [accessed 12 March 2018]

36. Brennand, 1994; Green, 2012

37. *South London Press*, 28 Sept 1895; 9 Nov 1895; 1 July 1899

38. Nisbet, 1905

CHAPTER 7: THE HOME FRONT

1. Power, 1910

2. Green, 2012

3. Dulwich College Archive, Board Minutes, 26 November 1908

4. Watt, 1919; Rackham, 2010

5. Power, 1910
6. Dulwich College Archive, Executive and Finance Committee Report, 10 Sept 1914
7. Dulwich College Archive, Executive and Finance Committee Report, 12 Sept 1919
8. Rawlinson, 1923
9. Storey, 2015
10. Gale, 2011
11. Dulwich College Archive, Board Minutes, 20 December 1917
12. http://www.auto-history.tv/monthly/archives/motoringinbritain1930s [accessed 26 May 2018]
13. Johnson, 1924
14. Martin, 1923
15. Griffin, 2004
16. Cocksedge, 1933
17. Swayne, 1934
18. Griffin, 2004
19. Logue & Conradi, 2010
20. Bousfield, 2014
21. https://www.dulwichsociety.com/local-history/379-the-wardens-post [accessed 23 September 2020]
22. https://www.dulwichsociety.com/newsletters/41-autumn-2006/245-home-guard [accessed 6 April 2018]
23. Gale, 2011
24. Logue & Conradi, 2018
25. https://www.dulwichsociety.com/local-history/379-the-wardens-post [accessed 23 September 2020]
26. Morgan & Glue, 1981
27. Self, 2014
28. *Lewisham Mercury*, 27 July 2011
29. *Croydon Guardian*, 2 June 2016
30. *Bromley Times*, 20 June 2017

CHAPTER 8: A DESIGN FOR LIVING

1. Robinson & Sutherland, 2002
2. Laybourn-Langton, Rankin & Baxter, 2019
3. Forshaw & Abercrombie, 1943
4. Abercrombie, 1944
5. Forshaw & Abercrombie, 1943
6. Logue & Conradi, 2018
7. Gale, 2011
8. https://www.dulwichsociety.com/2017-autumn/1535-fore-warned-is-forearmed-the-story-of-dulwich-s-nuclear-bunker-by-robert-worley [accessed 19 August 2020]
9. https://www.youtube.com/watch?v=nMcyogqF7lY [accessed 19 August 2020]
10. Oliver, 2003
11. Lousley, 1959
12. Lousley, 1960
13. *The Times*, 2 August 1966

CHAPTER 9: SAVE THE WOODS!

1. *Dulwich Society Newsletter*, April 1975, July 1975
2. *Dulwich Society Newsletter*, July 1976
3. *Dulwich Society Newsletter*, April 1979
4. Frith, 2012
5. *The Times*, 4 Decemeber 1984
6. *New Scientist*, 17 September 1987
7. *Hansard*, 8 February 1985
8. *Evening Standard*, 20 December 1984
9. *The Times*, 2 February 1985
10. *Dulwich Society Newsletter*, October 1985
11. *Dulwich Society Newsletter*, October 1985
12. Humboldt, 1848
13. Ruskin, 1884

14. Hulme, 2016

15. https://www.croydon.gov.uk/sites/default/files/articles/
downloads/beaulieu-heights-history.pdf [accessed 5 August
2018]

16. Griffin, 2004

17. *Dulwich Society Newsletter,* Summer 1988

18. *The Times,* 11 February 1988

19. *Dulwich Society Newsletter,* Winter 1988/89

20. *Dulwich Society Newsletter,* Summer 1989

21. *Dulwich Society Newsletter,* Winter 1989/90

22. *Dulwich Society Newsletter,* Spring 1992

23. *Dulwich Society Newsletter,* Spring 1992

24. Frith, 1999

CHAPTER 10: A NEW MILLENNIUM

1. Jones, 2002

2. Graham-Brown, 2006

3. Cirimele & Gallagher, 2005

4. https://www.croydon.gov.uk/sites/default/files/articles/down-
loads/6.2_Priory_School.pdf [accessed 9 September 2019]

5. https://www.croydon.gov.uk/sites/default/files/articles/
downloads/6.6-Virgo-Fidelis-Convent-School.pdf [accessed 9
September 2019]; *Sutton & Croydon Guardian,* 31 July 2012

CHAPTER 11: A TOUR OF THE WOODS TODAY

1. *Thornton Heath Chronicle,* 13 February 2020

2. https://www.newsshopper.co.uk/news/19028811.save-oaks-
southwark-will-not-fell-sydenham-hill-wood-trees [accessed 4
March 2021]

3. www.lewisham.gov.uk/myservices/planning/policy/LDF/
evidence-base/Pages/LDF-evidence-base-environment.aspx
[accessed 15 February 2019]

4. www.gigl.org.uk/online/site-Details.aspx?sID=So-BI03&sType=sinc [accessed 6 June 2018]
5. *The Times*, 20 February 2016

CHAPTER 12: WAYS THROUGH THE WOODS

1. Lawton et al., 2010
2. https://www.gigl.org.uk/keyfigures/#:~:text=How%20much%20of%20London%20is%20garden%20land%3F,domestic%20garden%20land%20(4). [accessed 12 December 2020]
3. Laybourn-Langton, Rankin & Baxter, 2019
4. Sánchez-Bayo & Wyckhuys, 2019, pp 8–27
5. www.ipbes.net/sites/default/files/downloads/summary_for_policymakers_ipbes_global_assessment.pdf [accessed 6 May 2019]
6. https://www.woodlandtrust.org.uk/trees-woods-and-wildlife/british-trees/how-trees-fight-climate-change [accessed 14 November 2020]
7. Spencer & Kirby, 1992.
8. https://assets.publishing.service.gov.uk/government/uploads/system/uploads/attachment_data/file/833726/landscapes-review-final-report.pdf [accessed 29 December 2020]
9. *Daily Telegraph,* 29 June 2020
10. See also Richard Smyth, 'Nature writing's fascist roots'. *New Statesman*, 3 April 2019. www.newstatesman.com/culture/books/2019/04/eco-facism-nature-writing-nazi-far-right-nostalgia-england [accessed 14 June 2019]
11. https://www.heritagefund.org.uk/blogs/black-and-brown-faces-green-spaces [accessed 4 Jan 2021]
12. London Borough of Lambeth Demography Factsheet 2017
13. London Borough of Croydon Annual Public Health Report, 2017
14. London Borough of Southwark Joint Strategic Needs Assessment Factsheet 2018

15. https://www.wildlondon.org.uk/equality-diversity and-inclusion [accessed 4 January 2021]
16. https://www.gov.uk/government/news/build-build-build-prime-minister-announces-new-deal-for-britain [accessed 5 January 2021]
17. *The Guardian*, 10 July 2020
18. https://www.ippr.org/research/publications/we-are-not-ready [accessed 26 July 2020]
19. https://www.globalcitizen.org/en/content/jacinda-ardern-goalkeepers-unga-2019/ [accessed 1 July 2020]
20. Lawton et al., 2010
21. *The Guardian*, 13 June 2019

BIBLIOGRAPHY

Abbott, Peter. *The Book of Penge, Anerley and Crystal Palace: The Community, Past Present and Future*. Wellington: Halsgrove, 2002.

Abercrombie, Patrick. *Greater London Plan*. London: University of London Press, 1944.

Adams, George. *Geometrical and Graphical Essays*. London: J. Dillon, 1797.

Adams, Ian H. (ed.). *Peter May, Land Surveyor 1749–1793*. Edinburgh: Scottish History Society, 1979.

Adeane, Jane Henrietta (ed.). *The Early Married Life of Maria Josepha, Lady Stanley: With Extracts from Sir John Stanley's 'Praeterita'*. London: Longman, Green, 1899.

Aldridge, W. *A Gossip on the Wild Birds of Norwood and Crystal Palace District*. Upper Norwood: Burdett, 1885.

Allen, Thomas. *History and Antiquities of the Parish of Lambeth*. London: J. Allen, 1826.

Anderson, Douglas. 'Noyfull Fowles and Vermyn: Parish Payments for Killing Wildlife in Hampshire 1533–1863'. *Proceedings of the Hampshire Field Club and Archaeological Society 60*, 2005, pp. 209–228.

Anderson, J. Corbet. *A Short Chronicle Concerning the Parish of Croydon*. London: Ballantine Press, 1882.

———— *Plan and Award of the Commissioners appointed to Inclose the Commons of Croydon*. Croydon: Printed for the Subscribers, 1889.

———— *The Great North Wood: With a Geological, Topographical and Historical Description of Upper, West and South Norwood*. London: Blades, East & Blades, 1898.

Aubrey, John. *Brief Lives*, ed. Richard Barber. Woodbridge: Boydell, 1982.

———— *The Natural History and Antiquities of the County of Surrey*. London: E. Curll, 1719.

Beasley, John. *Southwark Remembered*. Stroud: Tempus Publishing, 2001.

Beattie, William. *Life and Letters of Thomas Campbell*. New York: Harper, 1855.

Bell, Charles. *Letters of Sir Charles Bell: Selected from his Correspondence with his Brother George Joseph Bell*. London: John Murray, 1870.

Bickley, Francis B. *Catalogue of the Manuscripts and Muniments of the College of God's Gift at Dulwich*. Second series. Dulwich: The Governors, 1903.

Blair, J. *Early Medieval Surrey: Landholding, Church and Settlement Before 1300*. Stroud: Alan Sutton, 1991.

Blanch, William Harnett. *Ye Parish of Camerwell: its History and Antiquities*, London: E. W. Allen, 1875.

————*Dulwich College and Edward Alleyn: A Short History of the Foundation of God's Gift College at Dulwich. Together with a Memoir of the Founder*. London: E. W. Allen, 1877.

Bousfield, M. (ed.). *Dulwich LVD Log-Book 1940–1941*. London: Olympia, 2014.

Brabazon, Reginald. 'The Green Girdle Round London'. *The Sphere*, 20 July 1901.

Brayne, Martin. *The Greatest Storm*. Stroud: Alan Sutton, 2002.

Brennand, Tom. *Dulwich & Sydenham Hill: The Centenary History of a Golf Club, 1894–1994*. London: Dulwich & Sydenham Hill Golf Club, 1994.

Brereton, William. *Travels in Holland, the United Provinces, England, Scotland, and Ireland, M.DC.XXXIV.M.DC.XXXV*, ed. Edward Hawkins. London: Chetham Society, 1844.

Brigham, Trevor, et al. *The Archaeology of Greater London: An Assessment of Archaeological Evidence for Human Presence in the Area Now Covered by Greater London*. London: Museum of London, 2000.

Brooks, Alan, and Elizabeth Agate. *Hedging: A Practical Handbook*. Wallingford: The Conservation Volunteers, 1998.

Bull, G. B. G. 'Thomas Milne's Land Utilization Map of the London Area in 1800'. *Geographical Journal* 122 (1), March 1956, pp. 25–30.

Butlin, Martin (ed.). *Samuel Palmer: The Sketchbook of 1824*. London: Thames & Hudson, 2005.

Castle, Ian. *The First Blitz: Bombing London in the First World War*. Oxford: Osprey, 2015.

Cheesman, Beryl D. *Treetops and Terraces: A Bygone Era of New Town, Upper Norwood SE19*. Surrey: Theban Publishing, 1991.

Coates, Ben. *The Impact of the English Civil War on the Economy of London, 1642–50*. Abingdon: Routledge, 2016.

Cocksedge, W. C. 'The Great North Wood'. *London Naturalist* 12, 1933.

Coles, John, and Bryony Coles. *Sweet Track to Glastonbury: The Somerset Levels in Prehistory*. London: Thames & Hudson, 1986.

Collins, E. J. T. 'Changing Markets for Coppice Products and Coppice Management in England 1750–1914', in Salbitano, F. (ed.), *Human Influence on Forest Ecosystems Development in Europe*. Proceedings of a workshop in Trento, Italy 26–29 September 1988. Bologna: Pitagora Editrice, pp 331–334.

Collis, J. 'Field Systems and Boundaries on Shaugh Moor and at Wotter, Dartmoor'. *Proceedings of the Devon Archaeological Society 41*, 1983.

Cooper, Daniel. *Flora Metropolitana; Or Botanical Rambles within Thirty Miles of London*. London: S. Highly, 1836.

Coulter, John. *Norwood Past*. London: Historical Publications, 1996.

———— *Sydenham and Forest Hill Past*. London: Historical Publications, 1999.

Crane, Nicholas. *The Making of the British Landscape: From the Ice Age to the Present*. London: Weidenfeld & Nicolson, 2016.

Curnow, R. N., B. McEwen, and L. C. Miller, (eds.) *Colfensia No. 5*. London: Colfe's Grammar School, 1905.

Curtis, William. *Flora Londinensis, or, Plates and descriptions of such plants as grow wild in the environs of London*. London: The author, 1777–98.

Darby, William. *Dulwich Discovered*. Dulwich: William Darby, 1966.

Deakin, Roger. *Wildwood: A Journey Through Trees*. London: Hamish Hamilton, 2007.

Defoe, Daniel. *The Storm* [1704], ed. Richard Hamblyn. London: Penguin Classics, 2005.

———— *A Journal of the Plague Year* [1722], ed. Christopher Bristow. London: Penguin Classics, 2003.

———— *A Tour Through the Whole Island of Great Britain* [1724–26], ed. Pat Rodgers. London: Penguin Classics, 1986.

Dolley, R. H. M. 'Beulah Hill Treasure Trove 1953'. *Numismatic Chronicle 13* (43), 1953, pp. 115–122.

Donovan, Edward. *The Natural History of British Insects*. London: F. & C. Rivington, 1792.

Drew, Charles. *Lambeth Churchwardens' Accounts, 1504–1645 and Vestry Book, 1610*. Frome: Printed by Butler & Tanner for the Surrey Record Society and the Lambeth Borough Council, 1940–1950.

Ducarel, Andrew Coltée. *Some Account of the Town, Church, and Archiepiscopal Palace of Croydon.* London: J. Nichols, 1783.

Eden, Peter (ed.). *Dictionary of Land Surveyors and Local Cartographers of Great Britain and Ireland 1550–1850.* Folkestone: Dawson Publishing, 1975.

Edlin, H. L. *Forestry and Woodland Life.* London: Batsford, 1947.

————— *Woodland Crafts in Britain: An Account of the Traditional Uses of Trees and Timbers in the British Countryside.* London: Batsford, 1949.

Estienne, Charles, and Jean Liebault. *Maison Rustique, or The Countrey Farme,* trans. Richard Surflet. London: John Bill, 1616.

Evelyn, John. *Silva, or a Discourse of Forest-Trees and the Propagation of Timber,* 4th edn. London: Scott, 1706.

————— *The Diary of John Evelyn,* ed. Austin Dobson. London: Macmillan, 1908.

Forshaw, J. H., and Patrick Abercrombie. *County of London Plan.* London: Macmillan, 1943.

Foxe, John. *Acts and Monuments.* London: John Day, 1583.

Frith, E. 'A Croydon Quincentenary'. *Bulletin of the Croydon Natural History & Scientific Society* 93 (1&4), 1992.

Frith, Mathew. 'A Survey of the Stag Beetle *Lucanus cervus* in South London during 1997'. *London Naturalist 78,* 1999.

————— 'London', in Tim Sands (ed.) *Wildlife in Trust: A Hundred Years of Nature Conservation.* London: Elliott & Thompson, 2012.

Gale, John. *The Crystal Palace High Level Railway.* Lydney: Lightmoor Press, 2011.

Galer, Allan M. *Norwood and Dulwich Past and Present.* London: Truslove & Shirley, 1890.

Gaselee, John. 'Cutting and Laying a Hedge'. *Country Life,* 29 January 1959.

Gilchrist, Alexander. *The Life of William Blake*. London: Bodley Head, 1906.

Googe, Barnaby. *The Whole Art And Trade of Husbandry. Contained in four Bookes*. London: Richard More, 1614.

Gover, J. E. B., A. Mawer, and F. M. Stenton, . *The Place-Names of Surrey*. Cambridge: Cambridge University Press, 1934.

Graham-Brown, Sarah. 'Ancient Woodland Indicator Species and Ecological Change in Two London Woodlands'. *London Naturalist 85*, 2006.

Green, Brian. *Dulwich: The Home Front 1939–1945*. London: Dulwich Society, 1995.

———— *Dulwich: A History*. London: College Press, 2002.

Griffin, D. Betty. *Biggin Wood Norbury*. Streatham: Local History Publications, 2004.

Hannikainen, Matti O. *The Greening of London, 1920–2000*. Abingdon: Routledge, 2016.

Harris, Moses. *The Aurelian, or, Natural History of English Insects, Namely Moths and Butterflies . . .* London: The author, 1766.

Harrison, Melissa. *The Stubborn Light of Things: A Nature Diary*. London: Faber & Faber, 2020.

Hasted, Edward. *The History and Topographical Survey of the County of Kent*. Canterbury: H. Bristow, 1797.

Hemery, Gabriel, and Sarah Simblet. *The New Sylva: A Discourse of Forest & Orchard Trees for the Twenty-First Century*. London: Bloomsbury, 2014.

Hewitt, Rachel. *Map of a Nation: A Biography of the Ordnance Survey*. London: Granta Books, 2011.

Hewlett, Jan (ed.). *The Breeding Birds of the London Area: The Distribution and Changing Status of London's Breeding Birds in the Closing Years of the 20th Century*. London: London Natural History Society, 2002.

Hill, Dave. *An Atlas of Anglo-Saxon England*. Oxford: Blackwell, 1981.

Hodgson, Sidney. *Brief Notes on the History of the Hamlet of Penge with Anerley*. Penge: The Public Library, 1927.

Hoffman, Julian. *Irreplaceable: The Fight to Save our Wild Places*. London: Hamish Hamilton, 2019.

Hooper, W. 'Rocque's Map of Surrey'. *Surrey Archaeological Collections 40*, 1932. pp. 65–77.

Hughson, David. *London; being an Accurate History and Description of the British Metropolis and Its Neighbourhood* . . . London: J. Stratford, 1805.

Hull, F. 'Kentish Map-Makers of the Seventeenth Century'. *Archaeologia Cantiana 109*, 1991, pp. 63–84.

Hulme, Mike. 'Concept of Climate Change', in *The International Encyclopedia of Geography*. New York: Wiley-Blackwell/ Association of American Geographers (AAG), 2016.

Humboldt, A., E. Otté, B. Paul, and W. Dallas. *Cosmos: A Sketch of a Physical Description of the Universe*. London: Henry G. Bohn, 1848.

Johnson, Walter. *The Nature-World of London*. London: Sheldon Press, 1924.

Jones, Lucy. *Losing Eden: Why Our Minds Need the Wild*. London: Allen Lane, 2020.

Jones, Richard A. 'The Beetles and Other Invertebrates of Sydenham Hill and Dulwich Woods – Indicators of Ancient Woodland'. *London Naturalist 81*, 2002.

Kain, Roger, John Chapman, and Richard R. Oliver. *The Enclosure Maps of England and Wales, 1595–1918*. Cambridge: Cambridge University Press, 2004.

Knight, Mark. 'Excavating a Bronze Age Timber Platform at Must Farm, Whittlesey, Near Peterborough'. *Past 63*, November 2009.

Lawton, J. H., et al. *Making Space for Nature: A Review of England's Wildlife Sites and Ecological Network*. Report to Defra, 2010.

Laybourn-Langton, L., L. Rankin, and D. Baxter. 'This is a crisis: Facing up to the age of environmental breakdown'.

IPPR, 2019. www.ippr.org/research/publications/age-of-environmental-breakdown

Leman, Robert (ed.). *Calendar of State Papers, Domestic Series, of the Reigns of Edward VI, Mary, Elizabeth: 1547–1580*. London: Longman, 1856.

Lindley, Joseph, and William Crosley. *Memoir of a Map of the County of Surrey; From a Survey Made in the Years 1789 and 1790*. London: William Faden, 1793.

Logan, William Bryant. *Oak: The Frame of Civilization*. New York: W. W. Norton, 2005.

Logue, Mark, and Peter Conradi. *The King's Speech: Based on the Recently Discovered Diaries of Lionel Logue*. London: Quercus, 2010.

———— *The King's War*. London: Quercus, 2018.

London Natural History Society. *Birds of the London Area Since 1900*. London: Collins, 1957.

Lousley, J. Edward. 'Dulwich Woods: Relics of the Great North Wood'. *London Naturalist 38*, 1959.

———— 'Further Notes on Relics of the Great North Wood'. *London Naturalist 39*, 1960.

Lovegrove, Roger. *Silent Fields: The Long Decline of a Nation's Wildlife*. Oxford: Oxford University Press, 2007.

Lysons, Daniel. *Environs of London: Volume 1: County of Surrey*. London: Cadell & Davies, 1811 (first ed. 1792).

McCarthy, Michael. *The Moth Snowstorm: Nature and Joy*. London: John Murray, 2013.

McConnell, Anita. *Jesse Ramsden (1735–1800): London's Leading Scientific Instrument Maker*. Abingdon: Routledge, 2016.

Macnair, Andrew, Anne Rowe, and Tom Williamson. *Dury and Andrews' Map of Hertfordshire: Society and Landscape in the Eighteenth Century*. Oxford: Windgather, 2015.

MacNiven, Ian S. *Lawrence Durrell: A Biography*. London: Faber & Faber, 1998.

Magraw, Daniel, and Natalie Thomure. 'Carta de Foresta: The Charter of the Forest Turns 800'. *Environmental Law Reporter* 47, November 2017.

Manning, Owen, and William Bray. *History and Antiquities of the County of Surrey*. London: John White, 1814.

Martin, Edward A. *The Natural History and Antiquities of Croydon*. Croydon: Croydon Times, 1923.

Martyn, Thomas. *Flora Rustica: Exhibiting Accurate Figures of Such Plants as are Either Useful or Injurious in Husbandry*. London: F. P. Nodder, 1792.

Maurice, C. E. (ed.). *Life of Octavia Hill: As Told in her Letters*. London: Macmillan, 1913.

Meekings, C. A. F., and David Crook. *The 1235 Surrey Eyre*. Guildford: Surrey Record Society, 1979.

Merrett, Christopher. *Pinax Rerum Naturalium Britannicarum*. London: 1667.

Miles, Roger. *Forestry in the English Landscape*. London: Faber & Faber, 1967.

Mill, John Stuart. *The Collected Works of John Stuart Mill, Volume VI: Essays on England, Ireland, and the Empire*. London: Routledge & Kegan Paul, 1982.

Miller, Thomas. *Common Wayside Flowers*, London: Routledge, Warne & Routledge, 1860.

Mills, A. D. *A Dictionary of London Place-Names*. Oxford: Oxford University Press, 2001.

Morgan, R. A., and D. E. Glue. 'Breeding Survey of Black Redstarts in Britain, 1977'. *Bird Study* 28 (3), 1981, pp. 163–168.

Neville, L. S. C. *The Great North Wood*. London: London Wildlife Trust, 1987.

Newman, Jon. *River Effra: South London's Secret Spine*. Oxford: Signal, 2016.

Nisbet, John. *The Story of the One Tree Hill Agitation, with a Short Sketch of the History of Honor Oak Hill*. London: Enclosure of Honor Oak Hill Protest Committee, 1905.

Norden, John. *The Surveyors Dialogue. Divided into Five Bookes*. London: Hugh Astley, 1607.

Oliver, P. J. 'Ornithological Records from Dulwich Woods, 1959–1960'. *London Naturalist 82*, 2003.

O'Riordan, Christopher. 'Popular Exploitation of Enemy Estates in the English Revolution'. *History 78* (253), June 1993, pp. 183–200.

Orr, Mrs Sutherland. *Handbook to the Works of Browning*, 6th edn. London: G. Bell & Sons, 1885.

Paget, Clarence G. *By-Ways in the History of Croydon*. Croydon: Central Library, 1929.

Parikian, Lev. *Into The Tangled Bank: In Which Our Author Ventures Outdoors to Consider the British in Nature*. London: Elliott and Thompson, 2020.

Phillips, W. T. *Norwood in Days of Old*. 1912 (copy in Minet Public Library, Lambeth).

Piggott, Jan. *Charles Barry, Junior and the Dulwich College Estate*. London: Dulwich Picture Gallery, 1986.

———— *Dulwich College: A History, 1616–2008*. London: Dulwich College, 2008.

Pluymers, Keith. 'Taming the Wilderness in Sixteenth- and Seventeenth-Century Ireland and Virginia'. *Environmental History 16* (4), October 2011.

Power, F. D. *Ornithological Notes from a South London Suburb, 1874–1909: A Summary of 35 Years' Observations, with Some Facts and Fancies Concerning Migration*. London: Henry J. Glaisher, 1910.

Pryor, Francis. *The Fens: Discovering England's Ancient Depths*. London: Head of Zeus, 2019.

Rackham, Oliver. *Trees and Woodland in the British Landscape*. London: J. M. Dent, 1976.

———— *Ancient Woodland: Its History, Vegetation and Uses in England*. London: Edward Arnold, 1980.

————— *The History of the Countryside*. London: J. M. Dent, 1986.

————— *Woodlands*. London: William Collins, 2015.

Rawlinson, A. *The Defence of London, 1915–1918*. London: Andrew Melrose, 1923.

Rennie, James. *A Conspectus of the Butterflies and Moths found in Britain*. London: William Orr, 1832.

—————*The Field Naturalist. Volume 1: 1833*. London: Orr & Smith, 1833.

Richardson M., A. Cormack, L. McRobert, and R. Underhill. '30 Days Wild: Development and Evaluation of a Large-Scale Nature Engagement Campaign to Improve Well-Being.' PLoS ONE 11(2): e0149777, 2016. https://doi.org/10.1371/journal.pone.0149777

Robinson, Robert A., and William J. Sutherland. 'Post-War Changes in Arable Farming and Biodiversity in Great Britain'. *Journal of Applied Ecology* 39, 2002, pp. 157–176.

Rotherham, Ian D., Mel Jones, Lindy Smith, and Christine Handley. *The Woodland Heritage Manual: A Guide to Investigating Wooded Landscapes*. Sheffield: Wildtrack Publishing, 2008.

Roy, William. 'An Account of the Trigonometrical Operation, Whereby the Distance Between the Meridians of the Royal Observatories of Greenwich and Paris has been Determined'. *Philosophical Transactions of the Royal Society 80*, 1790, pp. 111–614.

Royden, E. B. *Three Roydon Families*. Edinburgh: R. & R. Clark, 1924.

Ruskin, John. *Fors Clavigera: Letters to the Workmen and Labourers of Great Britain*. Orpington: George Allen, 1871.

————— *The Storm Cloud of the Nineteenth Century: Two Lectures Delivered at the London Institution, February 4th and 11th, 1884*. Orpington: George Allen, 1884.

————Praeterita. Outlines of Scenes and Thoughts, Perhaps Worthy of Memory, in my Past Life. Orpington, Kent: George Allen, 1886–88.

Salmon, J. D., and J. A. Brewer. Flora of Surrey: A Catalogue of the Flowering Plants and Ferns Found in the County, with the Localities of the Rarer Species. London: John van Voorst, 1863.

Salmon, Michael A., Peter Marren, and Basil Harley. The Aurelian Legacy: British Butterflies and their Collectors. Berkeley: University of California Press, 2000.

Sánchez-Bayo, Francisco, and Kris A. G. Wyckhuys. 'Worldwide Decline of the Entomofauna: A Review of its Drivers'. Biological Conservation 232, 2019.

Saward, Arthur A. 'Reminiscences of Norwood'. Delivered at the Royal Normal College, Westow Street, under the auspices of the Upper Norwood Literary and Scientific Society, 10 April 1907 (copy in Upper Norwood reference library).

Scragg, Donald (ed.). Edgar, King of the English, 959–975: New Interpretations. Martlesham: Boydell & Brewer, 2008.

Sharp, William. Life of Robert Browning. London: Walter Scott, 1897.

Sheldrake, Merlin. Entangled Life: How Fungi Make Our Worlds, Change Our Minds and Shape Our Futures. London: Random House, 2020.

Sheppard, F. H. W. (ed.). Survey of London: Volume 26: Lambeth: Southern Area. London: Athlone Press for the LCC, 1956.

Sheppard, Francis. London 1808–1870:The Infernal Wen. London: Secker & Warburg, 1971.

Shower, Bartholomew. The Compleat English Copyholder: Or, a Guide to Lords of Manors, Justices of the Peace . . . London: Innys & Manby, 1735.

Smyth, Bob. City Wildspace. London: Hilary Shipman, 1987.

Snow, Robert. *Observations of the Aurora Borealis*. London: Moyes & Barclay, 1842.

Spencer, J. W., and K. J. Kirby. 'An Inventory of Ancient Woodland for England and Wales'. *Biological Conservation* 62(2), 1992, pp. 77–93.

Stace, Clive A. *New Flora of the British Isles*. Iver: Pemberley, 2019.

Standish, Arthur. *New Directions of Experience to the Commons Complaint*. London: 1613.

Stearns, Raymond Phineas. 'James Petiver: Promoter of Natural Science, c.1663–1718.' *Proceedings of the American Antiquarian Society* 63(2) Oct. 1952.

Steinman, George Steinman. *A History of Croydon*. London: Longman, 1833.

Stephens, James Francis. *Illustrations of British Entomology*. London: Baldwin & Cradock, 1828–32.

Storey, Neil. *Zeppelin Blitz: The German Air Raids on Great Britain During the First World War*. Cheltenham: History Press, 2015.

Sturzaker, John, and Ian Mell. *Green Belts: Past; Present; Future?* Abingdon: Routledge, 2017.

Swayne, F. G. 'Birds of the Norwood District', *London Naturalist 13*, 1934.

Tames, Richard. *Dulwich and Camberwell Past, with Peckham*. London: Historical Publications, 1997.

Thomas, David. 'London's Green Belt: The Evolution of an Idea'. *Ekistics, 17* (100), March 1964, pp. 177–181.

Thomson, Richard. *An Historical Essay on the Magna Charta of King John*. London: J. Major, 1829.

Thorndyke, Michael A. 'A Thriving Craft: The Art of Hedge-Laying'. *Country Life*, 22 July 1982.

Turner, G. J. 'The Justices of the Forest South of Trent'. *English Historical Review 18* (69), 1 January 1903, pp 112–116.

Tusser, Thomas. *Five Hundred Points of Good Husbandry*. London: Henry Denham, 1580.

Walford, Edward. *Old and New London: Volume 6 Peckham and Dulwich*. London: Cassell, Petter & Galpin, 1878.

Warner, George. *The Catalogue of the Manuscripts and Muniments of Alleyn's College of God's Gift at Dulwich*. London: Longmans, Green & Co, 1881.

Watt, A. S. 'On the Causes of Failure of Natural Regeneration in British Oakwoods'. *Journal of Ecology* 7, 1919, pp. 147–156.

Webb, Sidney. *The London Programme*. London: Swan Sonnenschein, 1891.

Weston, Richard. *A Treatise Concerning the Husbandry and Natural History of England*. London: T. Harris, 1742.

Whitehouse, Arch. *The Zeppelin Fighters*. London: Robert Hale, 1968.

Wilkinson, Samuel James. *The British Tortrices*. London: John van Voorst, 1859.

Willey, Russ. *Chambers London Gazetteer*. London: Chambers, 2006.

Williamson, Tom. *An Environmental History of Wildlife in England 1650–1950*. London: Bloomsbury, 2013.

Wilson, Michael I. *Nicholas Lanier: Master of the King's Musick*. Abingdon: Routledge, 2016.

Winterman, M. A. *Croydon's Parks: An Illustrated History*. Croydon: London Borough of Croydon, Parks and Recreation Department, 1988.

Wittich, John. *London Villages*. Shire, 3rd edn. 1987.

Wohlleben, Peter. *The Hidden Life of Trees: What they Feel, How they Communicate*, trans. Jane Billinghurst. Vancouver: Greystone Books, 2016.

Wood, William. *Index Entomologicus; or, A Complete Illustrated Catalogue of the Lepidopterous Insects of Great Britain, Containing 1944 Figures of Moths and Butterflies*. London: William Wood, 1839.

Woolf, Arthur L. *The Battle of South London*. London: Crystal Publications, 1945.

Wright, John. *A Natural History of the Hedgerow: And Ditches, Dykes and Dry Stone Walls*. London: Profile, 2016.

Young, W. *The History of Dulwich College*. London: 1889.

MAPPING THE NORTH WOOD

This chronological carto-bibliography lists both printed and manuscript maps showing all or part of the North Wood. Only printed maps based on original surveys, or which include significant new information, are listed. For manuscript maps, archival references are provided.

'Levehurst Manor: Inquisition (with plan)'. 1563–4. National Archives, Kew, E 178/92 m. 11.

Treswell, Raphe Snr.? 'Christ's Hospital Estates at Brockley Green, Lewisham. c.1600. London Metropolitan Archives, CLC/210/G/BKD/009A/MS22636/ 008.

Treswell, Raphe Jnr. 'A Rough Waste Percell of grounde full of hills and Fursyes as appeareth belonging to the Kinge's Majestye And Conteyninge 347 Acres'. 1606/7. National Archives, Kew, MPB 1/18.

Speede, John. *Surrey, Described and Divided into Hundreds. Described by the travills of John Norden. Augmented and performed by John Speede.* London: 1610.

'The plot of the mannor or lordshipp of Hatcham Barnes in the countyes of Kent & Surrye, part of the possessions of the Right Worshipfull Companye of Haberdashers.' Maunsell del. 1619. London Metropolitan Archives, CLC/L/HA/H/003.

Lane, Nicholas. 'The Plot of the Manor of Beckenham with the Demesne Lands Woods Pastures Meadows and Brooks Unto the Same Pertaining'. 1623. British Library, Maps 188.k.3(4.). This copy was made in 1768, but appears to be an exact reproduction of a lost original.

Janszoon, Jan. *Surria vernacule Surrey*. Amsterdam: 1646.

Mar, William. 'A Mapp . . . with the Lordships of the several Parishes of Lambeth and Croydon . . .' 1678. Museum of Croydon, GB-352-AR68.

Senex, John. *A New Map of the County of Surrey: Laid down from an Actual Survey*. London: John Senex, 1729.

Seutter, Matthäus. *Delineatio ac Finitima Regio Magnæ Brittaniæ Metropoleos Londini* . . . Augsburg: c.1730.

Rocque, John. *An Exact Survey of the citys of London Westminster ye Borough of Southwark and the Country near ten miles round / begun in 1741 & ended in 1745*. London: John Pine & John Tinney, 1746.

Rocque, John, and Peter Andrews. *A Topographical Map of the County of Surrey In which is Expressed all the Roads, Lanes, Churches, Noblemen, and Gentlemen's Seats, &c. &c., the Principal Observations, by the Late John Rocque, Topographer to His Majesty, Compleated and Engraved by Peter Andrews*. London: Mary Ann Rocque, 1768.

Andrews, John, Andrew Dury, and William Herbert. *A Topographical Map of the County of Kent in Twenty Five Sheets on a Scale of Two Inches to a Mile, From an Actual Survey* . . . London: A. Dury, 1769.

Cary, John. *Carys Actual Survey of the Country Fifteen Miles Round London on a Scale of One Inch to a Mile*. London: John Cary, 1786.

Faden, William. *The country twenty-five miles round London: planned from a scale of one mile to an inch*. London: 1788.

Lindley, Joseph, and William Crosley *Map of the County of Surrey, from a Survey made in the years 1789 and 1790.* London: 1793.

Milne, Thomas. *Milne's plan of the cities of London and Westminster, circumjacent towns and parishes &c. laid down from a Trigonometrical Survey taken in the years 1795–1799.* London: Thomas Milne, 1800.

Bainbridge, Thomas. *A Plan of the Parish of Croydon in the County of Surrey Shewing the allotments in the Common and Common fields as divided by Act of Parliament in the Year 1800.*

Mudge, William. *An Entirely New & Accurate Survey of the County of Kent, With Part of the County of Essex.* London: William Faden, 1801.

'A Map of the Manor of Lambeth in the County of Surrey: made in pursuance of an Act of Enclosure passed 46 Geo III.' Lambeth Archives, London. P 5/1.

Plan of Norwood Common as allotted by the Commissioners under the Lambeth Enclosure Act. London: G. Mills, 1806.

Doyley, John. *Plan of the Manor of Dulwich in the County of Surrey.* London: S. J. Neele, 1806.

Mudge, William. *Surrey* (Ordnance Survey Old Series VIII). London: William Mudge, 1816.

Waters, H. *The environs of London. Drawn & engraved by H. Waters. Published by Baldwin & Cradock, Paternoster Row, under the superintendence of the Society for the Diffusion of Useful Knowledge, February 1st, 1832.* London: Chapman & Hall, 1844.

'Camberwell Tithe Map, 1837'. Southwark Local History Library, London. 912.421 64 F(LS).

Davies, Benjamin. *London and its Environs. Containing the Boundaries of the Metropolitan Boroughs, the different Railroads & Stations, The New Cemetaries, Roads, Docks, Canals, and all modern improvements.* London: 1841.

Dewhirst, J. *Map of the Parish of St Giles Camberwell, delineating its Ecclesiastical & Parochial Districts*. London: W. Wheeler, 1842.

Plan of the Parish of St Mary Lambeth from a Survey Made in 1824. London: J. Allen, 1824.

Plan of the Manor of Dulwich in the County of Surrey 1852. London: Warrington & Son, 1852.

[Barry, Charles]. *Plan of the Manor & Estates of Alleyn's College, Dulwich, in the County of Surrey 1860*. London: Waterlow & Sons, 1860.

Stanford, Edward. *Stanford's Library Map of London and its Suburbs*. London: Edward Stanford, 1862.

Stanford, Edward. *Stanford's Library Map of London and its Suburbs*. London: Edward Stanford, 1872.

Barry, Charles. *Plan of the Manor & Estates of Alleyn's College, Dulwich, in the County of Surrey 1876*. London: 1876.

INDEX

Note

It is not possible to list every species found in the woods from the numerous surveys carried out over the past 400 years. Instead, key species are listed plus an index entry for the various categories of flora and fauna, giving references which lead to the results of the surveys. The relevant page references are as follows.

---

www.sandstonepress.com

Subscribe to our weekly newsletter for events
information, author news, paperback and e-book
deals, and the occasional photo of authors' pets!
bit.ly/SandstonePress

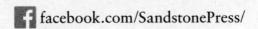 facebook.com/SandstonePress/

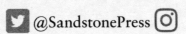 @SandstonePress